The Psychology of Education

CURRENT ISSUES AND
RESEARCH IN EDUCATION

GENERAL EDITOR *Harry L. Miller*
Hunter College

BOOKS IN THE SERIES

THE PSYCHOLOGY OF EDUCATION
Donald H. Clark

ELEMENTARY EDUCATION
Maurie Hillson

EDUCATION FOR THE DISADVANTAGED
Harry L. Miller

SOCIAL FOUNDATIONS OF EDUCATION
Dorothy Westby-Gibson

Fp

» DONALD H. CLARK

The
Psychology
of
Education

CURRENT ISSUES AND RESEARCH

THE FREE PRESS, New York
COLLIER-MACMILLAN LIMITED, LONDON

This book is dedicated to

Grace Rotzel

with great respect and affection. A quiet giant on the noisy battle-
field of Education, she knows that new is old and that each of us
does what he has to do.

Preface

THIS VOLUME IS ONE OF A SERIES INTENDED TO COPE PARTIALLY with the information explosion affecting all of the arts and sciences in recent years, a glut that has presented particularly severe problems for the field of education. Unlike the sciences and such applied arts as medicine, education has not had available a reliable network through which new ideas, experimentation, and criticism can be quickly gathered and disseminated. The field is only now beginning to establish centers for information retrieval to handle the vast expansion in educational activities that began in the 1950s.

Teacher training institutions for both graduates and undergraduates have themselves been forced to such a rapid expansion that they have had little energy to devote to helping their students keep up with the flood of new data. Instructors may choose the latest of texts, and most of them faithfully provide the traditional bibliography of recent journal articles; but education students, neither more nor less scholarly in their habits than those in other applied disciplines, can be expected to read those bibliographic entries that instructors have threatened to include on examinations, and no others. There is clearly a need for innovation in the struggle to keep up with a rapidly advancing field.

The *Current Issues and Research in Education* series substitutes for a bibliographical guide the current literature itself. Each volume surveys the most recent research findings, commentary on persistent issues, evaluations of ongoing experiments, and new ideas for the future and reprints the most significant among them in the form of excerpts, summaries, or entire articles. Frequent revisions will keep them up-to-date. Each selection represents a recognized expert's considered judgment of what is most significant in his special field; the editor helps readers to see each piece in perspective by providing historical background, an analysis of the article's relationship to general trends, or a critical assessment.

The series does not profess to substitute for basic texts in any of the fields it covers; the editors have made selections with the assumption that readers are already acquainted with the foundations of the particular field or, if they are students, that the collection supplements a general text.

All of us involved in producing the series are teachers of teachers; we hope that our perceptions of what our students need accurately reflect the perceptions of our colleagues.

H. L. M.

Introduction

This book looks forward from this moment. It does not review the past as does a text. It may be used as an introduction to classroom discussion of specific issues or to fill the gap between text and now.

Its function is more to agitate than to contemplate. It may give the college student a "head start" in preparing for the rapidly changing profession of teaching. I have tried to read the future by looking at the present. Hopefully, the teacher-in-training will take the same chancy look into the future and not agree with all my guesses.

D.H.C.

New York City

Contents

CHAPTER 1

The Disadvantaged

THE HOTTEST ISSUE IN THE PSYCHOLOGY OF EDUCATION TODAY IS the education of the disadvantaged child. The heat is beginning to produce light. We are beginning to see what must be done and how to do it. Certainly we have traveled a far road since *West Side Story* opened in 1957 and members of a street gang called the Jets stepped to the footlights and explained to Officer Krupke that they were very upset because they "never had the love that every child ought to get." Our culture has fretted for as long as anyone can remember about why some children seem bent on destruction. We searched for answers with lectures, corporal punishment, and "reform schools." When the Jets explained that they weren't delinquents but were misunderstood and that deep down inside them there was good, they were humorously reflecting the turn that our search had taken toward psychological and social explanations. These explanations are becoming increasingly sophisticated now because they draw on a rapidly expanding body of research.

One of the problems in this area, as in any other, has been finding words that all workers will agree to use in the same way. In the dazzling America of the 1960s every citizen owns a part of the strong and prosperous country. It is insulting to say that someone is poor. Writers and researchers in this field found that euphemisms, like flowers, are beautiful in first bloom but soon fade. They learned that people are equally insulted when called "lower class," "of lower socioeconomic status," "deprived," "products of the ghetto," "culturally deprived," "culturally disadvantaged," or even "citizens of the inner city." Rapid changes in terminology kept everyone hopping for quite a while. Things are settling a bit now, and oddly enough the term enjoying popular use is "poverty." It would seem that we have gone back to talking about the poor again, but the word "poverty" has a certain elegance that the word "poor" lacked.

This issue has become so important today partly because the federal government has been pouring vast amounts of money into research and action programs having to do with poverty. Researchers jokingly remind one another now that "There's a lot of money in poverty." The Civil Rights revolution of the 1960s is the other major cause and, obviously, these two are related.

Education, as usual, reflects the state of our culture. It is looking at problems of poverty with genuine professional interest rather than the magnificent condescension of past years. We have come to realize that Horatio Alger's prescription will not heal the hurts of today. In the world of the 1960s, education is dazed by the realization that it owns the key to gates that separate poor people from the rest of the population. An army of researchers are at work trying to determine the best ways to use the key.

The kind of research being done by Oscar Lewis helps us to keep an eye on the human being while studying the overall problem. Earlier, he gave us a warm acquaintance with the children of Sanchez and their problems. He is now at work studying the problems of Puerto Rican families on the island of Puerto Rico and in New York. His research technique of tape recording the words of the people whom he is studying permits us to see not only statistics, but humans. His book *La Vida* was published by Random House in 1966. A part of it is presented here.[1] Oscar Lewis describes Gabi:

1. From *La Vida*, by Oscar Lewis. © Copyright 1965, 1966, by Oscar Lewis. Reprinted by permission of Random House, Inc.

. . . an attractive, bright child with a ready smile. His experiences are typical of children who have grown up in the culture of poverty. They really have no childhood as we know it. Prematurely burdened by heavy responsibilities, exposed to violence, promiscuity, drunkenness and vice at a tender age and subject to unstable and immature adults, these children develop an incredible precosity and a superficial maturity which is damaging to their personality. Psychological tests suggest that Gabi is a lonely, confused and frightened child who depends upon cunning, denial, fantasy and escape to survive in his hostile and overwhelming world.

The most remarkable thing about Gabi is how well he manages to cope with a difficult and pathological environment. Those who define mental health as the ability to adapt would have to conclude that Gabi has excellent mental health. However, his adjustment is achieved at a high price. His own dream in which he sees himself at age twenty may foretell his sad destiny. Gabi's story illustrates the terrible abuse and waste of talent in human resources which are the real tragedy of the culture of poverty.

IN PART OF THE NARRATIVE, GABI (THROUGH LEWIS) TELLS US OF HIS arrival in New York City and his introduction to the urban school.

Felicita told me she was going to send me to New York to live in Uncle Simplicio's house. He wants me there. In New York, I can go to school and learn English to speak with Americans. Then I can get a job as a cook or get a job at the docks and earn lots of money. That way, when people are broke, I can give them money for food.

I want to grow up so they'll quit screwing me. Grown-ups are big bullies. When I'm grown up I can lift weights and drive cars because by then I will be earning money. And then I can get married. I'll find me a grown-up girl so I can be a real man and have sons and daughters. I'll have a job and give her money so she can make our dinner. When I get home from work, I'll hand her the money and kiss her. If she gets sick, I will send her to a doctor. When she's going to have a baby I'll take good care of her. And we will never quarrel or anything.

I told everyone I was going to New York and it was true. Felicita bought all new clothes for me. She bought me a suitcase and it was packed and ready. On Sunday we were supposed to go. I said, "Okay, I'm leaving." By seven I was all dressed.

I got to the airport at around nine. My grandmother, my *mamá*, and my Aunt Crucita went to see me off. When I said goodbye, I kissed my mother and grandmother and said to them, "Your blessing." Then I was sorry for them because they were crying. But I wasn't sad, I was happy.

I was thinking, "Maybe I'll never go back again so at Christmas and for Mother's Day, I am going to send my grandmother perfume and powder, the kind that smell a lot. Or maybe Uncle can save enough money to bring my grandmother up to New York for Christmas."

Well, the plane took off about ten and we didn't see each other anymore. The plane was so full that it looked as if it would fall down. I wasn't a bit scared because I wasn't alone. An American was taking care of me. And when we landed I'd be with my Uncle Simplicio and Aunt Flora.

I arrived at twelve. Oh, I felt happy! I didn't know what New York was like. In Puerto Rico the trees were full of leaves, all green and pretty. Here, they looked dried up, as if they had been through a hurricane. I asked Aunt about it and she said, "Oh, no. It's because of the cold."

"Ah," I said, "then it's all right."

We took a bus, which cost a lot of money—eight dollars. Eight dollars to get in! Then we had to get off and take a taxi for five dollars and finally change to another bus which charged six and took us all the way to Uncle's place.

I feel very happy here with Uncle and Flora. They treat me well. Here I dream that this is a royal palace and I'm the prince and that's why they love me so much. But my mother Felicita told me before I came, "Be careful what you say about me up there." She thought I was going to tell everybody that she spends her time hanging around bars and leaves us all alone. But I said to her, "Oh, no, I won't say anything. I'll tell lies there." I had forgotten all about it when she sends a letter here saying that at home I used to run off to the beach and never paid any attention to her. And she wrote too, "Goodness knows what he says about me up there."

She was scared, you see, because she was living with an American. Felicita thought I was going to tell that up here. But all I did was to tell my aunt, "When you write, tell that rat I'm not saying anything bad about her. Tell her too that I am never going back to Puerto Rico until I grow up and that I'm going to school already."

What I'd like is for Uncle and Aunt to have a baby in the house. I soon outgrow my shoes and if they had a little boy, he could wear them. I wish Angelito were here with me. My mother just has to send him because we are twins and if we aren't together we miss each other. I'd like to have lots of sisters too... nice sisters who would write to me. So that when I'm grown-up they'll be my family. But the trouble is that if my mother goes and has a lot more children, there won't be anybody to help her support them and then I won't be able to buy food for all of them.

Aunt Flora has a job at a factory. She sent for her sister Irene. She's not related to Uncle at all but he paid her fare over so that she could come take care of me. One hundred dollars it cost us.

I took all my things out of my suitcase so Irene could use it and I put my stuff in an old suitcase. I even went to meet Irene at the airport. And after all I did for her, you should hear the way she insults me now. She tells me to go to hell but I get right back at her. I say, "Go to hell yourself! I have more right to be here because I got here before you did. You shouldn't curse me like that because I'm not bad. I am a good boy. If I were bad, I would have kicked you out of here already."

She slept in my bed and I'd say to her, "You'd better lie with your head to the footboard and I'll lie with my head up." Then, after I fell asleep, she'd take my pillow away from me. What a witch!

They said someone had to go with me the day I enrolled in school, so she took me there. Then she went and said I was in first grade. I said, "No, I am in *second grade*." She didn't do anything right. And on top of everything, she beat me. She hit my fingers and made my nails black. She even cut me up.

I like going to school here because this place is new to me. The school would be really good if they spoke Spanish as well as English. I don't like to be spoken to in English because I don't understand it. People speak English in such a way that one can't understand anything. I tell the teacher, "*I don't speak English.*" If she gives me a paper and I don't understand what's written on it, I say, "*Teacher, I don't know.*" She gives me low marks because I don't know anything. There's one teacher who knows Spanish, but even she teaches in English. All, all of them teach in English.

The kids are bad as the Devil. They push me. There are all kinds of kids there, Americans, Chinese, Puerto Ricans, Negroes. Those Negroes hide so they can stick out their leg and trip you. The Chinese pull my ears. There's a real mean kid called Bushelman who grabs my little ass. So, you see, I don't have any friends in school.

There's a little girl called Karen—I wasn't doing anything bad to her, just touching her under the table, when she suddenly kicked me in the ribs with the heel of her shoe. I don't know how to speak with her because I don't know English. Then I called a little boy and told him, "Say something to her." You know what he did? He burst out laughing. "Haw, haw." I waited until school let out at three, then I really got hold of him. I hit him so hard, he bled. Teacher didn't see us. I never fight in front of her because if I did, she'd take me to the Principal's office.

I like it here, no matter if I don't speak English. I speak English just anyhow but now people understand what I say. I can ask to leave the room in English and then I go to the toilet. I repeat whatever I hear the other kids say and that way I learn quickly. I hear something today and keep repeating so by tomorrow I'll have learned it. A *gato* here is a "cat," the *mesa* is called "table." This morning I wrote, "Today is Monday" in English. "Monday" means *lunes*. They call the *ventana* "window," and the *casa*, "home." Isn't it true that I am beginning to learn?

In the afternoon I usually go with my Uncle Simplicio to his girlfriend's house. She lives way off in Brooklyn. You have to take the Lexington Avenue train. When we get there we find all the rest of them drinking. I would have liked to stay outside. I didn't want to see what went on in there.

I wish I were a grown man. I dreamed that I was twenty years old. I bought myself an apartment, a bed, and a chest of drawers with a mirror. The bathroom was next to the bed. I lived with Carmen Rosa and got up early to go to work.

Then it was Saturday and I went out to buy the food, corn flakes and oatmeal, meat and milk, chicken, canned spaghetti, sausage, bread, sugar, laundry soap, well, everything. After that, I went to pay the furniture store. And when my wife was sick, I did the cooking. I was always good to her. I'm telling you, though, if she does anything to me, I'll have a fight with her. You know what women are—when a man is all screwed up and doesn't have a house and lots of things, that is when they walk out on him. Well, if my wife does that to me, then I'll really beat her.

In my dream I walked and walked until I met some people. I asked them the way to the Bronx and they told me to turn and keep walking until I came to a hill. So I kept going until I got to Aunt Soledad's house but nobody was home. I went into several bars. In one of them I played pool. A man came and bumped against me.

I said to him, "No, no, I don't want to fight," because he had a gun. But I had a knife, so the other man gave up. I was big already.

WHILE "POVERTY" IS THE WORD MOST OFTEN USED IN THE POPULAR press, "disadvantage" is an increasingly useful word to researchers. More and more we speak of the ways in which a youngster is "disadvantaged" when he enters school. Benjamin S. Bloom, Allison Davis, and Robert Hess, of the Department of Education of the University of Chicago, are responsible for a masterful summary of research in this area, which was published as *Compensatory Education for Cultural Deprivation*. In it, they help to untangle the thinking behind such words as "disadvantage" and "deprivation." It is based on working papers contributed by participants in the Research Conference on Education and Cultural Deprivation and was published by Holt, Rinehart and Winston, Inc. in 1965.[2] The authors say: "Compensatory education as we understand it is not the reduction of all education to a least common denominator. It is a type of education which should help socially disadvantaged students without reducing the quality of education for those who are progressing satisfactorily under existing educational conditions." Several pages later they summarize research having to do with early experience.

Beginning very early, the child comes to perceive many aspects in the world around him. This perceptual development takes place through the sensory modalities such as vision, hearing, touch, and even taste and smell. This development continues in more and more complex ways as the child approaches the beginning of formal schooling at age six. Perceptual development is stimulated by environments which are rich in the range of experiences available; which make use of games, toys, and many objects for manipulation; and in which there is frequent interaction between the child and adults at meals, play times, and throughout the day. At the beginning of the first grade there are differences between culturally deprived and culturally advantaged children in the amount and variety of experiences they have had and in their perceptual development. Although differences in perceptual development are less evident by

2. Excerpts reprinted here are copyright © 1965 by Holt, Rinehart and Winston, Inc. Used by permission.

age nine, it is likely that the differences present at age six make for differences in school learning in the first few grades. The typical middle-class home provides a very complex environment for the child's early perceptual development, and this gives these children some advantage in the early years of school.

Linked to this perceptual development of the child is his linguistic development. As the child comes to perceive the world about him, he is able to "fix" or hold particular objects and events in his mind as he is given words or other symbols to "attach" to them. "Mama" and "Dadee" become representations of the important adults in his life. "Bottle," "cup," "dog," become symbols for appropriate objects in the environment. The adults in middle-class homes characteristically tend to use words so freely and easily that they teach them to the child at almost every opportunity. They encourage the child to say the word aloud, correct him when he says it incorrectly or applies it to the wrong object or event, and reward him when he uses the word or symbol correctly. This corrective feedback, which seems to be essential to the learning of languages in relation to experience, is more readily available to the culturally advantaged child than it is to other children.

As the child attempts to communicate with others, and especially with his parents, he uses a relatively crude and limited language. In many middle-class homes, the child's language is extended by the parent's responses to his statements and questions. In culturally deprived homes the parent is more likely to respond to the child with a monosyllable or to nod the head without using any words. The point of this is that one major difference between culturally deprived and more advantaged homes is the extension and development of the speech of children. Such differences have become very evident as a result of the studies done in various homes where parents are observed interacting with their children.

As a child develops more complex language, he becomes more able to perceive aspects of his environment, to abstract such aspects and to fix them in his memory, and to gain considerable control over his environment through the use of language. The frequent use of language in relation to his environment and the people in it enables the child to use words and language as tools for thought. Furthermore, the child becomes able to use language to express his own emotions, intentions, and desires. He is able to consider alternatives with regard to his emotions and to develop ways of delaying the gratification of his desires. Finally, the child develops his ability to compare, differentiate, and abstract aspects of his environment, as well as his own thoughts and emotions. Here again the child in the culturally advantaged home is given a great deal of opportunity to use language in these more complex ways, while the child in the disadvantaged home has less opportunity to develop it this way.

Put in other terms, the child in many middle-class homes is given a great deal of instruction about the world in which he lives, to use language to fix aspects of this world in his memory, and to think about similarities, differences, and relationships in this very complex environment. Such instruction is individual and is timed in relation to the experiences, actions, and questions of the child. Parents make great efforts to motivate the child, to reward him, and to reinforce desired responses. The child is read to, spoken to, and is constantly subjected to a stimulating set of experiences in a very complex environment. In short, he "learns to learn" very early. He comes to view the world as something he can master through a relatively enjoyable type of activity, a sort of game, which is learning. In fact, much of the approval he gets is because of his rapid and accurate response to this informal instruction at home.

"Learning to learn" should not be confused with the early teaching of the child to read, to spell, and even to do simple arithmetic. Such coaching in the home is merely trying to do the school's task before the child enters public education. "Learning to learn" is a far more basic type of learning than coaching the child on school learning. It includes motivating the child to find pleasure in learning. It involves developing the child's ability to attend to others and to engage in purposive action. It includes training the child to delay the gratification of his desires and wishes and to work for rewards and goals which are more distant. It includes developing the child's view of adults as sources of information, and ideas, and also as sources of approval and reward. Through such development the child changes his self-expectations and his expectations of others.

While all of this is not absent in the culturally deprived home, it does not play such a central role in child rearing in such homes. The size of the family, the concern of the parents with the basic necessities of life, the low level of educational development of the parents, the frequent absence of a male parent, and the lack of a great deal of interaction between children and adults, all conspire to reduce the stimulation, language development, and intellectual development of such children.

If the home does not and cannot provide these basic developments, the child is likely to be handicapped in much of his later learning and the prognosis for his educational development is very poor. Such a child is likely to have difficulty and to be constantly frustrated by the demands of the typical elementary-school program. His frustrations and disappointments in school are likely to have an adverse effect on his view of himself and his main desire must be to escape from the virtual imprisonment which school comes to represent for him.

LATER THE AUTHORS SAY THAT "CAREFUL STUDIES IN THE U.S. AND other countries demonstrate that it is possible to bring culturally deprived children up to satisfactory stages of readiness for the regular school learning. If this can be done on a broader base, then the regular learning procedures of the schools, which are now quite effective for the advantaged children, are also likely to be effective for the culturally disadvantaged children."

It was this kind of research evidence and reasoning that led to the availability of Federal funds to support Project Head Start. *Time Magazine*, in "Poverty—The War Within the War, Report on Head Start," May 13, 1966, described Head Start this way:[3]

Launched with a modest budget of $17 million and a target of 100,000 needy preschool children, the venture has proved the poverty program's best success. The response was nearly six times greater than anticipated, with 560,000 pupils in 2,400 communities attending classes for two months last summer. On the average, the children added eight to ten points to their IQs and 14 months to their intellectual performances. Not least of Head Start's achievements has been to nip budding health problems by giving its children complete medical exams—their first in most cases. In Boston, one-third were found to have major physical ailments or mental problems requiring clinical care, or both. Four out of five had advanced tooth decay. Of all the children enrolled nationwide, 100,000 needed glasses.

Lyndon Johnson has requested $310 million to train 700,000 students in fiscal 1967, but Powell's committee would like to give him $400 million to train 845,000. Exhilarated by the program's success last summer, the President announced plans to turn Head Start into a year-round program for 350,000 needy children, only to discover that it would have cost three times as much money as was available. The upshot was an administrative nightmare. Communities deluged Washington with applications, and OEO had to reject or pigeonhole scores of them.

THE DECEMBER 18, 1965 ISSUE OF THE *Saturday Review* CARRIED a series of articles on the Head Start program. In particular, one by Fred M. Hechinger, who is Education Editor of the *New York Times*, and one by Ivor Kraft, who is in the Division of Research, Children's Bureau, Welfare Administration, U.S. Department of Health, Education and Welfare, cast an evaluative eye on what they saw happening. These two articles are reprinted here in full. Mr. Hechinger's article was entitled "Head Start to Where?"[4]

The concept behind Head Start was disarmingly simple; disarming enough to make even hardened observers put aside legitimate doubts. The idea was to take great numbers of youngsters from disadvantaged neighborhoods—the polite new term for slums—and give them six weeks of pre-school experience plus physical care during the summer, just before they were to enter either kindergarten or first grade.

As such, Head Start was a massive, last-minute application of the new and increasingly accepted concept of pre-school education for deprived children, in an effort to help them overcome the handicap of not having grown up in a middle-class milieu prior to entering middle-class schools.

Based on this theory, last summer's Head Start was a cash as well as a crash program. It was expensive—in the neighborhood of $112,000,000. It was set up hurriedly. A Saturday morning committee meeting last spring, not long before the launching date found the educational and theoretical leadership largely groping in the dark. Nobody was even quite sure what the response would be—or, more important, who would respond.

Considering the late and the sudden start of Head Start, the turnout was highly gratifying in sheer numbers. Nearly 560,000 children took part, and they were enrolled at 13,400 centers in 2,500 communities. Some of the centers were run by public school systems, oth-

4. Reprinted with permission of *Saturday Review*, from the issue of December 18, 1965.

ers by parochial schools, private schools, child care centers, and every conceivable type of usable pre-school agency.

A preliminary report issued by the Office of Economic Opportunity showed that 70 per cent of a large sample of children who participated had their first medical and dental examinations during the summer. In one center, at Tampa, Florida, twelve tubercular cases were found and fifty youngsters turned out to have nutritional deficiencies. Without a doubt, many children had their first experiences with books, more or less sophisticated toys, organized music, art, and other educational activities.

Given all these facts, it may seem almost unpatriotic and antisocial to subject the program to critical analysis—even friendly scrutiny. It is like questioning Motherhood. But then—not all mothers are, despite the sentimental legend, entirely commendable, and even the total enterprise of Motherhood might be improved, just so long as an appraisal of its accomplishments or failures is not misinterpreted as being in the spirit of an abolition crusade. It is in a spirit of constructive skepticism, then, that Head Start is now being scrutinized.

Unfortunately objectivity is difficult because all Great Society programs are described in superlatives. In Johnsonian terms, every new education bill outshines the original Land Grant Act. Sargent Shriver's press agents view every antipoverty measure as more revolutionary than the entire New Deal. Project Head Start is no exception.

This is a pity. Not only because it makes reporters look extra hard for flaws and weaknesses—as part antidote, part self-defense; it is even more of a pity because it dwarfs the real achievements next to exaggerated claims.

President Johnson said, at the end of the summer, that the project "which began as an experiment, has been battle-tested—and it has proven worthy." Unfortunately, this is a misleading conclusion. It would be more accurate to say that Head Start as an idea is worthy, without any need of scientific proof or sociological study. But there is serious question whether the project started, in the proper sense, as an experiment. Many sympathetic experts complain that it lacked the kind of experimental preparation—pre-testing, careful study of the selected population, etc.—that makes valid conclusions possible.

What specific knowledge has been gained? The returns are very slow in coming in. Experts who have been analyzing the program admit privately that the official reports, based on a 10 per cent sample of the children in certain centers, are so sketchy and unscientific that it is questionable whether they will yield any comprehensive conclusions. At any rate, it will be at least another three or four months before the findings are available.

For the moment, therefore, the best instrument of appraisal is personal observation. Here, much of what can be recorded is gratifying indeed. Many teachers stress that the children who entered the formal classroom after Head Start fit far more readily into the school picture than those who came in from slum homes, without conditioning. They appear happier as well as more eager to learn.

"I have yet to speak to a teacher or parent who has anything but praise for what Head Start accomplished," said Dr. Seymour Gang, principal in a Harlem elementary school. One of his teachers added: "The Head Start children have adjusted better to school. They started the term familiar with the materials and were not frightened by the experience of going to school." Another teacher said: "It used to take me three weeks just to get them to stop crying and get into the routine. This time . . . the children were ready to learn. We were able to get off to a fast start."

Other teachers reported far greater sophistication among the Head Start youngsters. In one classroom, early in the term, a cockroach crawled across one of the tables while the children were sitting around with their paints. ("That's one of the Head Start legacies," smiled the principal. "The kids used to bring their food in here. But it's a small price to pay for what we gained.") The non-Head Start children either ignored the roach or seemed distressed. But several of the youngsters who had been in the summer program, spontaneously and with gusto started to sing "La Cucaracha," amid peals of laughter.

There were other gains—perhaps more vital, though even less tangible, than those to be measured in the classroom. Because the program took place outside the formal structure of education, it involved a far more diverse group of people. It was easier to get local neighborhood social workers as well as college students and even some high school seniors to join in the teaching and supervision. This, in turn, meant that the process was less forbidding to the parents—and they were more often drawn into the program.

A parent-coordinator in New York said: "We have made more progress in six weeks than we have been able to make with parents in four years." Another staff member reported: "Mothers came with baby carriages and stayed to help."

Indicating the deficiencies of "real school," one consultant delivered himself of this implied, devastating criticism: "School is a place that families have begun to trust as an institution for the first time" (since Head Start).

Such testimony is sufficient to proclaim that the initial year has been worthwhile—pragmatically, even without proper research data. But this does not mean that all the answers are in for the future. It does not even mean that the enthusiastic public-relations reports, unless tempered by facts and cautions, are not capable of doing some long-range harm.

Even on a matter of working detail, the complexity of the answers, and their interpretation, is worth thinking of. Take the enthusiastic response by Dr. Gang, an exceedingly able principal of a fine school in a predominately Negro area. In his instance, he was able to rely largely on his regular teaching staff to run the Head Start program. Since an able principal attracts able and happy teachers, the program was ahead of the game from the start. Furthermore, since the same teachers remain close to the Head Start youngsters after they enter school, the question of follow-up, which is such an important concern of the project's philosophy, is more easily resolved.

What if such an example led to the conclusion that it would be best to let the children's prospective regular teachers have an important hand in Head Start in every instance as a matter of course? An obvious danger would be that in the least successful schools with ineffective teachers—and they are often the crux of the problem in de facto segregated neighborhoods—the unsuccessful program would merely be given its own head start. Failure would begin a little earlier.

This instance is cited only to illustrate how difficult it is to translate the summer's experience into standard operating procedure and how misleading specific success stories might turn out to be.

But there are broader issues involved which call for unsentimental appraisal rather than uncritical enthusiasm. Dr. Martin Deutsch, director of the Institute for Developmental Studies and one of the pioneers of pre-school education as an instrument of social salvage, says bluntly that four-fifths of the program could have been much better, if only there had been as much preparation as enthusiasm. He charges that some of the programs were purely custodial. Others were good, and a few excellent. But, he warned, the poor programs "will only make children hate school sooner."

Perhaps some of the flaws of the first year's operation were unavoidable, and it is quite possible that from the social and political point of view it was more urgent and probably more beneficial to get a massive program off the ground, even at the risk of insufficient planning, than to satisfy Dr. Deutsch's more scientific and purist standards. But this should not lead to an aftermath of even the best-intentioned whitewash. Dr. Deutsch fears that educators, sociologists and psychologists, after going along with the demand for speedy mass-action, may not be ready to take a hard analytical look in retrospect—for political reasons. If this turns out to be so, the future effectiveness, not only of Head Start but of pre-school education in general may be seriously impaired.

Dr. Deutsch is not by any means a hostile critic. He stresses many of the achievements—with specific children and as a means toward changing patterns. In Houston, Texas, he points out, as an example, Negroes for the first time took an active part in a socio-educational effort. This vital by-product was confirmed by other observers who reported that integration in Head Start centers in the South was ahead of Southern public school integration in general.

First among the questions yet to be answered is whether the "Come and get it" approach can come to grips with the hard core problem of the vicious circle of ignorance, poverty, discrimination, and unemployment among the non-white minorities. Do the children who need pre-school education most really attend? Will parents who, because of their own ignorance and long-term disillusionment, place little hope in the schools, enroll their children? And what about the children with virtually no care by responsible adults? (It is here that the lack of sufficient pre-enrollment data may prove to be a most serious handicap.)

One expert who is sifting the presently available evidence said that from a medical point of view, despite some of the impressive single or localized case histories put out through OEO publicity channels, the children served last summer were far healthier than expected.

This may, of course, hint at a number of different conclusions. It is possible—although not considered likely—that the poverty-ridden population of the slums is healthier than is generally assumed. It may well be—and some observers have suspected this in a number of places—that the medical service provided in many Head Start centers simply was not of high enough quality to detect any but the most superficial or glaring defects. There is always the nagging doubt, as one expert put it, "that we missed the target."

Another possible clue, inconclusive but worth investigating, is the preliminary discovery that the mothers of Head Start children in some of the sampled centers had a more impressive educational background than had been anticipated—averaging eleven years of schooling. (Fathers averaged attendance only up to eighth or ninth grade, confirming the drastically lower educational status and opportunities for Negro men than for women.) What can be concluded? It is, of course, true that Head Start parents naturally are young and thus the part of a generation which has had the benefit of free and compulsory public education and growing education-consciousness. But again the nagging suspicion persists that the parents who were school dropouts may be more laggard in sending their children to a special education program—even though it is tailored to their needs.

A more fundamental question is how the Head Start concept and experience will be woven into the fabric of American education. It is on this point that even the most sympathetic observers comment with concern.

Dr. Kenneth B. Clark, professor of psychology at City College and, along with Dr. Deutsch, one of the pioneers in educational experimentation, has warned consistently that compensatory education for children of deprived minorities is no substitute for changes in the structure of education itself. Merely giving such children an opportunity to begin slightly ahead of the class is of little use if the regular schooling is not, at the same time, made relevant for them. There is little to be gained from surrounding these youngsters with loving and understanding adults in their pre-school taste of learning, if they subsequently are exposed to teachers who approach them with preconceived notions of limited potential. Nor is there much permanent consolation in parent participation in Head Start, if school itself does not continue to foster and nurture this new partnership.

The evidence of prior research, unrelated to the Head Start experiment, already shows conclusively that early compensatory education is of very limited, short-term benefit unless there is consistent follow-up. Children's pre-school gains in such experimentation have been shown to be spectacular as they entered first grade, but quick to erode within the next four years unless they are constantly reinforced. If there is a gap between pre-school education and kindergarten or first grade, the gains are minimal.

This may, however, be Head Start's most powerful promise. Dr. Deutsch, despite his skepticism and specific complaints about the project's operational limitations, underlined the importance of compensatory education as the spark that may impel the essential task of changing the structure of education.

There is now widespread agreement that a summer program is of little lasting value without follow-through. The White House Conference on Education emphasized this. President Johnson has already provided the basis for an official and fiscal follow-through. He has called for and made available the funds for year-around Head Start centers and for special programs to work with alumni of last summer's efforts.

This is not a simple task. There is a vast difference between staffing and running a summer program and doing so during the regular school year. While facilities are readily available during vacation time, they are likely to be already overcrowded during the school year. New York City is an example. To find room for a Head Start enrollment of about 26,000 in a city that normally teaches close to 1,400,000 in all its public and private schools is easy. To take care of a similar number during the academic year in a system that already runs on short and overlapping sessions requires exceptional ingenuity and a good deal of improvising—at least until pre-school education can be built into the over-all planning, budgeting, and construction.

Even more serious is the question of staff. The great majority of those who taught in the summer program—regular teachers as well as college students—are now again busy with their own work schedules. Perhaps even more important, during the summer it is relatively easy to be selective—to pick and choose the most suitable people out of a huge reservoir of available teachers.

The fact that the President has reduced the all-year target, at least for the moment, to an enrollment of 350,000 instead of the summer peak of 560,000, indicated that Washington is not unaware of the limitations. Even then, it is already clear that special personne' will have to be trained, and some such programs have since been inaugurated by a few teacher-training institutions, especially in the big urban centers.

It would, however, be fatal if the problem were to be thought of primarily in terms of numbers needed to staff conventional classrooms. The reason Head Start was successful with many children must not be attributed to some social or educational magic. The heart of the matter was that typically a Head Start class had only fifteen children, with a highly experienced teacher and several assistants—interns, college students, social workers, volunteers and others.

The secret unquestionably is in close personal relationships and individual attention, and this is exactly where the conventional schooling process has fallen down.

The inherent danger of any pilot project is that it may deceive the public into believing that an early success can easily be translated into routine—without the same investment of money, time and people on a regular, massive scale. It is a lesson painfully taught many times over—most recently by the initial success and long-term failure of New York City's "Higher Horizons" program, a special enrichment effort for children in slum neighborhoods. It worked like magic—but only as long as the extra teachers, extra funds, and extra care were forthcoming. Once institutionalized and watered down, the program faded into ineffective routine.

This is why the Head Start experiment—with all its fanfare and all its flamboyant publicity—holds out special hopes and conjures up serious dangers.

If the official oversell—and there is no doubt that OEO has been overselling in steamroller fashion—creates the public impression that an easy solution has been found and that the lucky Head Start children are safely on their way to salvation, then the eventual disillusionment will be cruel. Then, too, the most complacent school superintendents and boards are likely to settle back to do even less than in the past about tackling the year-round problems of the disadvantaged.

But if educators, together with their new allies in Washington, take hold and use the gigantic summer demonstration program as a means of pointing, not to what has been accomplished but to what might be done, then the project has been well worth both the fanfare and the expenditure.

Even the oversell may then have served a useful function. Out of the example of compensatory education, in the glare and publicity's spotlight, could come a real start in the rebuilding of the education system. Surely, for example, the community which has benefited from Head Start must have second thoughts if it does not yet have fully established kindergartens. And if the effect of well-staffed small classes is so demonstrably good, then the entire table of organization in the regular schools deserves a reappraisal, possibly a revolution. Finally, if something has been learned from the use of non-professional support personnel, how can an open-minded school superintendent fail to take official notice of such untapped potential?

Dr. Edmund W. Gordon, professor of psychology and education at Yeshiva University and Head Start's director of research and evaluation, said: "It is vital that the summer crash program not be regarded as a substitute for the regular and continuing education of disadvantaged children."

If these warnings are heeded, then even Washington's superlatives may have had their place. Hard-sell may be forgiven if it puts a sound idea across. Whether this approach is pardonable depends largely on the aftermath. Will it be merely self-congratulatory—an invitation to smug oversimplification? Or will it be the head start of a campaign to reform American education, heart and soul?

Last summer's project, even on the basis of such incomplete testing and records as are available, is believed by some reputable and honest experts to have raised the Intelligence Quotients of many rural children by between ten and fifteen points and those of urban children, who presumably started on a slightly higher level, by between eight and ten points. This is, by any yardstick, a considerable achievement. But just as those I.Q.'s were originally depressed by lack of development rather than lack of native ability, they may quickly slide back if the gains of a summer are thought of as safe and permanent. The eventual answer to the questions about this huge government-sponsored demonstration program will not be in until it is made unmistakably clear that a summer's enthusiasm will not turn, through neglect, into winters of discontent.

The key question will be whether Washington's pioneering fervor and salesmanship can be matched by the educators' steady, long-range follow-through and the people's commitment.

IVOR KRAFT'S ARTICLE IN THE SAME ISSUE WAS ENTITLED, "ARE WE Overselling the Pre-School Idea?"[5]

During the past year there has been a remarkable show of interest in nursery schools, especially for deprived, Negro children. In some ways this is gratifying, although it may result in over-investment and forced faith in what is at best a very limited kind of educational innovation. It may also hatch another educational albatross to hang

5. Reprinted with permission of *Saturday Review*, from the issue of December 18, 1965.

around our necks: tens of thousands of inferior custodial centers for small children.

Whether professional or lay people, most Americans believe that the first years of childhood are highly important in molding the well-adjusted personality, but this concern has never blinded us to what happens next. We have never settled for a "last chance" view of human nature.

For the good life beyond early childhood, schooling is essential in all advanced cultures, but no culture insists that three- four- or five-year-olds spend a structured part of the day in group outdoor play, indoor circle time, reading readiness, and so forth. Yet all cultures do seem to recognize that small children require freedom to play in benign surroundings and the more or less regular care of regularly available and responsible adults (usually the mother or a group of mother substitutes).

Group care of small children is often an enormous convenience to parents, and it can contribute a great deal to stable family life. Also, it makes all the difference in the world during emergencies. Nurseries fulfilled a vital role in Britain during the days of the blitz. During the Second World War we opened thousands of nurseries; while many of these centers were far from ideal, they made a great deal of difference for tens of thousands of American mothers who were working long hours in war industry.

Advocates of pre-schooling for "culturally deprived" children view it not as a baby-sitting service, but as a major compensatory device, a means of diminishing the inequalities of poverty. Theoretically, this is an attractive approach. But there is sometimes a chasm between theory and practice.

To begin with, many of our so-called "culturally deprived" families are not culturally deprived. They are merely poor. They need more money, better housing, more dignified jobs, increased respect as human beings regardless of race or ethnic origin. These needs will not be met by pre-schooling.

To what extent will the pre-schooling be genuinely compensatory? What happens when fifteen or so homogeneously deprived children spend a few hours a day in the care of an ordinary or even untrained teacher, and return to the same old environment? Can we expect to transform them into little scholars when we do not even attempt this with more "advantaged" youngsters? Can we do it on the basis of perhaps twenty or thirty minutes of deliberately structured intellectual experiences? (We have to allow for dressing and undressing, juice time, rest time, toileting, etc.)

It would perhaps be a different story if we were talking about an eight- or ten-hour day, highly skilled teachers, much individual attention, close contact with parents, and if we kept the children in this careful setting for not three months but for three years. Such a program would require an expenditure of at least $2,000 per child per year, and not a bargain basement budget of $200 to $500 per child.

We can assume that the pre-schools will produce certain measurable improvements in conventional school readiness and a rise in I.Q. test scores. What will happen next, when these children reach the first grade?

That all depends on what takes place in the first grade. And the second grade—and so on throughout the ensuing school careers of those children who live in low-income and slum neighborhoods. No responsible child development specialist could possibly claim that a few months of good pre-schooling will set the child up for life. Indeed, it is highly unlikely that it will set him up for much beyond the first few weeks of the first grade.

Unless we close our eyes to the massive evidence that keeps pouring out of our inferior elementary schools in the inner-city systems across the nation, we can easily predict that even the finest pre-school experience for deprived and segregated children will wash out and disappear as these children pass through the grades. Their I.Q. test scores will fall. Many of them will become functional illiterates. Thirty per cent of them will be dropouts by the ninth grade.

Top-quality early childhood education has an important role to play in American life, but there are pitfalls in overselling the pre-school idea. We may deceive ourselves into thinking that pre-schools can seriously offset the severer familial effects of poverty, when they can never substitute for the broad range of healthful, normative home and family experiences of small children. Also, we may be deflecting attention from the really crucial sectors in educational reconstruction, the primary and secondary inner-city schools. It is here that massive expenditures and profound efforts at innovating are needed, from the first grade through the twelfth. In devoting overly optimistic attention to pre-schools we are perhaps behaving like pastry cooks hard at work on the icing without having bothered to bake the cake.

It may be that just as we have never found pre-schooling an essential to future educational success for typical middle-class youth, so we will not find it an essential to school achievement for non-middle-class youth, once we provide this youth with really satisfactory buildings, teachers, curricula, as well as the genuine promise of future success in life.

INVESTIGATORS ARE LOOKING THROUGH ALL THE YEARS THAT THE disadvantaged child spends in school. They are looking for the special problems of the disadvantaged child in an attempt to find special techniques that will help him solve or at least live with these problems. One apparent reason that he is educationally disadvantaged is that he is likely to move more often. His new location may not be far from the old one nor much more desirable but it often puts him in a different school.

Joseph Justman, of the Bureau of Educational Program Research and Statistics of the New York City Board of Education, published an article in the *Journal of Educational Measurement*, 1965, entitled "Academic Aptitude and Reading Test Scores of Disadvantaged Children Showing Varying Degrees of Mobility."[6] He points out that there is a relationship between the amount of moving a youngster does and his experience in school. In his discussion of his research findings he writes:

It is evident that broad generalizations concerning the test performance of disadvantaged children must be approached cautiously. In the present study a large group of pupils drawn from schools located in disadvantaged areas but characterized by lack of mobility showed average or near-average functioning on intelligence tests and reading tests administered in the third and sixth grade. A comparable group, drawn from the same schools but showing a pattern of mobility from school to school, evidenced below average performance on the same tests. Moreover, progressively poorer performance was associated with increasing mobility. It is quite clear that mobility is a factor that must be considered before a blanket generalization can be advanced concerning the functioning of disadvantaged children. One may venture the hypothesis that uninterrupted school experience is an important element in the school performance of disadvantaged pupils.

THIS IS ONE EXAMPLE OF RESEARCH EVIDENCE PROVIDING A TOE hold for attempts to help the disadvantaged child. City school

6. Excerpt reprinted with permission of the *Journal of Educational Measurement*.

systems could relax area residence requirements sufficiently to permit many youngsters to stay with the same class and teacher at least through a full school year.

Other means of help are being sought with varying degrees of success. Murray Levine, who is at the Psycho-Educational Clinic at Yale University, published an article entitled "Residential Change and School Adjustment" in the *Community Mental Health Journal* in 1966. He describes a system whereby older students try to help newer students feel at home in their new surroundings. He points out, however, that such a program would be considerably more difficult to organize and to carry through in the kind of big-city school that is most troubled by transient students.

One of the most prominent investigators in this field, Frank Riessman, has often reminded us that while studying or working with the disadvantaged child, we must keep an eye on the positives as well as the negatives. We must not simply look for his special problems but also must look at his particular strengths and abilities. The clash between teachers' middle-class values and the values of their lower-class students has become legendary. The pointless debate about whose values are "better" has blinded us too often from the more productive question of how to make better educational use of whatever differences do exist. We are too often guilty of tailoring the child to meet the needs of the school rather than tailoring the school to meet the needs of the child. His article, "The Lessons of Poverty," published in the February, 1965 issue of *American Education*, is reprinted here.[7]

Wherever we look in the United States today, we see criticism of the school system, of the curriculum, of the teachers and administrators. The conformity of the system and the lack of real learning are constantly being attacked. At the same time the middle class in our country is being sharply criticized. Middle-class people are being portrayed as conformists who have lost their spontaneity, their convictions.

These criticisms are widespread. But there is one time when they seldom arise, and this is when the teaching of disadvantaged chil-

7. Reprinted with permission of the author.

dren is discussed. Suddenly, when we talk about these youngsters, we have a much more idealized picture of our schools and of middle-class life, and suddenly these children are to be made to conform to our suddenly wonderful ways.

I think that some important changes are beginning to take place in the schools and in the middle class. But a great deal has to be done, and I believe that these disadvantaged youngsters, with their own culture and their own style and their own positives, can help us change the middle class, the school system, and the society.

Before they can help, however, these children do need education. Most particularly they need teachers who take a new approach to teaching; and it is tremendously encouraging that the Federal Government, recognizing this, will next summer support several institutes for the training of teachers of the disadvantaged. These institutes, which were authorized by the 88th Congress when it added Title XI to the National Defense Education Act, will be conducted by colleges and universities, under contract with the Office of Education.

If I were to recommend one thing to the people who will be conducting these institutes, it would be this: Show teachers how to meet the disadvantaged on their own ground.

By this I emphatically do not mean that a teacher should compromise his standards or that he should condescend to his pupils. I mean that he should recognize that the culture from which these pupils spring has its own standards and its own sense of values and that he must work within these standards, in fact turn them to educational profit.

Specifically, I believe that the training of teachers for the disadvantaged should do four things for each trainee:

1. Develop in him a genuine interest in these children and a respect for them rather than simply have him acquire some knowledge about them.

2. Expose him carefully and thoroughly to the disadvantaged so that he can free himself of any negative preconceptions he may have had about these people.

3. Show him how to use teaching methods adapted to the learning style of the disadvantaged.

4. Develop in him an effective teaching *style*, as distinguished from method.

In naming these four objectives I am thinking of disadvantaged children who will be taught in integrated, multi-class schools and classrooms. Although my suggestions may be especially suited to low-income children, they should work well also with middle-class children by improving their styles of learning and broadening their general outlook.

Let us consider each of the four in order.

It is extremely important to respect disadvantaged children. It is the key to winning them to education. But in order to respect someone it is necessary to know something positive about him, and I find that too many of the people who talk about respecting these youngsters really see nothing in them to respect. This is why I think we should stress the good things in the culture, behavior, and style of the disadvantaged. We should stress, for instance, the freedom the disadvantaged enjoy from the strain that accompanies competitiveness; the equalitarianism, informality, and humor; the freedom from self-blame and parental over-protection; the children's enjoyment of each other's company; and the enjoyment of music, games, sports, and cards.

However, it is not enough to give people respect and knowledge; it is necessary also to change the *attitude* of teachers. You may think that this is a very difficult thing to do, but actually it may not be so difficult. The way to do it, I think, is by arousing the *interest* of the teacher in disadvantaged people and their culture.

Generally, teachers and other members of the school staff have not been especially interested in the makeup of these youngsters. They have seen the poor, for the most part, as an undifferentiated drab mass. In order to create interest, I would introduce considerable controversy and ferment about the poor and their psychology. The current proposals for providing teachers with a sociological analysis of disadvantaged groups, while valuable, are not sufficient for developing deep interest in and excitement about these people.

The time has come for teacher preparation to include reading of novels, seeing films, viewing art and dance, and hearing music of various low income groups, particularly the Negro and Spanish-speaking groups. So I would recommend, for example, that discussions take place around books like *The Cool World* by Warren Miller and movies such as *Nothing But a Man*. I think also a good deal of discussion about Negro history and Negro contributions in science, art, and engineering should take place in this kind of teacher training.

My second point is that we ought to take more thought in planning the "laboratory" programs we have for teachers. Many preparatory programs tend to stress visits to the homes and neighbor-hoods of the poor, visits which can actually reinforce existing steoreotypes about the disadvantaged. The simple and obvious reason is that teachers, like everyone else, see what they want to see, what they have been prepared by their training to see.

What I am suggesting here is a carefully directed, prepared expo-sure that will help teachers know *how* to look at the culture of the low-income groups. They won't see simply a family that is broken, for instance, but rather an extended female-based family which is in many ways highly organized, although organized very differently from the traditional family. They will learn to see the way in which functions are delegated and organized in this family, how child rearing is handled, how cooking is assigned, how members of the family take care of the house, and the way responsibility is divided.

The teachers will also have to be taught not to confuse the nor-mal and the pathological. The normal female-based family is not pathological. But pathology does occur in some families. In some middle-class strata, child rearing may have strong traces of parental overprotection, overindulgence, and the like. This may be the norm, just as less direct, less intensive loving is the norm in lower socio-economic groups. But neither pattern by itself is abnormal, even though the pathologies in both classes may well be related to the normative pattern.

Nor should the focus be on the environment as such—on the crowdedness, the lack of privacy, the lack of economic security. Rather, the focus should be on how these people struggle with this environment, how they have forged a culture in doing this, and how this culture and style can be utilized in the school situation. This calls for much more than "tours" and home visits.

The third point in my suggested program has to do with teaching methods. A number of techniques may have special value for low income children, but I shall confine myself to discussion of two—namely, role playing and the use of "hip" language.

Before I discuss these two techniques, however, let me simply list a few others that seem to hold promise for the disadvantaged:

1. The "organics" technique of Sylvia Ashton Warner (*The Teacher*) should be especially valuable in building upon the inter-ests and potentialities of the youngsters, and should guard against their being "acted upon." (The latter is the current trend in many programs designed for the disadvantaged, who are supposedly "defi-cit" ridden.)

2. The Montessori System, which places much emphasis on sen-

sory materials and on order, should be particularly congenial to low-income youngsters.

3. Various game techniques—"In the Manner of the Adverb," for example, and Robbins' "Auditory Set" game—may be valuable.

4. Lawrence Senesh's techniques for teaching economics to first- and second-graders seem promising.

The technique we call role playing owes a good deal of its success to the fact that participants feel free of tension. They act out various types of problems. A caseworker interviews a withdrawn client, say; or the manager of a housing project for low-income families interviews a tenant or a prospective tenant. Since they are "only acting," they can safely express their opinions about the situations they are dramatizing and safely try out new solutions to problems.

My own experience indicates that low-income people make an exceptionally positive response to role-play technology. For one thing it is physical, action-oriented. It is *do* vs. *talk*, and low-income people tend to work out mental problems best when they can do things physically.

The verbal performance of deprived children improves markedly in the discussion period following a role-playing session. Ask a juvenile delinquent who comes from a disadvantaged background what he doesn't like about school or the teacher, and you will get an abbreviated, inarticulate reply. But have a group of these youngsters act out a school scene in which someone plays the teacher, and you will start a stream of verbal consciousness that is almost impossible to shut off.

Role playing can have various beneficial results in the teaching of academic material in the school. If an inquiring student should wonder, for example, what Abraham Lincoln would think of our present civil rights policy, let "Lincoln" and "President Lyndon Johnson" stage a debate! The impossibilities of time and space are eliminated, and the civics lesson will be well-remembered.

The second technique I am recommending here—the careful use of "hip" language, sometimes combined with role playing—can be highly effective in teaching the disadvantaged. An article in the Syracuse, N.Y., *Herald-Journal* last November told how such a combination was put to good use in a ninth-grade English class at Madison Junior High School, which is participating in a program for the disadvantaged called the Madison Area Project.

A teacher had complained to Gerald Weinstein, the project curriculum coordinator, that her students "practically fell asleep" when she read a poem titled "The Magic Carpet" from a standard anthology. Weinstein went to the class armed with copies of the poem "Motto," by the Negro writer, Langston Hughes. It goes:

> *I play it cool and dig all jive.*
> *That's the reason I stay alive.*
> *My motto, as I live and learn*
> *Is: Dig and be dug in return.*

The students read the poem. After a long moment of silence— "Hey, Mr. Weinstein, this cat is pretty cool."

"It's written in our talk."

Discussion centered on the phrase "dig all jive." Weinstein asked the students how many kinds of jive they understood. They claimed that of course they understood all kinds, but when he launched into an abstract essay on the nature of truth, using all the big words he could find, they looked blank.

He asked them to try him with their jive. They threw six expressions at him, and he got five. "According to Hughes, who has the better chance of staying alive?" Weinstein asked, "You or I?" The class had to concede that he did because he dug more than one kind of jive.

The enthusiasm of that class session led the students into more of Hughes' poetry. Later they moved into other kinds of literature in more conventional language.

But the students, the newspaper article pointed out, were not the only ones learning from that exciting class. Weinstein learned, too. He learned the advantage of being familiar with the language of the children he was teaching, the advantage of establishing rapport with them.

I am not suggesting that teachers employ "hip" language in normal conversation with the underprivileged youngster, as a device for attempting to be friendly with the child. This would indeed be patronizing and dangerous. But the use of hip material in a *formal lesson plan* can become an excellent avenue to the style and interests of the disadvantaged.

There is great need for curriculum materials for use with disadvantaged youngsters. Both the Bank Street College of Education in New York City, through its proposed Educational Resources Center, and New York's Mobilization for Youth project have been developing laboratories in which such materials are created and tested.

Such laboratories should be closely related to the federally supported teacher institutes and should contain not only materials but also reports and films of positive experiments in the teaching of the disadvantaged.

The project conducted by Superintendent Samuel Shepard in the Banneker District of St. Louis is especially noteworthy as an experiment of this sort. He has demonstrated that disadvantaged youngsters at the elementary and junior high school levels can be quickly raised to their proper grade level. More comprehensive efforts than Shepard's might produce even more startling results.

Finally, teaching style—

We tend to assume that good teachers ought to be healthy, well-adjusted people. I am not sure it is that simple. I am not suggesting, of course, that we look for sick people and make them into teachers. I am suggesting that we think about the development of individual teacher style and that some of these individual styles may have significant non-healthy components.

In visits to schools in over 35 cities I have found at least one teacher in each school who according to all—children, parents, colleagues, and administrators—was a "good" teacher. These teachers differed vastly from one another in method and point of view. What I am saying is that there is no one best style.

Teachers attending NDEA institutes should have opportunities to observe teachers using various effective styles and to see films of them in action. They should even role play the classroom, the different problems that arise, the discipline problem, the disorder problem. Out of this role play, each will develop his own repertoire.

Only as he works at it—through such methods and procedures as I have suggested here—can a teacher learn to meet the disadvantaged on their own ground. And only as we meet them on their own ground can we hope to realize the contribution which, as I said at the start, the disadvantaged can make to our schools, our middle class, and society.

MANY DISADVANTAGED YOUNGSTERS SEEM BEYOND THE TOUCH OF education by the time they reach adolescence. Many have by then run afoul of our community rules for living and are more involved with policemen than with teachers. A unique research project reported by Ralph Schwitzgebel, in his book, *Street-corner Research*, published by the Harvard University Press in 1964, sought new research techniques suitable for juvenile delinquents.[8] The experimenters literally made contact with their subjects on streetcorners and offered to pay them by the hour to come to the laboratory and talk into tape recorders. They were free to talk about anything and everything. The lines between research, psychotherapy, and education soon became thin as these boys revealed more and more of themselves and thereby started on a difficult course of learning.

Schwitzgebel describes one boy, whom he calls Bill, who decided that he wanted to earn easy money by talking into a microphone. During his first session he tried to convince his prospective employers that he was qualified for the job by discussing his memories of reform school.

BILL: Yea. This other boy I was rooming with, he was a real brain, you know. Cause I was pretty smart but he was a brain. He could make keys to fit coke machines, paper machines, we'd just clean up on it, we had it knocked, break into parking meters, things like that . . .

During his fourth session with the tape recorder he described an experience from "back home."

I cut him from his navel around to his back. He was down on his knees yelling, "Help me, help me." I turned around and I just had to laugh—I don't know why. The next morning I read about it in the paper. I don't know why, but whenever I see something like that I have to laugh. Like if someone would fall out of that window, or whenever I see a wreck it's funny.

During his forty-third meeting with the tape recorder Bill said:

This is my happiest day in Massachusetts. This is the happiest day, the last thirty minutes is the happiest day in Boston or I could say in my life, I don't know. Because I can explain all of it. And, I left the house, and I wasn't, I wasn't thinking about it; I really wasn't, I wasn't thinking about it; and I started looking at people, I started looking at people and places. I looked at the cleaners, of

8. Reprinted by permission of the publishers. Copyright, 1964, by the President and Fellows of Harvard College.

how the guy was making his living. I looked at the car lots of how the people were making the easy buck off of cars. I looked at a man who was petting a cat. The guy was petting the cat. He looked like he didn't have a care in the world—probably had a thousand. I looked at the empty buildings that were businesses and I thought, said to myself that guy didn't make it here, I says, but I bet he went somewhere else and tried again. And I, I looked at all the businesses and all the people and I thought to myself. They made it and they didn't give up. And I walked along, and I think I reached two blocks down the street and I started crying. Happy tears, really happy tears! . . .

I saw the people that work in the factories, I saw the guys that had wives and I saw how happy they were and I knew, I felt how much trouble they had, and I felt like I could help them and I helped a dozen, at least twelve people I know with a smile. I smiled at them and they smiled back. I looked at the car lots, and the guys that were making the easy dollar on the car lots and I thought how much they went through to get there. And I told you I looked at buildings that were empty that they went somewhere else where they could make it . . .

And I want to tell you something that, that I never thought would happen to me. It feels great to be guilty; it feels great to be guilty and care for people. It really feels great to feel guilty, to, to know that I've hurt people so much and that I want to unhurt them and never hurt anybody else. And it feels great to be sorry for other people, and it feels great to be sorry for myself. Because, you remember the time that I, that I was downhearted and everything. That, that, those four days hurt me worse than I think ten years in prison could do. And I know you can. This thing is, is happening to me, and, and its something I, I'm not going to miss out on. I'm smart enough and I want to and I feel it and it's, it's something I pray for, that I, that I won't miss out on. It's something I love. This, to me, is more exciting; this is the excitement, this is the thing I've been looking for all my life. That's what I feel. The thing I've missed out on is to find myself and care and feel guilty and pray and, and not hurt anybody . . . But this is the only really good thing that's ever happened to me. And it's pushing me, it's pushing me, it's behind me, it's around me, it's in front of me, on top of me, on bottom, it's pushing me on as nothing has ever done before . . .

THIS DISADVANTAGED YOUNGSTER IS UNUSUALLY ARTICULATE IN explaining his thinking and feeling. His experiences in school apparently hardly touched him, though he surely was exposed to spelling, geography, arithmetic, social studies, and other areas of the traditional curriculum. His formal education was of little use to him and his transition in this unique research project suggests why. It is likely that the formal school experience was not well related to him and to his life as he understood it.

Failures of the educational system to meet the needs of the disadvantaged youngster are contributing to a rich variety of re-educational programs springing up everywhere these days. A fascinating one is reported in the MIND Monograph No. 2, published by the National Association of Manufacturers. The report is entitled "Industry and the Dropout: An industrial experiment in basic education at the National Association of Manufacturers" and is written by Charles F. Adams, Director of MIND, Dr. Sam Ball, of Columbia University, Dr. R. Lee Henney, of the Board for Fundamental Education, and Samaria Kimball, who is a research associate at MIND.[9]

The executive summary states:

On November 11, 1965, a six-week Basic Education Laboratory was begun in the MIND Project at the corporate headquarters of the National Association of Manufacturers, 277 Park Avenue, New York City.

Seven Negro and Puerto Rican high school dropouts were accepted to pursue a highly accelerated course in reading, writing, and arithmetic to discover:

1. whether or not such a training system could attract and hold selected high school dropouts;

2. how efficient the system might be; and

3. whether or not such a training system might be integrated economically with the profit-making structure of American business for solving industrial manpower problems.

Within six weeks the trainees averaged 2 to $3^{1}/_{2}$ grade level increases in word meaning, arithmetic computation, and oral reading ability. Significant and positive attitudinal changes were also observed.

Although the trainees had no visible means of support, they were not compensated for attendance, carfare, or lunch. The program

9. Excerpts reprinted by permission of the publisher.

was completely voluntary with no employment guarantees being given by the sponsoring organization or the trainees.

It appears, at present, that an instructional system designed to escalate the basic communications and arithmetic skills of under-educated adults rapidly and at a very modest cost could easily be integrated with the profit objective in America's business environment, and go far toward solving many industrial and social manpower problems. Additional laboratories are presently in session to document the feasibility of such a program.

This monograph was written to be of interest to the businessman and interested layman as well as to the teacher, the scholar, or the educational researcher.

ONE GETS A VERY GOOD FEEL FOR HOW THE TRAINING SESSIONS went from the teacher's description. (It appears here in condensed form.) Though she professes no qualifications as a teacher, many professionals will read her account with envy.

Classes were scheduled to start at the NAM on Tuesday, November 11, 1965. One of the first problems a trainer faces is the fact that the students might not show up at all. Many potential students had promised to come to recruiting sessions and had failed to do so. Suspicion of all white people, another academic failure, and the location of the National Association of Manufacturers far away from the familiar surroundings of Harlem or the Bronx were dominant influences on their behavior, I later learned from my students. This feeling of fear on my part lasted throughout the project as I rapidly learned that security is a luxury when working with this target population.

We had deliberately set the hours of instruction to correspond with the working hours of the personnel at the NAM so that the trainees would develop the discipline of getting to work on time. We had a time sheet posted on the wall of the classroom so the students could sign in and out each day.

Most of the students arrived before 9:00 A.M. the first day of the class. One did not come at all because his mother forgot to wake him up. She "did not think it was important for him to be on time" or present every day.

There were several steps we had agreed upon in consultation in forming a learning team which I carried out the first day of class. The first was to greet every person at the door when he arrived for class and show him where to hang his coat. Many of the men had not been in a large Manhattan office building before; and, as many people concede, the first visit is a frightening experience. Upon meeting each person I introduced myself again (they had already met me during recruiting) and introduced them to the others who had already arrived.

The seating arrangement in the room was pre-arranged. We all sat around a table so that we could face one another. There were reasons for doing this. Everyone who was in the class had failed in most of their prior educational experiences. They had very definite ideas about teachers, and the ideas were not positive. Previously the teacher had always been a symbol of authority. The traditional classroom presented rows of seats facing the authority figure in the front of the room. The student had to decide how he was to bridge that gap. If he approached the desk with too much familiarity, he was called "teachers pet" by his peer group. Some students rarely work up enough nerve to even attempt this because they are afraid of being humiliated in front of their peers. Therefore, by not having a teacher's desk in the classroom every one is seated on an "equal basis."

The second reason for this seating arrangement was the need to present a setting that was different in appearance from the traditional classroom in which they had failed and to accomplish what we later described as "teaching by exposure and observation." We felt that by conducting classes at the NAM offices and having a "conference room" arrangement, the young men would become aware of what would be expected of a person on a job. The students came in daily contact with the office staff and administrative officials of the NAM. They observed how they dressed, noticed their behavior toward each other and their work. They were learning what the industrial environment was all about.

Besides avoiding the prominence of the authority figure and the appearance of a traditional classroom arrangement, the physical arrangement gave the men an opportunity for eye contact and face-to-face conversation when speaking in class. They did not have the experience in this learning situation of only seeing the back of the head of the student in front of them.

After everyone had arrived, I began to explain to them what objectives we hoped to accomplish. "This class is being held to increase your skills in reading, writing and arithmetic. This is your classroom and you will make all final decisions as to who does or does not come into the room. You are free to come and go as you please. You are not required to attend any more than you would be required to go to work. However, you will not learn as much if you miss class just as you would not get paid if you did not go to work. This is your program, and you are responsible for its success.

"I am Miss Samaria Kimball, and I hope that you will call me Sam. I have never taught a class before and have not been trained as a teacher who would be qualified to teach in the public school system. Consequently, we will be going through this together; and I will learn as much from you as you do from me. This is a co-operative adventure. You have had experiences that I haven't had. We are going to share experiences with one another. We will all be teachers, and we will all be students. If you know something another doesn't know, you will be responsible for helping him. You are not going to be graded. All tests will be for your own information so that you will be able to see how much and how rapidly you are advancing. We are going to start where the tests, which you have already taken, indicate you should start. We are not going to leave anyone behind, but those of us who are better in some things will help those who have not learned them. Does this sound all right?"

Student A asked again if the trainees were to be paid. I replied negatively. There was little further comment so I continued.

"So far this morning I have done all of the talking. Now it is your turn. You know, every time I get with a group I like to know the person sitting next to me. I am sure you would like to know something about the person sitting next to you. Therefore, would you take the next fifteen minutes and interview the person next to you. By 'interview' I mean ask him his name, where he lives, what he likes to do, what his hobbies are, and why he came to this class. All right? Interview the person sitting next to you if you like; and, after you have finished, you can introduce that person to the rest of us."

There were several reasons for using this interviewing technique. It was of primary importance that an individual have a social and psychological success during the first class meeting so that he would return. A person is more hesitant about getting up and talking about himself to a group than he would be responding to questions from one individual. The interview enabled the person to find out more than just the name of the person sitting next to him. It was designed to let the person ask him questions and find out things about the other participants so that some peer group recognition could form. It enabled the students to know that they were all facing similar problems. It is often very difficult to admit to oneself, let alone others, that you are not adept at basic reading, writing, and arithmetic. I think this was demonstrated on the tapes where the students were talking about being "just rusty" in these skills. . . .

This method also gives the trainer the chance to find out some of the reasons the students came to the class so she will know whether or not the class, as it stands, is going to fulfill the objectives of the students. In this situation I did not have to ask them why they were here because they were asking each other.

After 30 minutes had elapsed there were two voices dominating the conversation—Student A and Student D. The other men were listening to them. I turned around and faced the class, and everyone immediately became silent.

I asked them if they had learned anything about the person next to them. They all indicated they had by either shaking their head or with a gesture of their hand. I asked Student A to introduce Student B to the group. I deliberately selected Student A to go first since he had been the one who seemed more sure of himself than any of the rest. He had talked a great deal before the class began.

In a tone of formality that was entirely foreign to his apparent nature Student A said, "I would like to introduce Mr. (Student B) who lives in the West end of that section of this place called Harlem. Mr. (Student B) likes to play basketball and likes to take out girls. He belongs to the Young Life group in Harlem and came to this class because he wants to learn more so he can go into I.B.M. machine operator training. He left school after he had done three terms of high school because he wasn't learning anything. I thank you." There was general laughter around the table. I said thank you and asked Student B to introduce Student A.

Student B did not know where to start, and he did not start. I asked him what Student A's name was and where he lived. He talked in a very soft tone, apparently afraid that he was going to make a mistake. He did say that Student A lived in the North part of Harlem and that he liked all types of sports. He told us that Student A had a job once in a "nice big office building" but left it to go back to school. He never got back to school because it was too much trouble. He came to this class because he didn't have anything better to do with his time.

We carried on around the table with the men getting more open about talking about each other. They would make comments about the introductions and began to warm up to the situation. The tension which had preceded the opening of the class had given way to a relaxed type of verbal exchange about how they had been treated in school and what was wrong with the school system.

It was about noon by the time we had finished the interviews. I mentioned this to the group to see if they wanted to break for lunch or go on to the next part of the class. As was going to happen for the next few days, Student D took the floor and made an elaborate presentation saying that he had come here to learn, that all they had accomplished to this point was talk, and that he didn't even know what the class was all about yet. Therefore, he thought that I should at least tell them what they were going to do so they could decide whether or not they wanted to stay. This speech seemed to impress the rest of the group so I tried to explain again.

I said that the class had been set up so that they could learn to read, write, spell, and work math problems well enough to pass entrance tests for company training programs or jobs. The class was to help them prepare themselves to enter the labor market.

Student D interrupted me at this point and asked, "What's your game? Why are you doing this and what does this organization get out of it?" Here I began to get a picture of what they thought about all programs. No one does anything without getting something out of it, and they wanted to know our "angle."

It had taken a lot of courage for them to come to the class in the first place because they were strangers to the NAM and to each other. I decided at this point to be very truthful with them. "We have no game. Many people in our society say that you people do not want to learn and that you are too stupid to learn. They also feel that you would rather live on welfare than go out and make an honest living like everyone else has to do. They feel that you are lazy and no good. We think that you want to learn, that you want to get jobs and be self-supporting, and make something out of yourselves. Therefore, we decided to offer this course to give you an opportunity to show people that you will come to a learning situation and that you will stay in it even if you are not paid because of your desire to learn and make something of yourselves. Are we right in assuming that you do want to learn and get a job?" The class was very much in agreement that this is what they wanted and that it would be good to have this experience. However, the suspicious attitude remained with the class for the first week.

· · ·

The weekend came, and everyone showed up for class on Monday. I felt that the class was going very well. We had perfect attendance that week. Student D announced to the class that he had spent Saturday and Sunday looking at his book. "I couldn't seem to put it down. That's the first time that ever happened to me," he said. Students A and F brought newspapers to class. Student C, who was at a higher beginning level than the rest of them, was getting bored. However, it was soon convenient for him to be the leader of the group for reading; and he became quite involved in teaching the others.

During this week, part of a taped discussion made by the trainees was on how they had made their living before they entered the class. Whether or not the statements made in this discussion are completely accurate, they do give a clue as to the attitude the men had about life. They seem to consider only themselves and their families. With the exception of one student, all seemed to be very close to their families.

This family relationship was exemplified by Student F when he said that he did not drink, smoke or use drugs because his mother would kill him if she ever caught him doing anything like that. Student E also indicated that the family was meaningful when he described his situation: he was the oldest member of a large family; a four-month-old baby was left to the care of her brothers and sisters; the father was of no use in the house because he was continually drunk; and the mother was in the hospital with a nervous breakdown. Student E's main concern was that the baby get the right things to eat. The rest of the group got support from their homes even though it was sometimes negative support. I asked Student B what his parents thought of his being in the Project. He said, "They like it O.K."; but his mother said he would "drop out of it like he did everything else." Student B did not drop out of the Program. He later accepted a position on the MIND staff as a Project Assistant (teacher) for BEELAB-III.

Everything was going very well in the class. All the men were coming to class on time and working very hard. They were proud that they could get the spelling words right; and there was evidence that they were studying at home at night, an activity that was not required.

Since a section of *System for Success* covered material on the Air Force, I asked the students if they would like to have some Air Force recruiters come and speak to them. They all agreed, so I scheduled it for the following day. There was very little interest in the lecture, and one student slept throughout the entire presentation. The class froze when they were allowed to ask questions. This was the first time an outsider had entered the room since the beginning of the program. When the students did respond there was a general lack of courtesy. The recruiters were discussing the advantages of the military, and Student D responded with, "Yeah, like Viet Nam." Since I was not playing the role of an authority figure, I sat, smoked furiously, and stared at the wall hoping circumstances would never force me to seek employment with the Air Force after this episode.

• • •

One December day, we found that a stop watch was missing. It had been on the table in the room; and, when the men left, it was gone. We had people who would steal. However, I had known this before class ever started. Three of the men had police records, and they had made no bones about telling us this was partly how they had stayed alive. I had never thought very much about it, really. Coming from a small Western town where a person seldom thinks about theft, I habitually left my purse lying around and had never missed a penny.

The next day the stop watch reappeared in the room. It had been "picked up by accident." That was the only thing that was ever missing through the entire course. The man who had borrowed the stop watch told another member of the MIND staff that he had "used it," and he did not want to let me know that he had used it.

During the NAM's Annual Congress of American Industry at the Waldorf-Astoria, we had the opportunity to see astronaut John Glenn. However, the men chose to stay in the class and study. They decided that they would rather not miss their spelling test and math lesson. Strange decisions!

That afternoon we went to the Waldorf-Astoria to see an oceanography show. The men were afraid to go but were extremely courteous to me and the people to whom they were introduced after we got there. Their dress and manners had improved a great deal since the beginning of the class. Student A had said that he always dressed in his jeans and a tee shirt and was not going to change just because he was coming up to this "big ass" building. He was now in pressed slacks and a sweater. It was becoming apparent that peer pressure and individual pride was having an effect on the men's conduct, conversation, and dress. This was the greatest success that was brought about during the program. The general attitude towards life was forming, and they could see that *something* they were doing was effective. Student B reported that even his mother had become interested in the project. He would take his book home and talk with her about what was happening. He was having real communication with her for the first time in his life. He was also doing something successful and staying with the program, which was a new experience for him.

The season for colds came, and we started to pass a virus around the room. I was buying aspirin for myself and the group, but three of the men had been out two days. We were moving slowly. We went to hear Richard Nixon speak, again at the NAM's annual event at the Waldorf; and the men on their own went up, shook hands with him, and told him it had been a wonderful speech. I stood in awe of them since this behavior had been unsolicited by me. I would have been terrified to do it myself.

•   •   •

The curriculum had been completed by the last week of December. We decided that December 29th would be the date for post-instruction tests. Class was nearing an end. I was delighted at the results as far as the people were concerned. What had entered as bitter, hostile men were now anxious, part-time gentlemen who talked of employment and future education. They wanted to go to work. We had told them at the beginning of the course that we would only direct them to places where they could put in their applications. We were not going to find jobs for them.

•   •   •

We filled out work history forms and typed them up so that the men could have something to take with them as they started to seek employment. It was a different group of men that returned on Wednesday to take the final test than the group who had arrived on November 11. I concluded, as I had felt all of the time, that, if given an opportunity to learn, these men, the "outcasts" of society, would come to a learning situation, would attend on their own, and would find their own means of maintaining themselves in the program. It has been an exciting and rewarding experience. My vocabulary has increased one-hundred fold. Perhaps it is fortunate that I cannot share it with you on the printed page.

THE EDUCATION OF THE DISADVANTAGED IS A RELATIVELY NEW business. Not that disadvantaged students are new, but our attempts to find special ways to help them gain a useful education are relatively new.

Will the public school ever be a place where *all* children can learn? Must all children use the teacher's dialect in order to communicate or can teachers meet them part way by making use of the child's dialect? Will Project Head Start make lower-class children into junior-middle-class children who are then suitable for the kind of school we know how to teach? Can school be a place where "advantaged" children learn something worthwhile from "disadvantaged" children? Can we, as educators, adjust to more casual attitudes about punctuality and the virtue of neatness? Must our students dress as we do (with neckties or white blouse)? Can a teacher appear in a classroom in a sweatshirt and still promote learning?

We have done an increasingly better job of finding customers who thrive on the educational food we serve but now we are beginning to realize that we must do a better job of preparing foods that will satisfy all our customers. In this country we are dedicated to the ideal of education for all. That means many customers and it means many different kinds of customers. It's going to mean a very interesting search for a widely varied menu.

CHAPTER 2

Intelligence

THE CONCEPT OF INTELLIGENCE AND THE CULTURAL CASTE MARK OF IQ are currently caught in the tides of controversy. We humans have always been interested in finding out which children have what talents. We are anxious to find the talent, polish it, and refine it, so that it may be used to the advantage of the future community. One of our difficulties now is that in today's rapidly changing world it is hard to say what talents will be useful in the next generation or even in the next decade. We can no longer simply select children who we think will do well in school because we are questioning whether the school is doing well. We suspect that some talents our schools have been polishing will prove useless in the years ahead, while other needed talents are being neglected. To complicate matters further, we now suspect that we have even done a poor job of selecting those children with potential to do well in the kind of schools that we have today.

When the New York City Board of Education decided to abandon group intelligence testing, the repercussions were felt at the farthest borders of our nation and beyond. Joseph O. Loretan, of the Board of Education of New York City, carefully explained the reasons behind the move in an article called "The Decline and Fall of Group Intelligence Testing," published in the October, 1965, issue of *Teachers College Record*.[1] The article is reprinted here in full.

The validity of the group intelligence test, used extensively all over the nation, is being widely questioned; and New York City, with the largest public school system in the country, has recently discontinued its use. Although the concept of the IQ has long been taken for granted, it is actually only within the last four decades that intellectual development has been measured by group tests.

Traditionally, individual teachers bore the responsibility for assessing their own students' mental characteristics as they watched them struggle to accomplish assigned tasks and saw how some succeeded and some did not. Their judgments were based on observation; and, although they sometimes miscalculated, one teacher's assessment could always be balanced against another's, and great damage was seldom done.

Then, early in this century science intervened with new ideas about the measurement of intellectual development. In 1904, Alfred Binet was appointed to a commission in the city of Paris which had been asked to recommend methods of picking out mentally incapable schoolchildren. He had worked out some tasks that middle class children could be expected to perform routinely. They included such activities as buttoning clothes, obeying simple commands and copying simple drawings, knowing left from right. On the basis of his observations of individual children set to such tasks, he came to some tentative conclusions about the comparative development of intellect. These, coupled with an interest in psychometrics, led him to devise the first "measurement of intelligence" instrument.

But "intelligence," for Binet, was educable. "A child's mind," he wrote, "is like a field for which an expert farmer has advised a change in the method of cultivating, with the result that in place of desert land we now have a harvest. It is in this particular sense, the one that is significant, that we say that the intelligence of children may be increased. One increases that which constitutes the intelligence of a school child, namely, the capacity to learn, to improve with instruction" (6).

Binet's testing procedures survived, but not his belief that what was being measured was educable. James McKeen Cattell, Henry Goddard, and Lewis Terman, concerned with either retarded or

---

1. Reprinted with permission of *Teachers College Record* and the author.

gifted children, took the tasks developed by Binet and incorporated them into the instrument we have been using for forty years. Binet's notion of "a field of cultivation" was completely reversed in the textbooks on measurement written after the development of the Stanford-Binet test in 1916.

The textbook writers tended to the view that the IQ was to be considered a constant, since, in each individual case, intelligence was conceived to be fixed. By intelligence, psychologists suggested, they understood "inborn, all round intellectual ability" (9), an inherited, general mental quality susceptible to accurate and easy measurement. Almost universally, the popular press and the parents and teachers of America began speaking of intelligence as something children possessed in fairly fixed amounts.

GROUP TESTING BEGINS

The advent of the group test was what led to the greatest misconceptions. The group IQ test was descended from Binet's individual test; but, unlike a biological descendant, it possessed few of its ancestor's characteristics. Modified by psychologists at Columbia, Stanford, and Chicago, it was intended for low-cost use in various-sized groups, since individual testing was (and is) prohibitive in terms of time, personnel and expense. The test-makers, it is true, were men of good conscience; and care was taken to preserve as many as possible of the aspects of the individually administered test. The first group mental ability tests, in fact, took four hours to administer and included many of the elements of the original individual test. But even the most enthusiastic proponents of the four hour device realized that four hours were too much for youngsters in classroom situations. So the test was whittled away until it was reduced to one that could be administered in forty-five minutes.

In such a brief span, then, a youngster is tested on verbal meanings, spatial concepts, reasoning, number concepts, and word fluency. He is subjected to this, moreover, at whatever time is administratively convenient for his particular school system. The test is usually administered to him by a teacher untrained in testing, whose only qualification is the ability to read the "Directions to Teachers" on the first page of the manual.

By these means, he is identified, labelled, classified, and placed, more often than not, in a class with youngsters of "equal ability." As more than one teacher has said, "Once you know the child's IQ, you tend to see him through it, and you adjust your teaching to his ability or level of intelligence—as revealed by the test." In this manner, the IQ becomes a self-fulfilling prophecy to a child as well as a teacher. It begins to signify something "given," as if it were a part of the body; and, too often, it is taken to be a clue to what a child is "worth." The effect of this on the initiative of teachers and the self-images of children is appalling to contemplate. What is even worse, the general public seems to think that the IQ means the brain power a person was born with, and that nothing can be done about it in future life.

Yet we know through experience that the IQ score is not unchanging. Glenn Heathers, Director of the New York University Experimental Center, states that some children's IQs may vary as much as 40 points from one period of their lives to another. This was dramatically demonstrated in the New York City Demonstration Guidance Project not long ago. Children who were in the project from 1956–59 gained an average of 8 points in IQ. Those in the project from 1957–60 gained an average of 15 points. The range was from a gain of 5 points to 40 points.

Study after study is proving that the IQ can be elevated with good teaching and increased student motivation, for all the fact that many people still consider the IQ score to be stable and predictive. Henry C. Dyer, a recognized expert in testing, writes that ". . . the 'IQ,' which is a type of derived score attached to intelligence tests, is now generally frowned upon by experts in measurement because the assumption on which it rests differs from one test to another and from one standardization group to another. The common meaning it appears to have across tests and populations is quite unreal and misleading" (4). Kenneth Clark, psychologist at City College of the City University of New York, says that IQs based on the usual group tests "are worse than meaningless; they are misleading." He goes on to explain that an IQ score is meaningful only under controlled conditions "of individual testing by a specially trained psychologist who can draw out the best in a child and who can remain sensitive to the level of the child's motivation during testing."

When one looks at studies of the distribution of intelligence, as measured by group tests, one finds that only five to ten per cent of America's students rank as "superior." If this is so, the chances of national survival are slim. But, in reality, we have never learned to recognize or develop more than a portion of the potential in this country because we have imposed strait-jackets through our measurement devices, set limits, sat in judgment.

ON CAPACITY AND ACHIEVEMENT

Consider the observation made in the HARYOU report to the United States Office of Education: that median IQs dropped 4 points from grade 3 to grade 6 in 25 Central Harlem schools. What inferences ought to be drawn from this? Can it be that, the longer some children stay in school, the "less intelligent" they become? Or can it mean that we are simply testing achievement with respect to a narrow range of abilities?

Chauncey and Dobbin, in a recent book (2), state that intelligence tests only measure *capacity for learning.* They do not measure latent intelligence, nor do they trick people into revealing how much brilliance or stupidity they possess. The basic idea of an intelligence test is that of the "work-sample," since it confronts a student with tasks (or standard jobs) on which he can demonstrate his skills and then compares his work with that of others who have been set to the same tasks.

In addition, they can only measure mental ability, not in terms of some inborn power but in terms of something already learned. ". . . even though 'native intelligence' is suspected to exist, the intelligence tests we use" can only measure "a developed ability in which the innate ability and learned behavior are mixed in unknown proportions." Moreover, the writers go on to say, intelligence tests provide *comparative* estimates of learning capacity, rather than measures of capacity in absolute units.

Although similar in concept, intelligence tests tend to differ from publisher to publisher; and different types of ability may be associated with intelligence in different schools. Nevertheless, the tasks on which children's skills are tested tend always to be those most appropriate for children in an "average" cultural environment; and they are almost always "schoolish," if not "bookish" in nature.

Recent research, like J. P. Guilford's on the specific abilities required for scientific research, and Jacob Getzels' on creativity, indicates clearly that the abilities commonly measured do not include the ability to think of original scientific solutions, nor do they include the skill of "divergent thinking" which creative people characteristically possess. With considerable justification, Robert L. Ebel of Michigan State University has pointed to the danger associated with the use of a single test or test battery in selective admission procedures and in awards of scholarships. This may foster, he says, "an undesirably narrow conception of ability and thus tend to reduce diversity in the talents available to a school or to society" (5).

Important as verbal and quantitative skills may be, Dr. Ebel suggests, "they do not encompass all phases of achievement." It is operationally simpler to use "a common yardstick" for all students, but overemphasis on the single test may well lead educators "to neglect those students whose special talents lie outside the common core."

THE USES OF ACHIEVEMENT TESTS

Having found +.80 correlations between high school grades and freshman college grades in a study conducted for the Educational Records Bureau, Geraldine Spaulding concluded that there was considerable evidence for the stability of student grades throughout four years of high school, and that a high correlation exists even between ninth year grades and college freshman grades. Studies such as hers suggest the possibility of longitudinal studies based upon school grades supported by standardized achievement tests (11).

Benjamin Bloom, in a recent book (1), writes of "correlations as high as +.83 between high school grades and college grades (scaled), with the average correlation being approximately +.78." The evidence seems to be reliable enough to suggest the use of school grades as a "measure of academic prediction," when further longitudinal evaluations are made.

Another possible measure is to be found in standardized achievement tests like those reported by Learned and Wood (8). Again, high correlations were found between the results of tests at the end of the 14th and 16th years of school. Similar results were reported by Lanholm (7), after giving the General Education portion of the Graduate Record Examination to 1,000 college students when they were sophomores and again when they were seniors. Where elementary and secondary school students are concerned, there are studies like those of A. E. Traxler (12), who gave reading comprehension tests to 7th grade students in four schools and repeated the tests in the 12th grade with a correlation of +.85. D. P. Scannel (10) conducted Iowa Tests of Basic Skills in the 4th, 6th and 8th grades and gave the Iowa Tests of Educational Development to the same students in the 9th and 12th grades. Again the correlation (between, for example, the scores at the 4th and 12th grades) was high.

As Vaughan J. Crandall reports (3), achievement behaviors tend to be consistent across situations and time; and evidence of achievement efforts during elementary school age and early adolescence tends to be predictive of adult behavior. Also, achievement testing combined with teacher judgment have the value of showing continuing growth. The student has the opportunity to compare himself against an achievement test mark—and move up from where he started, if he can. Unlike IQ tests, achievement tests offer hope for improvement and serve as starting lines, not limits or goals. There is considerable agreement among teachers as well as psychologists that, as Kurt Lewin once pointed out, successful goal striving renews motivation for more striving.

INNOVATION IN NEW YORK

New York City has initiated a comprehensive program of achievement testing to supplement class grades. Not only is there substantial evidence that, with appropriate help, achievement scores tend to soar; there is the sense that the new programs may counteract the fatalism fed by beliefs of inherent inferiority, based on misinterpretations of the meaning of the IQ.

Beginning in September, 1964, reading tests have been administered to every grade from the 2nd to the 10th. Achievement batteries are planned for three points in each pupil's educational career, in grades 3, 6, and 9. Mathematics tests are to be given in grades 2, 3, 6, and 8. The following skills are to be repeatedly tested: spelling, capitalization, punctuation, usage, map-reading, graphs and tables, reference tables, arithmetic concepts, and problem-solving, constituting a range of abilities considerably wider than those traditionally tested by IQ group tests.

In the spirit of this new approach, an action research project has been undertaken and is being conducted cooperatively by the New York City School System and the Educational Testing Service. The project deals with the problem of assessing the intellectual ability of young children; and 2,250 first graders in 25 schools are involved. It grew out of the conviction of the author and Henry Chauncey, President of ETS, that teachers' judgments would be more reliable than group IQ testing in gauging diverse first graders' intellectual ability, especially if certain guidelines were established, and if the judgments were supplemented by achievement testing.

It was thought necessary to show teachers *how* to assess their pupils' intellectual development on the basis of observations in the classroom; and a variety of principles were developed. Teachers were provided with sensible guides to observation, so as to know precisely what to watch for; and a few ground rules were defined for recording and interpreting the observations made.

Equally significant was the structuring of a theoretical model or point of view. A unifying theory does not have to be totally or uncritically accepted to benefit a project of this sort; but there are great advantages in using a single model as a set of working assumptions, so that the project can proceed "all of a piece" rather than as a series of unrelated activities.

The source of the model was largely discovered in the now familiar work of Jean Piaget, modified by ETS staff members and by relevant observations of such psychologists as Jerome Bruner, J. P. Guilford, and others. The three basic assumptions are (1) that intelligence is mostly acquired in a sequence of stages which is about the same for every individual; (2) that it is acquired through interaction between the child and his environment; and (3) that it is revealed by the child's behavior—to the person who knows what to look for.

The first step in putting a theory to work in education is to translate it into terms which can be used by teachers; and the logical starting point for our project was found in the work of Jean Piaget himself. If, it was asked, the working assumptions are tentatively considered to be true, what are the behavioral clues to intellectual development to be used by the first grade teacher in improving his or her understanding of the individual child? The answer had to satisfy two criteria: each clue was to have a demonstrable connection with the child's intellectual development and each clue taken was to be a kind of behavior potentially visible to the teacher who knew what to look for.

Specific descriptions of behavioral clues to intellect among children between five and seven were drawn from the research observations of Piaget, Guilford, Bruner, and others. Contemporary empiricists like these men, no matter how their observations are phrased, always describe development in terms of behavior, or in terms of what the child *does* that is visible to someone else. Those concerned with the project were able to mine a rich vein of research into the nature of intellect and the evidence of learning, and to compile a list of behavioral "signs" of intellect as observed by many professional researchers. This list was called the "researchers' list" of clues to intellect.

TEACHERS' CONTRIBUTIONS

The second source was the primary grade teacher. The project team, an ETS staff, and a headquarters "task force" consulted 75 teachers in 25 New York City elementary schools and asked them about the behavioral signs of intellect they could see in their classrooms. After being given an explanation of the project, each teacher was encouraged to talk about specific occasions when particular children, by their behavior, provided insights into their intellectual development. Occasionally, two or three teachers meeting together would recall behavioral clues provided by the same child, filling out a rounded picture of an intellectually able child. All those interviewed were asked to do all their describing in terms of behavior and to concentrate on positive, not negative clues to intellect.

The candor and thoughtfulness of the teachers interviewed may be suggested by the following:

Teacher A: "Juan seldom speaks in class, apparently doesn't know much English, and will fall out of the bottom of the readiness tests, BUT . . . he can take the right bus to get him across town with the laundry, work all the right buttons in the laundromat, and go home again on the bus in rush hour. No matter what the IQ tests show, Juan is a bright six year old in my book!"

Teacher B: "Grace can't or won't do much in language or arithmetic, but in art she reveals perceptions and understandings that would be a credit to a child twice her age."

Teacher C: "If children at this age can communicate well— with each other and with me—I suspect they are pretty bright. Not all the bright ones can communicate, of course, but all the good communicators seem better to me than average in mental alertness."

Hundreds of behavioral clues were gathered from these conversations with teachers. Each suggestion was written on a card immediately after each session with a teacher; and no attempt was made to eliminate duplication until all the material had been gathered.

When the teachers' suggestions were finally edited and categorized, it was found that a rich "teacher list" of behavioral clues to intellectual development could now be evaluated against and compared with the "researchers' list." A staff jury did this work and discovered that most of the clues suggested by the teachers fitted into the original list at least once. The outcome was a long list of behavioral clues to intellectual development in six year olds which conformed to the theoretical model.

Because of the unfamiliarity of Piaget's terminology, a set of categories appropriate to the teachers' list of clues was developed for the try-out materials, and the researchers' list was fitted into the categories defined. Like all categories, they are simply "handles" for efficient use of the behavioral statement, and the primary purpose of the organization is to help teachers find their way through the list of behavioral descriptions. The categories are:

    Area 1: Concepts of Space and Time
    Area 2: The Growth of Logical Reasoning
    Area 3: Understanding Mathematics
    Area 4: Oral Communication
    Area 5: Learning About the World
    Area 6: Imagination and Creativity

The combined researchers' list and New York teachers' list of behavioral clues to intellectual development have been printed in the booklet *Let's Look At First Graders: An Observational Guide for Teachers,* for try-out in the school year 1964–65.

CLUES AND OPPORTUNITIES

From the very beginning of the project, when the ETS staff was combing the research papers of Piaget and others for the specific behavioral evidence of intelligence, it was apparent that not all of the behavioral signs of growing maturity could be seen just by waiting for them to happen in the classroom. Some of the more important signs appear so infrequently in the ordinary course of events that the teacher might watch for months and never see them. The water-volume demonstration that Piaget was so fond of illustrates the point. This is a simple experiment that children think is fun to watch, and it permits the individual to exhibit his level of development in two different intellectual characteristics. However, lacking this simple but artificial *opportunity* for a child to reveal such development, the teacher might never be able to see what the child is like in these respects.

So the project was planned by the author's direct staff and the ETS policy group and project staff to consist of three phases or elements:

Element I: This phase is to concentrate on behavioral clues to intellectual development likely to be exhibited naturally in the course of planned classroom lessons and playground activities following usual curriculum guides. The teacher is to observe clues without special provision for eliciting them. The eventual outcome of this phase of the project is to be a guide to the observation of six-year-olds for the purpose of estimating their intellectual development. The try-out form of the material in this phase is *Let's Look at First Graders.*

Element II: This phase is to concentrate on lesson materials and ideas for *eliciting* intellectual behavior so that it can be observed by the teacher. If, for any one of several reasons, the teacher is not able to "see" certain children engaged in appropriate intellectual tasks, she can use prototype lessons suggested as part of Element II, as well as puzzles, tasks, and games, to make sure that they have opportunities to demonstrate their development.

Element III: This element of the project is concentrated upon developing special tasks for first-graders to perform in approximately "standardized" circumstances. That is, even though the project emphasizes the role and the skill of the teacher in observing and assessing pupils' intellectual development, there remains a need for a means of *comparison* among children so that the teacher may retain a fairly stable set of ideas about what bright children at age six can do. Though the materials produced in this phase of the project will *not* be standardized "tests" in the traditional meaning of that term, they will have more of the characteristics of tests than the materials in either of the other two phases.

There are no assurances that *Let's Look At First Graders: An Observational Guide for Teachers* will be a valid assessment of the intellectual ability of young children. It might just live up to its name, "an observational guide for teachers"; and this alone might represent a giant step in education, especially if it directs teachers' attention to the actualities of behavior.

Jerome Bruner, Director of the Center of Cognitive Studies at Harvard University, suggests that the objective of testing should be to discern what the far limits of man's capacities are—how much a child can make of the best hints we might give him. He goes further and suggests that we should teach and test and teach and test, and only then can tests serve us with a benchmark, not of where a child *is* but of where he is capable of *going*.

It is on this premise that we should build: that there is no upper limit to what people are capable of doing with their minds. Back in 1900, before Binet had turned most of his attention to psychometrics, he concerned himself with the educability of intelligence, taking five or six aspects of intelligence that he thought could be trained. We have moved little in sixty years. It is time for educators to concern themselves with educability once again.

REFERENCES

1. Bloom, B. S. *Stability and change in human characteristics.* New York: Wiley, 1964.
2. Chauncey, H., & Dobbin, J. *Testing: Its place in education today.* New York: Harper & Row, 1963.
3. Crandall, V. J. Achievement. In Stevenson, H. W., *et al (Eds.) Child Psychology: Yearb. nat. Soc. Stud. Educ.*, 1963, 62, Part I, Pp. 416–459.
4. Dyer, H. What intelligence tests don't test. *University, A Princeton Magazine,* 1964 (No. 20), 4–5.
5. Ebel, R. The social consequences of educational testing. ETS Annual Meeting, 30 October, 1964.
6. Hunt, J. McV. *Intelligence and experience.* New York: Ronald, 1961.
7. Lannholm, G. Educational growth during the second two years of college. *Educ. psychol. Measmt.,* 1950, 10, 367–370.
8. Learned, W. S., & Wood, B. D. *The student and his knowledge.* New York: Carnegie Fnd. Adv. Teach., 1938.
9. Moody, W. and others. *How the mind works.* London, Eng.: George Allen, 1945.
10. Scannel, D. P. Differential prediction of academic success from achievement test scores. Unpbl. PhD dissertation, State Univer. Iowa, 1958.
11. Spaulding, G. Another look at the prediction of college scores. Unpubl. rep. for the College Entrance Examination Board. New York: Educ. Rec. Bur., 1960.
12. Traxler, A. E. Reading growth of secondary school pupils during a five year period. *Educational Records Bulletin.* New York: Educ. Rec. Bur., 1950, No. 54, Pp. 96–107.

IN THE JANUARY, 1966 ISSUE OF *Teachers College Record,* HARRY B. Gilbert, of the Board of Examiners of the New York City

Board of Education, responded to Joseph Loretan's article. His rejoinder, "On the I.Q. Ban," is printed here in full.[2]

TO THE EDITOR:

I have just read Dr. Loretan's article, "The Decline and Fall of Group Intelligence Testing" in the October *Record*; and it has prompted me to respond with a very different point of view. What follows has been adapted from a paper read at a panel of the New York State Psychological Association meeting last May; and I hope you will consider it for publication.

It was on February 26, 1964 that a directive was sent to the 800 public school principals in New York City, informing them that group intelligence tests would no longer be administered to their pupils and that "an extensive achievement testing program is being substituted. . . ." Despite vigorous objection by school supervisors to this ban, the prohibition has remained in force and even been extended to include intelligence tests intended to be used for research purposes by research personnel.

Criticism of intelligence tests, as you may know, is not new, particularly criticism of the use of such tests on culturally different children. In 1923, the London Board of Education published a report of a study of "underprivileged, isolated, and often illiterate children" of English canal-boat families, whose mean Stanford-Binet IQ was found to be 69.6. This study was cited as a warning to test-users in many textbooks on testing.

In more recent years, of course, the problem of testing culturally deprived children, particularly from minority groups, has come to the fore. We are all familiar with the "Guidelines for Testing Minority Group Children," published in 1964. This handy guide presents a temperate and cautious approach to the use of intelligence tests with minority children. But it does not suggest total elimination of tests for all minority children, much less all children.

Attempts to create "culture-fair" or "culture-free" tests have failed. One of the best known is the "Davis-Eells Games," which Thorndike and Hagen have reviewed as "laborious to give and relatively unreliable. . . . We must conclude that it does not appear very useful as a measurement tool at the present time." In short, although there has been extensive criticism of misuse of tests on minority children, nobody had imposed a total interdiction against their use until New York City took its drastic action.

2. Reprinted with permission of *Teachers College Record* and the author.

What is the rationale for the ban? The directive to the schools states, "Present group measures of intelligence provide an inadequate base for judging the instructional needs of children." It goes on to point out that high scores do not necessarily insure success and that low scores do not necessarily denote incapacity for learning. Therefore, since group intelligence tests can present misleading pictures of student abilities, they are to be discontinued and achievement tests given instead. Furthermore, it is promised, experimentation will be conducted to develop aids to improve teachers' judgments of children's intelligence.

One gains little understanding of the rationale from the directive. It would be difficult indeed to find teachers or supervisors in any appreciable number who use a group intelligence test as a *sole* basis for judging children's instructional needs. However, personal inquiry has revealed that the basic motivation was one of assumed unfairness of intelligence tests for culturally deprived children and a belief that school personnel in general adhere to the notion that the IQ is somehow a fixed, static, and genetic measure of learning capacity. Be it noted that all previous instructions to teachers and supervisors with respect to administration of group intelligence tests have always cautioned against using such tests for children who are handicapped verbally, culturally, physically, socially or emotionally. Furthermore, ample caution is advised with respect to utilizing all data about children including intelligence and achievement test results, teacher judgment, informal tests etc. I do not believe it is possible to find support for the pure genetic IQ concept in any textbook written in the past 30 years. The straw man persists, however.

Let me review the reasons for using group intelligence tests in our schools.

1. They are an aid to individualization of instruction in a mass educational enterprise that sets as its goal the full development of each pupil.

2. They serve as an aid in screening pupils for individual examination, whether they are suspected of being retarded or gifted or are presenting learning or adjustment problems.

3. They serve as a basis for guidance of pupils, particularly if there is a cumulative record of tests and teacher judgments over a period of years.

4. Finally, it must be emphasized that they are only useful as part of a total battery of information about pupils and must be used in conjunction with all other estimates of pupil ability, achievement

tests, informal assessments, health records, etc., and particularly over a period of time. By way of example, a child who attains an IQ of 107 on the Pintner-Cunningham in the first grade and who progressively attains lower IQs in later grades on tests dependent upon reading, has given his teacher and counselor useful information that can no longer be obtainable under the ban.

Let me now comment on the concept that such tests are unfair to all minority children. We are in a climate of great generalization regarding culturally deprived or culturally different children. With much more sentiment than sense, contemporary bandwagon passengers characterize such children as coming from broken, impoverished homes with little sensory, verbal or experiential stimulation. It is small wonder that these slum children never have a chance when they come to school to be taught by middle-class, non-understanding teachers, and fall progressively further behind year by year. So goes today's line.

Now I am not denying that the slums are full of pathology for their inhabitants, or that there is a high incidence of broken families, alcoholism, drug addiction, prostitution, disease and many other sad concomitants of poverty. Nevertheless, I insist that the process of lumping all Negro children who live in the slums as a homogeneous group is a new form of racism. Indeed it is erroneous to classify all slum children as though they were a homogeneous group, regardless of ethnic origin. There are many families of sufficient strength to combat the effects of slum dwelling, and the children of these families reflect their home strengths in their school performance and adjustment to life.

Joseph Justman, Acting Director of Educational Program Research and Statistics of the New York City Public Schools, has studied the records of 934 pupils drawn from 16 "special service schools" in New York City. Most of the children were Negroes from Harlem and Bedford-Stuyvesant. All were in the 6th grade; 395 of them had been in the same schools since the 3rd grade; the remaining 539 had been transferred 2, 3 or 4 or more times. Thus test results could be compared for the no-transfer or "stable" group as against the "mobile" groups with 2, 3 or 4 or more school admissions. The results are both heartening and sobering and should serve as a warning to the over-generalizers of our day. The mean IQ for the stable group was 100.8 in grade 3 and 102.4 in grade 6, a difference statistically significant at the .05 level but operationally not significant. For the other 539 children, the mean IQ in grade 3 was 94.2 and in grade 6 it was 92.9, again a difference significant statistically at the .05 level but not operationally significant. When the sub-groups are analyzed more carefully, a progressively larger decrease is noted in both 3rd and 6th grade IQ as number of admissions increases. In other words, the more the pupil mobility, or transfer from school to school, the lower the initial IQ and the lower it drops. For children with 4 or more admissions, for example, grade 3 mean IQ is 88.0 and grade 6 mean IQ is 84.0, a difference significant at the .01 level. Justman repeated the study, using achievement test results; and, as expected, the reading and arithmetic trends are the same as the intelligence test trends.

The significance of the Justman findings are that we err seriously in generalizing on so-called effects of minority status on intelligence test results when we lump all test data for the large group. Clearly there is a difference when we separate stable sub-groups from mobile sub-groups as defined by Justman. All that has been demonstrated is the differences. Their causes remain to be discovered. One could speculate, based on considerable personal, clinical experience, that the mobile group contains a high incidence of social and family pathology. The stable group contains a high incidence of family strength. However, this is speculation and still does not get at cause, which might be of great importance in diagnosis on the road to therapy. There is no doubt that intensive, case study analysis is imperatively needed as a follow-up.

There are other professional voices now being heard in opposition to today's sentimental over-generalizations. Fifer of Hunter College reported on "Social Class and Cultural Group Differences in Diverse Mental Abilities" by using tests of verbal reasoning, numerical and spatial abilities on middle and lower class groups of Chinese, Jewish, Negro and Puerto Rican children. In all cases he found that "the data reveal sharp test-performance differences between middle and lower class groups regardless of ethnic group. . . ." The obvious caution, therefore, is against assuming homogeneity because of ethnic or religious grouping.

Rosenhan delivers a sharp castigation to the cultural deprivation opportunists. He says "the term cultural deprivation and the so-called theories that have grown from it are vague notions and catchwords that have an extraordinarily high noise-to-content ratio." He points out that among culturally deprived children there are many problems such as school retardation, poor verbal ability, unstable identification figures and unstable community ties, etc. However, it has erroneously been assumed that the correlation is evidence of causality. This has not been demonstrated, and Rosenhan proceeds to cite his research based on theories which point up hopeful leads to the education of culturally deprived children. His report is highly recommended as an antidote to such popular treatises as Reissman's "The Culturally Deprived Child," a prime example of hastily assembled super-generalizations.

I should like to cite a point made by Trachtman of New York University in a splendid paper, "The Evils of Educational Change." Although mainly concerned with the contemporary fetish of assuming that educational change is itself proof of improvement, he cites the New York City test ban as an example of going through the motions of form rather than content presumably to help children.

May I now call to your attention a leaflet entitled "Testing and the Culturally Disadvantaged Child" by Roger Lennon. Among the many salient comments, I select the following. "If these tests seem to favor the middle or upper-class child, it is because they place a premium on types of abilities important for success in academic work. If there is a question of bias, it concerns the nature of the tasks set by the school, and only secondarily the tests." It is worth keeping this in mind. The basic curriculum in our public schools reflects middle class values, and everything we hear today indicates that our complex society will require better educated citizens in verbal and mathematical skills. Our group intelligence tests are highly predictive, precisely in these areas and their usefulness in educational planning is bound to increase. The test ban is a regressive step unless we want to follow it with a ban on many aspects of our curriculum.

I deplore the notion that teachers and school administrators are ante-diluvian test users, rooted in a concept of the IQ as a hereditary, fixed and absolute quantity. Nevertheless, I feel that the ban will have served a useful purpose, provided that the following steps are taken:

1. *Institute a major educational program on the uses and limitations of intelligence tests.* I have received assurance of cooperation from many distinguished experts in measurement. I have in mind such a proposal as a well conceived TV course to be followed by discussions and exercises on a local level, with small groups of teachers and administrators led by school psychologists, research personnel or guidance counselors.

2. *Restore the use of group intelligence tests but drop the con-*

cept of the IQ. Indeed the tests should properly be called tests of scholastic aptitude. The IQ is an outmoded concept. It no longer is a quotient; it is a deviation score. Use percentiles, or standard scores, or stanines. I would leave the designation to a high level committee of advisers but I would strongly propose using a term that is not too familiar, or even a coined term, similar to the stanine. The advantage of a novel term would be to force attention to its meaning and to add to it the concept of a probability range, or band, instead of a unitary score idea.

3. *Stress that all decisions about tests should be made with one paramount consideration: the welfare of the child.* If the overwhelming majority of measurement experts agree that group intelligence tests can make a contribution to children's education, even though the contribution in itself is only minor, then the tests should be used. In the long run, the very notion that *all* culturally deprived children are handicapped in test taking in and of itself is a vicious labeling. The facts belie this doctrine. Maintenance of this policy will inevitably fix the notion that the entire group is inferior, but must be protected from tests by a ban on tests.

MEANWHILE, RESEARCH CONTINUES TO SORT OUT OUR KNOWLEDGE in this area. The study reported by Fifer, which Harry B. Gilbert referred to earlier, was published in monograph form in 1966 with the title, *Mental Abilities of Children from Different Social-class and Cultural Groups.* The work was done by Gerald S. Lesser, of Harvard University, and Gordan Fifer and Donald H. Clark, both of Hunter College of the City University of New York. The report casts some light on the profound influences of social-class and cultural identity in determining how a child is likely to use his mental talents. A few excerpts from that lengthy report follow.[3]

The purpose of this study was to examine the patterns among various mental abilities in young children from different social-class and cultural backgrounds. The patterns among four mental abilities (verbal ability, reasoning, number facility, and space conceptualization) were studied in first-grade children from four cultural groups in New York City (Chinese, Jewish, Negro, and Puerto

3. Reprinted by permission of the Society for Research in Child Development from *Monographs of the Society for Research in Child Development, 1965, 30,* 4(102).

Rican), with each cultural group divided into middle-class and lower-class groups.

Perhaps the most important implications of this research on patterns of mental ability in young children relate to the practical efforts to determine the optimum educational conditions and the most valid assessment instruments for children from diverse backgrounds. The loss of outstanding intellectual talent in groups labeled "culturally deprived" has been a source of increasing concern. American society is dedicated to the development of intellectual ability wherever it is found. However, before talent can be developed, it must be located and identified. In the last few decades, intellectual ability has been located primarily with the aid of a few popular tests of intelligence (e.g., the Revised Stanford-Binet Intelligence Scale). For better or worse, we have, in practice, defined "intelligence" in terms of the most popular tests that presume to measure it.

These intelligence tests have been frequently criticized for being too heavily loaded with verbal items that are both unfair to certain groups within our population and too narrow as assessments of intellectual functioning. A score based on a test that is heavily loaded with one factor can tell little about the quality and quantity of the various talents that an individual has. Perhaps because of such intelligence measures, or for reasons as yet undiscovered we are failing conspicuously to discover outstanding talent in certain strata of our society. It is clear from the research literature that lower socioeconomic groups and certain cultural groups do not contribute their proportion of intellectually productive individuals.

Teachers must make both immediate and continuing educational decisions about children from different social-class and cultural backgrounds in order to provide effective classroom instruction. There is, however, a serious lack of valid information available regarding the abilities of these children. When a child is classified on the basis of a single, global score, such as a general-intelligence quotient (even if the test is appropriate and valid for his social-class and cultural group), much remains to be known about the range and operation of his abilities. However, if that single global score is not only too narrow but is also inappropriate and invalid for his group, the information available to the teacher becomes even more obscure and less useful.

The study of cultural differences in mental abilities attacks a fundamental, persistent problem for education and psychology:

How do we provide valid psychological evaluation of children from widely dissimilar cultural groups? There is no doubt that one of the most pressing needs expressed by teachers and school administrators is for testing instruments that will provide fair, accurate, and broad assessment of the abilities of young children from cultural backgrounds other than those typical of our total school population.

School personnel in "underprivileged areas" contend that their children cannot possibly perform well on the available psychological tests because the tasks required of them are either unimportant or alien. The claim has often been made that intelligence tests (such as the Stanford-Binet Intelligence Scale) were originally designed to measure those aspects of mental ability in which middle-class children excelled, ignoring those other aspects of mental ability in which the lower class, through its culture, encourages its children to perform favorably. This is understandable since intelligence tests were developed to answer the need for prediction of performance in school. As long as schools function to train children who are best able to understand and work within standards that are based on middle-class, white, urban values, such tests should do a reasonably good job of predicting those children of superior academic "ability."

We are no longer satisfied with such limited educational goals, however. We must educate children who can contribute to our changing society in ways that we may well not be able to anticipate today. This means we must broaden our definition of "ability" or "talent" to include behaviors based on values that, thus far, have not been prominent in middle-class culture. We must be able to identify relative intellectual strengths *within* an individual, and we must be able to identify his individual intellectual strengths, no matter what his social-class or cultural identity may be. Having done this psychological assessment job, we must develop educational techniques that will help the most talented children develop their talents fully, although radical departure from traditional educational procedures may be necessitated thereby.

Before the psychological assessment job can be begun, however, information is needed on the possible variations in the *patterns* of diverse mental abilities as they relate to variations in social class and culture. In order to understand the relative strengths of an individual child's mental abilities, we must have information on how children of a particular background (e.g., middle-class Puerto Rican or lower-class Chinese) tend to express their intellectual abilities, in contrast to how the majority of the school population tends to express its intellectual abilities. Perhaps intelligence tests can then be developed that will yield intra-individual profiles of scores for the various mental abilities of children, with contrasting normative profiles for children of similar social-class and cultural identity and for children in the entire nation.

No effort to add to our knowledge about social-class and ethnic-group effects upon mental ability will have tangible or socially useful educational outcomes unless accompanied by simultaneous, co-ordinated efforts to develop curricula, train teachers, modify school organization, and improve methods for establishing public policies for our schools. Each of the many educational efforts that affect children from culturally diverse groups—issues of measurement, curriculum, teacher training, school organization, etc.—has remained almost entirely divorced from the others. These studies seem to spin in their own orbits, each remaining theoretically or methodologically discrete, profiting little from each other's existence, and failing to feed any really useful information to the practitioner conducting daily classroom instruction. When innovations are attempted, they are introduced in one or another of these educational areas singly, with insufficient concern for how an attempted innovation in any one area will affect all the other parts of the educational system.

The present attempt to construct suitable testing procedures for studying children from culturally diverse groups has not yet departed from this traditional isolation of educational efforts. We have not yet incorporated considerations of curriculum development, teacher training, and school organization as essential aspects of our test development, and our results, consequently, have little immediate, direct applicability to the solutions of these problems.

The present study however, has taken the first step toward contributing to the solution of the broader educational problems: We have shown that several mental abilities are related to each other in ways that are culturally determined. We have been interested in identifying these abilities as distinct from the motivations, aspirations, and individual attitudes of the subjects. However, we have not yet attempted to relate these patterns of ability to school performance but have proposed, instead, that the identification of relative strengths and weaknesses of members of different cultural groups is a basic and vital prerequisite to making enlightened decisions affecting the educational process and aims. The attempt to apply the present findings to the building of new school programs and the adaptation of old school practices to fit the knowledge of the patterns of abilities in culturally diverse groups is the most compelling extension of this research.

IN DISCUSSING THE FINDINGS, THE AUTHORS SPEAK OF "PATTERNS" and "absolute level" of mental abilities. "Patterns" refers to the relationship between scores on the four tests of mental ability (verbal, reasoning, number, and space). "Absolute level" refers to how high or low the score is on each of the four tests considered by itself, rather than in relation to the other three scores.

The major findings were as follows:

1. Differences in *social-class* placement *do* produce significant differences in the absolute *level* of each mental ability but *do not* produce significant differences in the *patterns* among these abilities.

2. Differences in *ethnic-group* membership *do* produce significant differences in *both* the absolute *level* of each mental ability and the *patterns* among these abilities.

3. *Social-class* and *ethnicity do* interact to affect the absolute *level* of each mental ability but *do not* interact to affect the *patterns* among these abilities.

. . .

The following other specific results were found:

1. Regarding social-class effects upon mental abilities, middle-class children are significantly superior to lower-class children on all scales and subtests.

2. Regarding ethnic-group effects upon mental abilities: (*a*) On Verbal ability, Jewish children ranked first (being significantly better than all other ethnic groups), Negroes ranked second and Chinese third (both being significantly better than Puerto Ricans), and Puerto Ricans fourth. (*b*) On Reasoning, the Chinese ranked first and Jews second (both being significantly better than Negroes and Puerto Ricans), Negroes third, and Puerto Ricans, fourth. (*c*) On Numerical ability, Jews ranked first and Chinese second (both being significantly better than Puerto Ricans and Negroes), Puerto Ricans third, and Negroes, fourth. (*d*) On Space, Chinese ranked first (being significantly better than Puerto Ricans and Negroes), Jews second, Puerto Ricans third, and Negroes, fourth.

3. Regarding sex differences, boys were significantly better than girls on the total Space scale, on the Picture Vocabulary subtest

(but not on the total Verbal scale), and on the Jump Peg subtest (but not on the total Reasoning scale).

4. Regarding the interactions of social class and ethnicity, two effects combined to produce the statistically significant interaction effects upon each scale of mental ability: (a) On each mental-ability scale, social-class position produced more of a difference in the mental abilities of the Negro children than in the other groups. That is, the middle-class Negro children were more different in level of mental abilities from the lower-class Negroes than, for example, the middle-class Chinese were from the lower-class Chinese. (b) On each mental-ability scale, the scores of the middle-class children from the various ethnic groups resembled each other to a greater extent than did the scores of the lower-class children from the various ethnic groups. That is, the middle-class Chinese, Jewish, Negro, and Puerto Rican children were more alike in their mental-ability scores than were the lower-class Chinese, Jewish, Negro, and Puerto Rican children.

5. Regarding the interactions of sex and ethnicity, the significant interactions for both Verbal and Space reflected the higher scores for boys than for girls in all ethnic groups, except for the Jewish children; Jewish girls were superior to Jewish boys for both Verbal and Space scales.

It was concluded that social-class and ethnic-group membership (and their interaction) have strong effects upon the level of each of four mental abilities (verbal ability, reasoning, numerical facility, and space conceptualization).

Ethnic-group affiliation also affects strongly the pattern or organization of mental abilities, but once the pattern specific to the ethnic group emerges, social-class variations within the ethnic group do not alter this basic organization. Apparently, different mediators are associated with social-class and ethnic-group conditions. The mediating variables associated with ethnic-group conditions do affect strongly the organization of abilities, while social-class status does not appear to modify further the basic pattern associated with ethnicity.

These findings allow a reassessment of the various proposed explanations of cultural influences upon intellectual performance. The importance of the mediators associated with ethnicity is to provide differential impacts upon the development of mental abilities, while the importance of the mediators associated with social class is to provide pervasive (and not differential) effects upon the various mental abilities. This conclusion allows selection among the several explanations offered to interpret cultural influences upon intellectual activity; the explanations based upon natural selection, differential reinforcement, motivation, problem-solving tactics, work habits, and so forth, were re-examined in the light of the present results.

In summary, the findings lend selective support to Anastasi's premise that "Groups differ in their relative standing on different functions. Each . . . fosters the development of a different *pattern* of abilities." It seems true that social-class and ethnic groups do "differ in their relative standing on different functions." However, ethnic groups do "foster the development of a different pattern of abilities," while social-class differences do not modify these basic organizations associated with ethnic-group conditions.

The present effort to construct suitable testing procedures for studying children from culturally diverse groups must now incorporate the broader educational considerations of curriculum development, teacher training, and school organization. We have shown that several mental abilities are related to each other in ways that are culturally determined. We propose that the identification of relative intellectual strengths and weaknesses of members of different cultural groups must now become a basic and vital prerequisite to making enlightened decisions about education in urban areas.

No DISCUSSION OF TODAY'S ISSUE OF "INTELLIGENCE" WOULD BE balanced without noting that the federal government's dollar influence has strongly encouraged focused attention on the less intellectually talented members of our society. Our concern here is not simply with clearly identifying level of ability. Papers presented at the 1965 Annual Meeting of the American Orthopsychiatric Association in New York City, in a panel entitled "Needed: A Revolution in the Care of the Mentally Retarded in Institutions," give the flavor of today's concern. These papers were later reprinted in the *American Journal of Orthopsychiatry* during 1965. One of the papers, entitled "Shared Responsibility of the Mentally Retarded—One Approach to the Prevention of Institutionalism" by Martin B. Loeb, who is Professor of Social Work at the University of Wisconsin, is reprinted here.[4]

---

4. Copyright, the American Orthopsychiatric Association, Inc. Reproduced by permission.

The overwhelming impact of a need to assume life-long care for a mentally retarded child has moved many parents to seek early institutionalization. Such parents are often encouraged by physicians, lawyers, friends and relatives to apply for institutional commitment. Without knowing what institutions are like, these advisors point out that the child will be better off with all that trained personnel to look after him; the jeers of neighborhood children can be avoided; siblings will be better off not having to bother with or be bothered by someone unable to look after himself. Besides, caring for the retardate is too difficult a task for a mere family. To add to the pressure of the argument there is the final punch of, "Who will take care of him after you've gone?" In spite of these admonitions, there are those parents who carry their burden bravely, heroically and without any help. Neither of these choices will maximize the development of the retarded child nor of the parents and siblings. Yet these are frequently the only choices: either give over custody and complete care to the state or sustain the responsibility alone. In most instances, legal and social institutions allow only for this either-or approach. Given the shortage of bed space, any chance to get the retarded child into an institution is an added pressure on the parents.

Of course, there are also experts to help the family make the decision on institutionalization in a more studied manner. Social workers, particularly, often help parents sort out their feelings and face up to realities. Yet in times past the social worker has floundered about in a psychotherapeutic pond, assuaged guilt feelings and neglected the realities of the social situation. Most often, however, even with the best of social workers involved, the feelings remain in massive confusion, and the realities are overwhelming. The problem is to find useful alternatives to permanent or long-term institutionalization which realistically can meet the needs of the retarded child, the family and the community (and which can also be clear and straightforward enough to reduce a sense of panic).

In planning for the mentally retarded we have tended to deal in rather strict categories and to let these rigidities determine the limitations of our programs. Out of trying to avoid this rigidity, we now have come up with a proposal which looks as if it might be able to overcome some of the worst features of either present-day institutionalization or overardent home care. We call this new concept *shared responsibility*.

The proposal is that children who are clearly in the severe mentally retarded group and who ordinarily would be considered for institutionalization should be given a status by the state government which would *guarantee* life-long care. The parents would be asked to assume as much responsibility as they could with the help of professional staff provided by state and local agencies. Parents need to know the details of their responsibilities and learn how to care for their special child and how to get along with relatives, neighbors and friends. As they are taught how to do these things they can continue to assume many of the usual parental responsibilities. A major help for the parents is directing them to the community resources and directing them to ways of helping their communities develop new and better resources as needed. Parent groups are an important resource. In this way the state, the community and the family share the responsibility both for the child and for developing resources to provide for his needs in some planned way.

We are firmly convinced that present institutions are poor places in which to be brought up. We are further convinced that institutional living, at least as presently carried out, is deleterious and in effect inhumane. The disorder caused by the "total institution" is often worse than the original defect. This "institutionalism" is a disease about which we can do something. To be sure, some children are so crippled mentally and physically that they require the constant care and protection that a hospital can afford, and we are not proposing that we prevent institutionalization by eradicating institutions. Those not severely physically handicapped (this includes most retardates) have a better chance of developing their potentials in a family in a community, especially during their formative years. The modern family, however, has some great vulnerabilities, and the stress of a mental retardate in the home can be too great unless some of the stress can be diffused. The urban American family is not closely tied to an extended kin group which can be helpful when needed. It lives in rather cramped quarters in an environment which is essentially dangerous. The mentally retarded child is then a constant burden, and there are only the parents, mostly the mother, to carry the burden.

If the family is to assume its responsibility for the retarded child, the community must develop resources which can give the family relief from its constant burden. If it does not, then these families will demand more and more colonies and training schools.

What is needed? First, good consulting service consisting of well trained professionals in the hospital when the baby is born and from that time on to help the family make its decisions. Every court needs the services of such consultants before commitments are made. Day care services and nursery schools are needed which take children when quite young (about 18 months). These should not be of the cooperative variety as it is necessary to let the mother have her respite. A nursery school with trained teachers and volunteers from the rest of the community is one successful type.

For children who are over four there should be some residential center to provide intermittent care so that families can enjoy vacations or house guests or deal with other crises and can at those times leave their crippled child in good hands. These can be special units, or other local resources can be used. In Wisconsin we have county mental hospitals; some communities have built special residences. There also may be a select list of foster families.

Special classes in the public schools should be available for both the educable and the trainable. There could be better use made of dormitory type schools for some periods of the formative years, especially adolescence. There should be sheltered workshops for the older mental retardates. These well might have attached to them some kinds of hostels for supervised living of the adult retardate. Many adult retardates will need economic subsidy in one form or another hopefully without a means test.

There are, of course, many other possibilities, and many communities have some of these services now. The parents at the very outset should know about these possibilities and what they themselves can do to promote the development of needed services. The decision-influencers, such as physicians, psychologists, social workers, lawyers, ministers, teachers and counsellors, also need to become aware of the community potentials and family strengths.

In shared responsibility the state assumes the responsibility for life-long care, the community develops its resources and the family assumes responsibility for its child to the greatest extent possible. It seems to be a simple solution but to make it work laws have to be changed, attitudes of professional people have to be changed and both the potentialities and the limitations of family life have to be realistically assessed.

The alternative is more and bigger institutions. The pressure for these will be great, especially as there is even less chance for the retardate to assume a more or less normal place in the job market and the suburban neighborhood, with increasing automation and the virtual urbanization of the whole population. Institutionalization cannot be prevented simply by keeping people out and on waiting lists. The demand for more institutions will be clamorous and successful if there are not other pathways available such as shared responsibility.

AND SO THE ISSUE OF *intelligence* CONTINUES. AS WITH "DISAD-vantaged," the definition of the word troubles us. It's a handy word. "I.Q." is even handier but both have gotten us into considerably troubled and muddy waters because different people have meant different things while still using the same word in superficial agreement.

Why should any youngster show an apparent continuing *drop* in I.Q. as he spends more years in school? Obviously it is not his native potential that is decreasing. It is a score on a test that reflects his increasing disadvantage in the classroom situation and elsewhere. This can be altered by making a test that asks different questions and/or by arranging a classroom experience that permits the child to use his native potential in ways that fit his life style.

Not the least of our difficulty rests on the educator's lack of sophistication about the meaning of intelligence test scores, achievement test scores, or any other scores. Teachers leave training programs with the unjustifiable belief that intelli-gence is a talent for success in school (*and in life!*) that is re-flected in the score called "I.Q." Far too many assign similar magic properties to scores on achievement tests. If these scores were viewed as similar to any other test score they would be considered no more confidential than last week's spelling tests, which are displayed on the bulletin board.

It is clear that social-class and cultural experiences early in childhood influence the ways in which one shows off his tal-ents. A child's early learning inhibits or enhances his various talents. Every child has a right to an education that helps him use *his* talents to build a satisfying life. This is equally true for the relatively "bright" child and for the relatively "dull" or retarded child. Each has talents that can be trained to pro-mote his welfare.

We see that we must take a closer look at an individual child and his early experiences. Knowing that a child is Negro does not tell his story. Knowing whether he comes from a lower-class or middle-class background doesn't tell the story either but it is one more giant step in that direction.

There is absolutely no doubt that the search for talent will continue, as will the shifting of words and battle positions. The problem for the school remains, however, how to prepare tomorrow's citizens for tomorrow's world. Since we know very little about tomorrow's world we are stuck with the problem of grooming talents that we may not recognize today.

The problem begins to point our direction. We are back at an age-old cliché. We must help the child to develop all his talents. We can no longer benignly nod agreement to the cliché, however. If we do not begin to encourage the development of unseen talents or even those that are seen but considered useless or distasteful, we will find ourselves living in a world that has left us behind, a world that we cannot manage because we haven't the talents.

CHAPTER 3

Creativity

WE TAKE OFF OUR HATS TO CREATIVITY JUST AS WE DO TO INTELLI-
gence. It's one of those talents that helps civilization progress
and therefore deserves profound respect. One reason we lift
our hats to it is that we are unsure what else to do about it.
Happily we are agreed that we're for it. The word creativity
conjures up delicious remembered or anticipated experiences
with music, drama, sculpture, poetry, paintings, dance, and
literature. America in the 1960s has time and money to indulge
an increasing thirst for art. If there is something that can be
done in school to encourage it, by all means, everyone agrees
it must be done.

As with intelligence, however, the more closely we look at
this talent called creativity, the more puzzled and troubled we
become. It was easier when we believed that it was simply a
gift given to a few clearly superior people, a bonus from the
gods. We didn't have to worry much about it then because
if someone was *really* creative it would show. Jacob Getzels'
and Philip Jackson's research report, entitled *Creativity and
Intelligence*, published by John Wiley & Sons in 1962, made
an explosion that is still echoing. Their evidence indicated,
they declared, that intelligence and creativity could be viewed
separately. Indeed, they were able to experimentally isolate
some youngsters who were not strikingly high in intellectual

ability but who were high in creative ability, who had been commonly referred to as "overachievers."

The quarrels continue about their study, their methodology, and their interpretation, but the fact remains that this book gave educational psychology a much-needed shot in the arm. Certainly the tide had started long before, but there is now a virtual flood of articles, letters, opinions, and even some research in the area of creativity. Much of the writing and the research relates creativity in some way to other talents such as intelligence. Like other talents, apparently it is present to some degree in all of us.

There is a developing consensus that it is the able person, usually labeled especially "intelligent," especially "creative," and favored by the stars in other ways, who makes outstanding contributions. This is some comfort to those vexed by the rapidity with which old truths are changing. But now we are increasingly aware of the importance of the common garden variety of creativity in industry, science, teaching, politics, and everywhere else in the human scene.

A book by one clearly talented individual, writer Arthur Koestler, made its appearance in 1964, published by The Macmillan Company. Its title is *The Act of Creation*. In it, Koestler pointed to his understanding of the nature of creativity, no matter in what area it is seen. Gordon W. Allport of Harvard University wrote an excellent review of the book. It was called "Like Apollo Amok" and appeared in the February, 1966 issue of *Contemporary Psychology*. It is reprinted here.[1]

My advice to the reader of this enormous volume is first to fix its one and only theoretical contribution firmly in mind, and then to abandon himself to an enjoyment of the voluptuous potpourri of these astonishing pages. History, anecdote, myth, art, literary criticism, information, and obiter dicta crowd 24 chapters of Book I and 18 chapters of Book II. Taken together they provide the reader with a liberal if untidy education.

The single theoretical contribution is, in my opinion, original and valuable in spite of its vaguely familiar ring.

1. Reprinted by permission of *Contemporary Psychology* © 1966 American Psychological Association.

Simply stated: the creative act is in essence one and the same thing whether it crops up in humor, in scientific discovery, or in art. All creativity is 'bisociation'—a process whereby an item at first belonging in one matrix (context) is suddenly perceived as belonging to a second, entirely different matrix. In the author's words, "When two independent matrices of perception or reasoning interact with each other the result (as I hope to show) is either a collision ending in laughter, or their *fusion* in a new intellectual synthesis, or their *confrontation* in an aesthetic experience" (p. 45). Illustrations may help.

The pun is an elementary creative act. Two frames containing a common single homonym collide. Thus "the aging libertine feels his old Krafft Ebing."

In science, when Kepler perceived the fit of astronomical facts to an "oval" orbit rather than to the traditional circle (harmony of the spheres) it was a creative act of great significance. The inventions and discoveries of Faraday, Darwin, Edison, and countless others demonstrate the same point.

In art, bisociation again is the essence of creativity. For millennia Egyptian art portrayed the human body within a rigid frame (front view of the torso, profile of the face). It took a creative act to wrench the body loose from this routine matrix.

The Rorschach inkblot illustrates the theory. Possible bisociations of the blot's form with subjective frames of meaning are inexhaustible. The subject who sees a landscape in the blot is bisociating and thus creating. Having made this point Koestler does some bisociating on his own. In the eighteenth century, he tells us, the English landscape painter Alexander Cozens recommended using inkblots for inspiration. Still earlier Leonardo da Vinci had the same idea; so too the philosopher Pliny; not to mention Chinese artists from the eleventh century onward. All this information makes tasty fare but is not easily digestible, especially when in the same mouthful we are offered Hamlet's clouds, the interpretations that psychotics give to ornaments and decorations, not to mention practices of Greek, Byzantine, cubist, and Zen artists. All this in less than a page—and there are over 700 pages of such over-rich plum pudding.

In a general way the central proposition of the book restates, with extensive illustration, Bartlett's contention (in *Thinking*, 1958) that the most important feature of original thought is the discovery of overlap and agreement where formerly only isolation and difference were recognized.

While Koestler cites Bartlett, and offers a general bibliography of breathtaking length, he has many serious blind-spots. Nowhere is there a discussion of the Deweyesque stages of felt hitch, incubation, illumination, verification. (Koestler deals almost exclusively with illumination.) Nowhere does one find reference to the work of Bruner, Ghiselin, Crutchfield, Getzels, Gollan, Guilford, MacKinnon, Mednick, Merton, Stein, Torrance and many others who have poured forth empirical studies of creativity in recent years. Koestler draws his evidence from the history of science, art and literature, rather than from contemporary research.

Motivation to sustain the creative act comes from an exploratory tendency; its energy is of a playful or "ludic" order. Tension reduction as a theory is inadequate, whether couched in Hullian or Freudian terms. "Just as Freud's libido-theory had no room for dalliance, so learning-theory has no room for curiosity or learning-by-play" (p. 496). The emotions involved in creativity are of the gentle order. Psychologists have missed them in their preoccupation with the rugged "adreno-toxic, hit-run-mate-devour" emotions. "Laughter and tears, awe and wonder, religious and aesthetic feeling, the whole 'violet' side of the rainbow of emotions was left to the poets to worry about; the so-called behavioral sciences had no room for them" (p. 286).

I find it odd that a person who has written novels of situation should neglect the importance of the social setting in his psychological theorizing. Laughter, for example, is above all else a social phenomenon—a fact never faced by the author. He deliberately rejects the role of situation in creative thinking. Even when times are ripe for multiple inventions (and he admits the evidence), he insists that the creative act is still solitary bisociation. No doubt, for the process itself; but surely the available matrices, the pieces of the puzzle, and the incentive, are conditioned by the *Zeitgeist*. Nor does personality receive mention excepting in an Appendix entitled "Some Features of Genius" where one finds a few condensed biographies of great creators.

Another neglected problem concerns the validity and value of creative acts. Many eureka experiences, we all know, are mere bloopers. Dreams are highly creative but most of their intersecting planes produce nothing but nonsense. How, for example, shall aesthetic productions be judged? The author tells how at a certain masquerade ball a prize was offered for the best representation of Charlie Chaplin. It so happened that Charlie himself was present at the party incognito. He won third prize (p. 402).

Koestler, of course, recognizes the distinction between trivial bisociations and those of world-shaking significance, operating, "on the highest level of the hierarchies of existing knowledge" (p. 658). But he does not solve the problem of value and validity. Whether the criteria should be expert opinion, accepted canons of excellence, long range impact, or subjective certainty, we are not told. We are told, however, that there are no absolute criteria. "Any attempt to get a direct grasp at naked reality is self-defeating" (p. 343). All creativity, even scientific, is only "tentative" (p. 246). Koestler would probably say that it is his job to identify process and not worry too much about its axiological relevance. This formula for escape is also invoked by most psychologists when they find themselves confronted by metaphysical or ethical challenge.

Book II (almost as long as Book I) is a technical filling in of the basic argument. It is titled "Habit and Originality"—a broad caption that allows the author to tell how our routine matrices are built up (through genetic inheritance, imprinting, learning, memory) as well as how occasional breakthroughs occur.

Once again he complains that S-R is inadequate to account for creative departure from networks previously woven of repetition and reward. All associationism deals traditionally only with connections within a single matrix, and not with the "simultaneous activity of two conceptual cycles."

Gestalt theory fares no better. Not only is it preoccupied with visual organization, but its concept of "insight" (a visual term) implies too much conformity to a solution already resident in the nature of things. Gestalt does not deal with the bisociation of independent matrices. Unfortunately, Max Wertheimer's contributions are not mentioned.

Yet it seems to me that Koestler's theory is at bottom a blend of these two rejected schools. The eureka experience is certainly a kissin'-cousin of insight. Further, even classical associationism could admit that a sensory core that normally arouses Context A may under special circumstances activate also Context B. It would be better for the author to advocate a synthesis, rather than a rejection, of these traditional schools.

He is, however, entitled to credit for bringing together the three planes of humor, science and art into a fruitful trisociation. Like all creative acts this one engenders, as Bruner would say, "effective surprise." Another point to his credit: although association and Gestalt are implicit in his theory, the author goes beyond them in perceiving the need for at least "two simultaneously acting conceptual cycles" to account for the creative act.

As we might expect, Koestler is at his best in dealing with literary creativity—with character and plots and with poetry. All lives are lived in a conflict of matrices, and the theme of literature is human conflict. Yeats said, "We make out of our quarrels with others rhetoric, but of our quarrels with ourselves poetry."

It is clear that we are dealing here with a major production in "literary psychology." Its impact is jolting but wholesome. I know of no book that illustrates so well what James called "an electric aptitude for analogy." From Juvenal to Jung, from Tycho de Brahe to Tinbergen, from gene-function to sign-Gestalten—one idea races with another. Analogies run wild. Bisociation doesn't express it; his associations are infinite.

The book is fun to read—in snatches. The reader enjoys the master's leaps from one idea, from one metaphor to another—like fireworks—like a wayward encyclopedia—like an Apollo amok.

OUR LOVE AFFAIR WITH CREATIVITY OFTEN COMES TO A SCREECHING halt in the classroom. This is one of the places where the differences between *convergent thinking* and *divergent thinking* take clear form. These terms are used by many workers in the field to indicate the difference between what we usually think of as intelligence (convergent thinking that seeks *the* right answer) and creativity (divergent thinking that seeks as many alternative answers as possible).

If everyone has some degree of each of these talents and if both talents can be trained, the problem is in the training. There are exceptions, but the rule of the school is to find the right answer. Centuries of critics have hardly dented this rule. It is one reason why intelligence tests can do a fairly good job of predicting school success.

Like most current issues in the psychology of education, this one is not confined to the United States of America. A. J. Cropley of the University of New England in Australia, published an article called "The Relatedness of Divergent and Convergent Thinking" in the September, 1965 issue of the *Alberta Journal of Educational Research*. It is reprinted here in full.[2]

2. Reprinted with permission of the *Alberta Journal of Educational Research*. This

Psychologists and educators have recently begun to place great emphasis on the concept of creativity, since it is argued on the one hand that man's creative faculties restore his dignity in a computer-dominated age (Bruner, 1962), and on the other, that human creativity is mankind's greatest asset (Toynbee, 1962). Torrance (1963) has also suggested that the proper exercise of creative talents is important in maintaining mental health.

There is increasing agreement that conventional tests are concerned mainly with the ability to reproduce the already known rather than the capacity to "invent and innovate" (Guilford, 1950). However, a number of writers (Guilford, 1950; Lowenfeld, 1958; Getzels and Jackson, 1962; Torrance, 1963) have suggested that there are, in fact, two distinct aspects to intellect which may appropriately be labelled "convergent thinking" and "divergent thinking" (Guilford, 1950). Conventional intelligence tests are usually held to be useful measures only of the first kind of capacity and to ignore the second kind, which may even be inhibited (Getzels and Jackson, 1962; Torrance, 1963) in the classroom, with its emphasis on finding 'correct' answers.

However, as Burt (1964, pp. 13–15) has pointed out, there is no complete agreement among theorists as to whether there is a separate intellectual capacity appropriately labelled 'creativity' or divergent thinking. Burt's view is that individual differences in scores on divergent thinking tests result more from differences in 'general ability' than from differences on some separate and distinct intellectual skill appropriately identified by the label 'creativity.' Vernon (1964) has suggested that the usefulness of conventional tests could be extended by adding divergent thinking sub-tests to them.

Although the Getzels and Jackson (1962) study is frequently cited as supporting the notion of two distinct and independent kinds of thinking, many of the correlations between their divergent thinking measures and the test of conventional IQ were larger than correlations within the battery of divergent thinking tests. Furthermore, factor analyses of the Getzels and Jackson correlation matrix (1962, p. 20) carried out by both Thorndike (1963) and March (1964) indicated that, although there was a factor defined by the divergent thinking measures, this factor owed much of its variance to the tests of convergent thinking.

study, carried out while the author was a student in the Department of Educational Psychology in the University of Alberta, was partly supported by an A.C.E.R. grant and was conducted under the supervision of Dr. C. C. Anderson, to whom the author wishes to express his grateful thanks.

In fact, many studies have indicated the existence of significant correlations between divergent and convergent thinking. Getzels and Jackson (1962, p. 5) reported correlations ranging from .02 (Andrews, 1930) to .27 (Welsh, 1946), while they obtained correlations ranging from .131 to .378 (1962, p. 20) from their own data. A number of other recent studies have reported significant correlations between divergent and convergent thinking (Meer and Stein, 1955; Ripple and May, 1962; Richards, Cline and Needham, 1964), while Ketcham and Kheiralla (1962), in comparing scores on the WISC, the Stanford-Binet and the Primary Mental Abilities Test with scores on a battery of divergent thinking tests, obtained 54 out of 64 correlations significant beyond the .05 level.

Taylor (1964) has summarized the relationship between divergent and convergent thinking by pointing out that although correlations may be very low, or even negative, when samples are homogeneous with regard to either variable, selection of heterogeneous samples usually leads to significant correlations. Vernon (1964) has extended this point by suggesting that the two may become independent once some minimum IQ level (threshold) has been reached.

The purpose of the present study was to examine the relationship between scores on tests of convergent thinking and tests of divergent thinking obtained by a sample of Edmonton schoolchildren. The major question which the study sought to answer was: Are divergent thinking and convergent thinking really substantially independent of each other as some authors have suggested, or do the two kinds of thinking overlap?

METHOD

Sample. The sample consisted of the entire Grade Seven population of a large metropolitan Junior High School. Of 354 children enrolled, 320 completed the entire test battery. The full sample, whose mean age was 13 years 6 months with a SD of 16.9 months (range—11 years 1 month to 16 years 1 month), had a mean verbal IQ on the appropriate Lorge-Thorndike test of 114.3 (range—79 to 150; SD = 14.5). The sample included 170 boys, for whom the mean verbal IQ was 114.7 (range—70 to 148; SD = 15.2), while the corresponding figure for the 150 girls was 113.8 (range—88 to 150; SD = 13.6). The mean age of the boys was 13 years, 10 months (SD = 16.6 months; range—11 years 1 month to

16 years 1 month), and of the girls 13 years 2 months (SD = 17.3 months; range—11 years 7 months to 16 years 1 month).

Tests. Tests employed in the study included the appropriate levels of the Lorge-Thorndike tests of verbal and non-verbal intelligence. Scores were also obtained on the following 5 measures of divergent thinking—Seeing Problems; Tin Can Uses; Consequences; Symbol Production; Circles. In general, these tests were taken from the work of Guilford (French, 1963) although Tin Can Uses and Circles have been revised and developed by Torrance (1962).

Procedure. The tests were all administered on the same day and in the same room to the 320 subjects, who had been gathered in the school gymnasium for that purpose. Administration was according to the published specifications (French, 1963; Torrance, 1962), while scoring was for originality in all cases except Symbol Production, where total number of appropriate symbols was recorded as a subject's score.

Correlations between the various measures were calculated for the full sample, for the 170 boys alone, and for the 150 girls alone.

RESULTS

The intercorrelations between the various tests of divergent thinking and the two measures of convergent thinking are shown in Table I, for the full sample.

Table I—Correlations Between Convergent and Divergent Thinking

	Seeing Problems	Tin Can Uses	Conse- quences	Circles	Symbol Production
Verbal IQ	362*	194	351	145	263
Non-verbal IQ	303	231	350	171	302

*All decimal points have been omitted.

With 318 degrees of freedom, the critical value of the correlation coefficient for significance at the .01 level is .145. Hence, it can be seen that every one of the correlations obtained in the case of the full sample, was significant at or beyond the .01 level of confidence.

Correlations obtained using the boys' data only are shown in Table II.

With 168 degrees of freedom, the critical value of the correlation coefficient for significance at the .01 level is .198. Hence, it can be

Table II—Correlations Between Convergent and Divergent Thinking
(Boys Only: N = 170)

	Seeing Problems	Tin Can Uses	Conse-quences	Circles	Symbol Production
Verbal IQ	306*	103	333	259	288
Non-verbal IQ	323	174	405	247	369

*All decimal points have been omitted.

seen that 8 out of 10 boys' coefficients are significant beyond the .01 level of confidence.

Girls' correlations are shown in Table III.

Table III—Correlations Between Convergent and Divergent Thinking
(Girls Only: N = 150)

	Seeing Problems	Tin Can Uses	Conse-quences	Circles	Symbol Production
Verbal IQ	406*	264	365	064	253
Non-verbal IQ	290	281	312	133	253

*All decimal points have been omitted.

In this case (df = 148) the critical value of the correlation of co-efficient for significance at the .01 level is .210. Again, 8 of 10 coefficients obtained are significant beyond the .01 level of confidence.

DISCUSSION

Almost all correlations between the two tests of convergent thinking and the five measures of divergent thinking were significant. Hence, the present data do not support the notion that convergent thinking and divergent thinking are completely independent aspects of intellect. In this respect, they are consistent with other studies which have reported significant correlations between convergent and divergent thinking.

Theorists too have stressed the essentially overlapping nature of the two kinds of thinking. Maslow (1954) argues that, although some kind of coding (convergent thinking) is essential to handle the masses of incoming stimuli which the individual processes, creativity involves the capacity to master and go beyond conventional ways of coding data. A similar point has been made by Pribram

(1964, p. 107) who points out that there is no neurological basis for regarding convergent and divergent thinking as separate processes, but that divergent thinking arises out of convergent thinking. Finally, in a similar vein, Gordon (1961, p. 9) stresses the importance of thorough knowledge of basic material, pointing out that the 'moment of insight' described by Ghiselin (1955, pp. 29, 30) can only arise out of a thorough knowledge of the field, a knowledge acquired, clearly, through the exercise of convergent thinking.

Hence, the data obtained in this study suggest that the relationship between divergent thinking and convergent thinking may be summarized in the following way. The two skills represent overlapping aspects of intellectual functioning which probably interact in creative productions. Divergent thinking may well arise out of convergent thinking, which constitutes a base on which higher level activity rests.

In this conception, the correlations between divergent and convergent thinking are seen as reflecting the extent to which convergent thinking underlies divergent thinking, either as some kind of threshold as Vernon (1964) has suggested, or perhaps as a necessary precursor to divergent activity. Nevertheless, correlations between the two kinds of tests do not account for more than a small portion of their respective variances. To the extent that scores on tests of divergent thinking are not predictable from conventional tests, divergent thinking may be regarded as a separate aspect of intellect not sampled by the kinds of measures most often used in assessing students' potential. That these aspects of intellect are worth measuring and are important to the teacher is made apparent by the fact that conventional IQ tests usually account for only about one quarter of the variance of achievement measures (Getzels and Jackson, 1962, p. 2).

REFERENCES

Andrews, E. G. The development of imagination in the pre-school child. *University of Iowa studies in character*, 1930, 3.

Bruner, J. S. *On knowing.* . . . Cambridge, Mass.: Harvard University Press, 1962.

Burt, C. Preface in Koestler, A. *The act of creation.* London: Hutchinsin, 1964.

French, J. W., Ekstrom, R. B., and Price, L. A. *Manual for kit of reference tests for cognitive factors.* Princeton: ETS, 1963.

Getzels, J. W., and Jackson, P. W. *Creativity and intelligence.* New York: 1962.

Ghiselin, B. *The creative process.* New York: Mentor Books, 1955.

Gordon, W. J. *Synectics.* New York: Harper Bros., 1961.

Guilford, J. P. Creativity. *Amer Psychologist,* 1950, 5 pp. 444–454.

Ketcham, W. A., and Kheiralla, S. Creativity in relation to intelligence and school achievement. In *Collected papers of the Inter-institutional seminar.* Education Department, Henry Ford Museum, 1962.

Lowenfeld, V. Current Research on creativity. *J. nat, educ. Assoc.,* 1958, 47, pp. 538–540.

Marsh, R. W. A Statistical reanalysis of Getzels and Jackson's data. *Brit. J. educ. Psychol.,* 1964, 34 pp. 91–93.

Maslow, A. H., *Motivation and personality.* New York: Harper, 1954.

Meer, B., and Stein, M. I. Measures of intelligence and creativity. *J. Psychol.,* 1955, 39, pp. 117–126.

Pribram, K. H. Neurological notes on the art of educating. In Hilgard, E. R. (Ed.) *NSSE Yrbook.,* LXIII, Chicago: University of Chicago Press, 1964.

Richards, J. M., Cline, V. B., and Needham, W. E. Creativity tests and teacher and self judgments of originality. *J. exp. Educ.,* 1964, 32, pp. 281–285.

Ripple, R. E., and May, F. Caution in comparing creativity and IQ. *Psychol. Rep.,* 1962, 10, pp. 229–230.

Taylor, C. W. (Ed.) *Creativity: progress and potential.* New York: McGraw-Hill, 1964.

Thorndike, R. L. The measurement of creativity. *Teach. Coll. Rec.,* 1963, 64, pp. 422–424.

Torrance, E. P. *Education and the Creative potential.* Minneapolis: University of Minnesota Press, 1963.

Torrance, E. P. *Guiding creative talent.* Englewood Cliffs: Prentice-Hall, 1962.

Toynbee, A. Has America neglected its creative minority? *Calif. Monogr.,* 1962, 72, pp. 7–10.

Vernon, P. E. Creativity and intelligence. *Educ. Res.,* 1964, 6, pp. 163–169.

Welch, L. Recombination of ideas in creative thinking. *J. appl. Psychol.,* 1946, 30, pp. 638–643.

WHETHER CONVERGENT THINKING UNDERLIES DIVERGENT THINKING or vice versa, educators now want to train people to look for the right answer and *also* to look for all possible answers. Naturally, if one gets in the habit of looking for all possible answers, he begins to suspect that there is no one right answer. Also, the teacher who believes he is having a creative discussion with his class when quizzing them to elicit the key words in his memorized lesson plan is in for an unsettling experience.

The teacher, as usual, is crucial. Much depends upon his own creative talent and training. E. Paul Torrance is one of the most active workers in this field. He and Ethel Hansen, of Wisconsin State College, published a study in *Psychological*

Reports in 1965, entitled "The Question-Asking Behavior of Highly Creative and Less Creative Basic Business Teachers Identified by a Paper-and-Pencil Test." It is reprinted here.[3]

One of the most common and persistent characteristics of the creative person is his tendency to ask questions about the things that puzzle him. Since he is attracted to the puzzling, the unknown, and the unusual, the creative child's questions are numerous, provocative, and frequently embarrassing. Such questions are rather severely punished and this type of questioning tends to drop out of the behavior of all except the most stubbornly creative persons of our society.

Even among the most creative persons of modern history, rather severe punishment has resulted from a tendency to ask questions about the unknown and the puzzling. Tom Edison's teacher did not like the kind of questions Tom asked. As a result, Tom spent many of the mornings during the three months that he attended school on the low stool in the corner of the schoolroom. After three months, the teacher decided that young Tom was mentally "addled." The teacher became enraged one morning when Tom asked why water ran uphill in some rivers instead of downhill as in most rivers. Albert Einstein also received a great deal of punishment for asking questions about the things that puzzled him. In his early school years he was sometimes thrashed for asking such questions at school. Before graduating, he was asked to withdraw from school and became a dropout simply because he asked his teachers too many embarrassing questions. Of course, no one at that time knew the answers to some of Einstein's questions and he himself discovered the answers to some of them in his maturity. Fortunately, Edison, Einstein, and other creative people continued asking questions about the unknown and the puzzling.

In considering the requirements for a more creative kind of education, educators at least since the days of Socrates have recognized the need for asking provocative questions. Studies of classroom behavior, however, indicate that provocative questions are rarely asked at any level of education. One study (Fowlkes, 1962), for example, showed that over 90% of the questions asked by junior high social studies teachers called only for the reproduction of textbook information. When efforts have been made to encourage teachers to ask provocative questions, it has become obvious that few teachers possess such skills. Presumably, they stopped practic-

3. Reprinted by permission of *Psychological Reports.*

ing these skills at an early age and find it difficult even deliberately to ask other than factual questions about the knowns.

In this study, an effort is made to ascertain whether or not a group of highly creative basic business teachers identified on the basis of a paper-and-pencil test of creative thinking ability manifest question-asking behavior in the classroom different from that of their less creative peers who were identified by the same battery of paper-and-pencil tests.

PROCEDURE

Data for this study were obtained as a part of a larger study which involved the administration of a battery of creative thinking tests known as Test of Imagination, Form DX, and developed by the senior author. Ss were the entire population of ninth and tenth grade basic business teachers in the Twin Cities and selected suburban schools in Anoka, Forest Lake, Bloomington, and Spring Lake Park, Minnesota.

Form DX (Torrance, 1965) includes the following tasks: Product Improvement Test (requiring the production of clever, interesting, and unusual ways of improving a stuffed toy dog so that it will be more fun for a child to play with), Unusual Uses (calling for the listing of interesting and unusual uses of this same toy), Unusual Uses of Tin Cans, the Ask-and-Guess Test (calling for the production of questions about the unknowns in a picture, hypotheses about preceding causes, and hypotheses about subsequent effects), and the Circles Test (calling for the sketching of varied and unusual objects with a circle as a main element). Testing time was 50 min. A total of 29 teachers were tested and their responses were scored by experienced scorers under the supervision of the senior author. Responses were scored for fluency (number of relevant responses), flexibility (number of different categories of responses or approaches to the problem), and originality (statistical infrequency and creative strength of responses). On the basis of total raw scores, two criterion groups (the six highest scoring teachers and the six lowest scoring teachers) were identified.

The names of the 12 teachers in the two criterion groups were given to the observers, two graduate students in business education, without identifications as to high or low creativity. An observation scale devised for use in a larger study being conducted by the two observers was used for recording the classroom behavior of the 12 teachers. Observations were made at the end of every 30-sec. interval throughout each of five class sessions randomly selected over a semester for each of the 12 teachers. Observer reliability was established at a highly satisfactory level (Hansen, 1965). Included among the observations was a record of the questions asked by each teacher during the five class sessions observed.

Using a scoring system developed and validated by Burkhart and Bernheim (1963), labeled "Divergent Power," each question was assigned a score. This scoring system assigns heaviest weights to questions that call for divergent responses and are self-involving. Least credit is given for simple answer questions and factual questions (other than those calling for divergent responses). To qualify as divergent, a question must call for a basic alteration, the projection of the self into a new world, or a projection of the self into an object or situation. Questions are considered self-involving when they make use of "you" and rely upon personal experience, perception, opinion, attitude, or thought for an answer.

Questions were also classified as "Divergent-Provocative" or "Factual-Reproductive." A question was classified as "Divergent-Provocative," if it met the criteria outlined above and required productive thinking beyond textbooks and lectures. It was classified as "Factual-Reproductive," if it called for the reproduction of facts included in the textbook, lecture, or the like. There were few disagreements in classifications by two independent judges.

RESULTS

The mean Divergent Power score of the six highly creative teachers was 58.83 which was compared with the mean of 2.67 for the six less creative teachers. The *t* ratio of this difference in means is 2.89, significant at between the .01 and .02 levels of confidence.

A total of 330 scoreable questions were asked by the six highly creative teachers and 243 were asked by the six less creative teachers. The percentage of factual questions asked by the highly creative group was 36.67 compared with 76.13% for the less creative teachers. This difference in percentage is significant at the .01 level.

The percentage of divergent questions asked by the highly creative teachers was 10.91, with 0.82 for the less creative teachers. This difference, too, is significant at better than the .01 level.

DISCUSSION

From the data that have been presented, it is very clear that the criterion groups of basic business teachers participating in this study differ markedly in their question-asking behavior in the classroom. The highly creative teachers by comparison with their less creative peers achieved significantly higher scores on the Divergent Power measure devised by Burkhart and Bernheim; a smaller proportion of their questions are of the factual-reproductive variety and a larger proportion of them are of the divergent-provocative variety.

The data have the obvious limitations of a small sample of teachers in a single subject-matter area. The question-asking behavior of a teacher deals with only one aspect of his creative behavior. The data have certain virtues, however. The criterion groups were carefully selected and differ fairly markedly on the creativity dimensions assessed by the paper-and-pencil test battery whose reliability and validity has been discussed in detail elsewhere (Torrance, 1965). The observations were carefully made by two well qualified observers experienced in the field of instruction in question and skilled in shorthand and other observational skills. The criterion groups were selected from the total population of basic business teachers in the geographical area accessible to the observers.

Even in the group of highly creative teachers in this study, it is interesting to note that the percentage of divergent-provocative questions is rather low, just slightly above 10%. The less creative teachers asked almost no questions in this category, less than 1%. These findings are in line with results from other studies analyzing classroom questions (Fowlkes, 1962), the objectives of teachers (Torrance, 1963), and college admissions (Mednick, 1961).

REFERENCES

Burkhart, R. C., & Bernheim, G. *Object Question Test Manual.* University Park, Pa.: Dept. of Art Education Research, Pennsylvania State Univer., 1963. (Mimeo)

Fowlkes, J. G. *The Wisconsin improvement program for teacher education and local school systems.* Madison, Wis.: College of Education, Univer. of Wisconsin, 1962.

Hansen, E. A comparison of the teaching behaviors of highly creative and less creative basic business teachers. Unpublished doctoral dissertation, Univer. of Minnesota, 1965.

Mednick, S. A. Development of admission criteria for colleges and universities that will not eliminate such applicants as the bright nonconformist, the underchallenged, and the individual with highly specialized ability. In *Goals for higher education in a decade of decision.* Washington, D.C.: Assn for Higher Education, 1961. Pp. 86–88.

Torrance, E. P. *Education and the creative potential.* Minneapolis: Univer. of Minnesota Press, 1963.

Torrance, E. P. *Rewarding creative behavior: experiments in classroom creativity.* Englewood Cliffs: Prentice-Hall, 1965.

THE CURRENT TREND OF LITERATURE SUGGESTS THAT THERE IS A possible happy marriage in the classroom between convergent and divergent thinking. It seems that after having gone off on divergent kicks, one must pull himself or his thinking together to make the convergent answer to the question of the moment. Productivity is apparently a blend of convergent and divergent. The convergent harnesses the energy of the divergent. We may have to learn to send a child hunting in all alleys, including blind ones, and then to help him sort through his findings for his usable answer of the moment. This may mean the death of lesson plans that presume to anticipate children's answers to "stimulating" questions. It may mean that a teacher's lesson plan will simply indicate an area to be covered and some hopeful stimulants to be offered along the way.

Torrance's book, *Rewarding Creative Behavior: Experiments in Classroom Activity,* published by Prentice-Hall in 1965, was reviewed by David Hawkins of the University of Colorado in *Contemporary Psychology* in 1966. Hawkins discusses the meaning that this research has in the classroom. His review, "Reward or Facilitation?" is reprinted in full.[4]

In a series of studies carried out over the past seven or eight years, the author and his collaborators have concerned themselves with various problems relating to creativity in children and its educational implications. The book is concerned primarily with investigating ways in which schools inhibit or encourage creativity in children. There are two appendices. One is an account of the Minnesota Tests of Creative Thinking, the other a pamphlet used in several of the studies.

The first group of studies center around the use of the pamphlet referred to on "Rewarding Creative Thinking." The general conclusion is that the advice, activities and exercises conveyed by the pamphlet are without significant effect. The most significant result is found when teachers are grouped on the basis of their own scores

4. Reprinted by permission of *Contemporary Psychology* © 1966 American Psychological Association.

on Minnesota Tests. The author's special conclusion from studies in this group is that the opportunity to engage in activities and exercises intended to strengthen creativity have little effect unless the reward systems and evaluative practices of teachers are such as to reinforce and support the kind of performance aimed at. Four later studies are concerned with aspects of this hypothesis. Two involve spare-time activities of a fairly extensive kind, one a weekly literary magazine in an elementary school, the other a high school Saturday Seminar that sounds lively and imaginative. They show educationally significant results. The third study is concerned with the influence of peers as shown by different ways of grouping children. A final study in the set concerns the evaluative practices of trial teachers in SMSG mathematics, rather clearly showing the predominance of "trouble shooting evaluation" characteristic of the most effective teachers, as against praise-and-blame tendencies of the least effective ones.

There is a study of sex-typing as related to opportunities for creative performance. There is a study comparing educational stereotypes from five countries (the U.S., Germany, India, Greece, the Philippines), as correlated with the judgments of a "panel of experts" (American psychologists, no Buddhist sages!) on creativity.

The theoretical component of the book is contained in an initial discussion of definitions, a running commentary on the studies, and a final synoptic commentary. "Creativity" has been a controversial term, of course, and the author presents some diverging views as well as a pragmatic justification of his own position. His interest is in differences as pedagogically induced, and in the use of tests (which he has helped create). As a result he does not really talk about creativity, but about a complex of traits and aptitudes which are more or less plausibly involved in or concomitant with creativity. There is no discussion of the classical literature on the subject, from Plato to Polya. The real subject, however bannered, is the effect of school atmosphere and teacher style on the normal capacities of the human child for evolving certain kinds of excellence.

Whether "creativity" is a good banner, I do not know. At any rate I stand with Professor Torrance in the major tendency of his thinking about schools. Since, however, the chips are not down, let me put a few more in the air. The first trouble, I think, is a style of empirical investigation found in several of the studies. It would be unfair to Prof. Torrance not to add that the style is endemic. My concern is not that of the tough-minded methodologist, sniffing out contaminating variables, or of the zealous graduate student who wants to "clean it up." It is about a genre of investigation that produces only small perturbations or aims to find only small contrasts in an otherwise undefined milieu. Such investigations quite predictably reveal only weak relationships, quantitatively minor, statistically significant but of indeterminate significance.

An example is the experimental study of grouping, which puts children in a "creative" situation which is ad hoc, of fifty minutes duration, extrinsically motivated, with an immediate and merely quantitative output. The result is then taken to imply a very general conclusion to the effect that heterogeneous grouping (either by I.Q. or "creativity" scores) is more stressful than homogeneous grouping for the highly creative child. The experimental situation not only produces small contrasts, but it represents a one-point sample across a wide universe of possible teaching situations, and, I would hope, a vanishingly rare one. Skillful professional teachers group in many ways for many purposes, and they *evolve* these groupings by criteria that would be quite impossible to predict by such lumped, noise-diluted indices as tests provide, useful as these latter may be for some purposes. Where grouping is evolved in terms of children's complementary strengths, it is highly unlikely that such groups are homogeneous by this or that single scoring device. Such conclusions are *already* known. Would it not be better science to study, and learn from, the people who know them?

The literary magazine study, the seminar study, and the comparison of mathematics teachers' ways of evaluating are more significant. Perturbations and contrasts are stronger, although still weak as measured by the standards implicit in optimal teaching. Must we perhaps face up to the implication that as we work toward educationally more significant investigations in learning and creativity, our task becomes indistinguishable from that of major, though radically self-critical, educational innovation?

My second line of criticism is related to Professor Torrance's lack of discussion of what creativity—or children's normal learning capacity—is. My criticism concerns the title notion of "reward," which seems to be located all in the human environment, and none in the act or activity. What is called "reward" and what is called "evaluation"—as I read between the lines—are properly aspects of the facilitation of learning. This is the *direct* implication of the study of the effective mathematics teachers. Professor Torrance's distinction between creative activities and the reward system weakens his implicit thesis, or at any rate the thesis I would like him to put forth: that so-called "creative activities" without genuine facilitation of children's work (based, as the author well says, on *respect* for their capacities) are sham, just "twenty minutes of creativity." When genuinely and artfully facilitated, children's success needs no supplement, in the first approximation, by way of external and terminal reward. The essential reward is intrinsic, esthetic, or, in Dewey's old term, consummatory. Good teaching anticipates such experience and shares in its enjoyment, amplifies the enjoyment, and invests it with a larger meaning; but not with impertinent "rewards." Hence I would add to Prof. Torrance's maxim of "respect for the child" the maxim "respect for genuine subject matter." For it is only that which can liberate and discipline and reward; and it is only through common absorption in such subject-matter that children and teachers can meet effectively or help each other in their respective vocations.

WE SEE QUITE CLEARLY NOW THAT CREATIVITY IS NOT SIMPLY RE-stricted to the arts. It is essential to our survival as a civilization. With traditional teaching techniques, the most creative child in a class is often the biggest pain in the neck to the teacher. It seems obvious, however, that unless we retool— that is, develop new teaching techniques that will permit creativity to flourish along with other talents (while managing some content at the same time)—we may have quite a pain in our civilization.

Developing new teaching techniques means exercising professional creativity. It means taking chances and daring to try something new. Teachers face administrators and administrators face the community, but daring that permits teacher creativity to flourish is our only hope for tapping the larger reservoir of creative talent in students.

Perhaps the handful in each generation with striking creative talents would creatively surmount the barriers of traditional teaching as they have in the past and would go on to their great accomplishments. The problem is that the handful that was sufficient in the nineteenth century and the handful that managed to help us this far into the twentieth century may be spread too thin to solve our multiplying complex problems in the twenty-first century.

CHAPTER 4

Emotional Resources

THE TITLE OF THIS CHAPTER WAS PURPOSELY CHOSEN INSTEAD OF "Mental Health" or "Mental Hygiene." The former term suggests a contrary condition to illness and the latter suggests brainwashing or "a cerebral douche before breakfast," as a student once charmingly put it. We have supposedly been too busy with the usual classroom curriculum to take classroom time for psychological problems unless a youngster was officially "disturbed." Any observer in a usual classroom, however, knows that this is not true. Five minutes of a teacher's lesson plan is good for at least fifteen or twenty minutes if the children are alive and breathing because they are so busy licking emotional wounds or doing calisthenics with emotional resources in an attempt to get stronger. So the teacher is forced to deal with psychological factors in a haphazard manner. Unfortunately, in the haphazard process, emotional liabilities grow stronger.

Progressive education has paid a great deal of attention to these matters for the past few decades, though the scattered results have not been impressive. The mainstream of education has, as it often does, picked up keywords and gone through the motions. It is now commonplace to see "guidance lessons" though it is rare to see one that touches the youngsters' emotions any more deeply than the lesson on geometry that precedes it or the one on the structure of the national governmer that follows. Helping children to develop emotional assets just doesn't fit into a neat half-hour lesson.

The push is on now to get this important area competently covered by teachers. This involves increasing the teacher's sensitivity to emotional nuances. But resistance to the push is great. Some educators are morally opposed and some feel inadequate.

Not the least of the problem is the tradition of viewing things mental in terms of health or illness. One of the most articulate current writers in this field is T. S. Szatz who has been waging a fierce battle against "the myth of mental illness." His writings may be found in book form as well as in journals of psychiatry, psychology, social work, law, and education.

The general issue has never been more eloquently stated than by Ivor Kraft, who is quoted earlier, in the chapter on the disadvantaged. He makes the point that prevention is an enormous social task. The teacher is one of the key professionals involved, and the *only* professional in our culture who has more than fleeting contact with every growing child. His article, entitled "Preventing Mental Ill Health in Early Childhood" appeared in *Mental Hygiene* in 1964. Excerpts from it are reprinted here.[1]

Among the many excellent aphorisms in the English language, few are as popular and often repeated as this: "An ounce of prevention is worth a pound of cure." From the earliest days of scientific medicine, when the Greeks assigned cure to the god Aesculapius and prevention to the goddess Hygeia, wise men have recognized the essential difference between these two activities among healers and teachers of men.

We have recognized their difference but also their interdependence. It was always known that if one was a faithful worshiper of Hygeia, then perhaps one would not have to call on powers of Aesculapius. But we have always been much more awed by the potency and magic of the healer and curer than we have by the pedestrian wisdoms of the preventer. When Aesculapius became

1. Reprinted from Vol. 48 (1964), pp. 413–423, by permission of the National Association for Mental Health, Inc.

so mighty in his healing powers that he even succeeded in reviving the dead, Zeus had him put to death. Apollo intervened and persuaded Zeus to resurrect Aesculapius in the form of a God. It was not the first nor the last time that death yielded transfiguration.

Thus, we have always regarded with awe and mystery the powers of the healer. As for the patient and unassuming protectors of the public health, we have held them in a much more casual light. Unless my knowledge of Greek mythology fails me, I am not aware that anyone ever tried to kill Hygeia for her extravagant successes.

Yet it is only right that Hygeia, too, should have been elevated to godhood. The ounce of prevention, no matter how hard to come by, is certainly worth the pound of cure. Today, with our many recently undertaken studies in the epidemiology of mental illness, we are more aware than ever of the great need to eliminate this agonizing problem.

The recently issued volumes of the Joint Commission on Mental Illness and Health present us with a wealth of documentation establishing the proliferating roots of mental ill health and its connection with a multitude of related social problems, such as delinquency, poverty, and alcoholism. A recent study of mental health in Manhattan concludes that as many as one out of four adults has levels of mental ill health requiring treatment.

It is clear that mental disorder has now emerged as our leading public health problem. We have all but wiped out general paresis. Soon we will defeat arteriosclerosis, senile deterioration, cancer, heart diseases, and certain varieties of mental retardation. All of these may one day be eliminated from the crucial roster of medical concerns, just as blacksmithing, once a flourishing trade in America, has all but disappeared in the farms and villages of our country. Just as the automobile replaced the horse, so the disenchanted mind is about to replace the deteriorating flesh. Perhaps we may look forward to the day when the sad state of our immortal souls will preoccupy us more than the agitated condition of our mortal minds.

It should be said at the onset of this presentation that it is a serious mistake to assign the achievement of mental well-being exclusively to the clinical professions. No profession and no discipline has a monopoly on that phenomenon we call the mind. Physicians, surgeons, neurologists, psychologists, psychiatrists, psychiatric social workers—no one of these acting alone or in concert can secure among men those benign relationships which are the only guarantee of mental well-being. Mental hygiene must be a major concern of economists, administrators, sociologists, statesmen, and above all, educators.

With more than one-third of our families compelled to get by with incomes that lead to violation of the minimum standards of physical health,. nutrition, housing, and all the rest, how can we expect positive mental health to prevail in the land? What good will it do if we erect a friendly neighborhood mental health clinic on the corner of every city block—right next to the friendly neighborhood saloon—as long as we continue to have rat and cockroach infested slum housing, and parents who are so preoccupied with keeping body and soul together that they simply do not have the spiritual strength and peace of mind necessary for good childrearing?

The ever-present contradictions, the blatant antithesis in our culture and styles of living in the United States contaminate all efforts at making neat biological or psychological assessments. Poverty and disease, miserable slums and job insecurity, malnutrition and primitive cultural aspiration—all these clash with luxury and precious neurotic drives, gaudy suburban dwellings and inane occupations, overnutrition and pseudocultural pursuits.

There are those who have neither the time or inclination to search for values or even to know what such a search is all about, and there are those who seek continually and never find. In the United States we sanctimoniously worship a God of loving-kindness and feverishly devise monstrous weapons designed to destroy all life on earth in as much time as it takes to read this paper.

We are all of us besmirched by these terrible contradictions, and by our inability to live consistently above the animalistic level. Is it truly possible to speak of good mental health and primary prevention in such a world?

Our society is so constructed that it deliberately violates one of the basic insights about human nature. There is nothing new about this insight. It is as ancient and venerable as the roots of scientific medicine and the origins of systematic philosophy. It was known to Hippocrates and is embodied in the oath which carries his name. It was known to Plato and Epictetus, to Avicenna and Maimonides, to Johann Weyer and Philippe Pinel. It was made the cornerstone of Harry Stack Sullivan's psychiatry, although Sullivan certainly did not invent it.

This powerful insight asserts that it is the relationships which prevail among men as individuals and as members of a structured society that ultimately determine their basic states of mental health and spiritual well-being. It is possible to have a strong and healthy mind in a weak, even a tortured and devastated human body. The example of Helen Keller comes to mind. But to have strong and healthy *collectivities of minds* we must have healthy social relationships.

We shall be forever doomed to failure if we persist only in seeking to invent techniques of prevention, only in weaving subtle theories of human personality that will reveal the vulnerable crisis points, only in forwarding still newer and more fanciful fashions in psychotherapy. We are merely reshuffling the deck; the cards remain the same. Until we learn to prevene as well in the social order, there will be no real primary prevention.

In the United States today we do not yet possess a true philosophy of primary prevention, because we do not yet have clear convictions on how we must prevene in the social order. We do not yet have genuine programs of primary prevention because we are so committed and over-committed to symptomatic treatment methods.

We seem powerless, each of us in our own professional identities, to move in the direction of collective efforts, to regroup social forces with fearlessness and selflessness. At bottom, with the prominent exception of certain vital social security measures inaugurated in the 1930's, we in the United States are still operating in a framework of nineteenth-century concepts of charity, although we heatedly deny this.

What is needed is the strength, the audacity and the courage to sustain the broadest possible vision of man's ultimate potentialities, of his proved capacity to remake his own nature, while at the same time working within the contemporary framework and its incredibly flexible limitations. So much is possible, and so much is impossible.

We must have the courage to plunge into action despite the waves of ignorance and despair which pound all around us, despite our painful awareness that it is the destiny of man not to leap from ignorance and evil to wisdom and goodness, but rather to traverse an unknown road from error and limited vision to less error and less limited vision.

As teachers, nurses, counselors, parents, physicians, we too plod along this endless path which began in the times when the ice covered our planet and a frail thinking creature emerged to fashion tools and to be fashioned by them. It is our task to carry this creature another step along the path and, while so doing, to diminish pain, to remove obstacles, to forestall error and failure.

But this is work not of prevention but of promotion. In the last analysis we will prevent those nonbiological failures, dysfunctions, errors and miseries of behavior which we lump together and call mental illness only if we are bold and courageous in promoting those still tenuous and primitively developed capacities of man for tenderness, empathy, altruism and selflessness.

What, then, is true prevention? It is the continual creation and re-creation of a world which fosters these capacities among men.

SYLVIA ASHTON WARNER IN HER BOOK, *Teacher*, SPEAKS OF CHILdren as having two vents, one for aggression and one for creativity. If one is sealed the other becomes more active. Educators have been actively, if not always pleasantly, aware of aggression for a long time. It has been bottled, dammed, channeled, and observed like water. Educators have admired it, realized our dependence on it, and feared it.

The book *On Aggression*, by Konrad Lorenz, has enjoyed almost uniformly positive reviews. Grace Rotzel, who was director of the small but educationally influential School in Rose Valley from its inception until 1966, wrote a review of this book for the June, 1966 issue of the *School in Rose Valley Bulletin*. In it she points to the need of educators to help young developing humans understand their own aggression. Her review is reprinted here.[2]

A new book by Konrad Lorenz is an event for those who enjoyed the account of his pet jackdaws and greylag geese in *King Solomon's Ring*. Now, fifteen years later, his increasing concern about man's predicament has moved him to describe what the natural scientist has discovered about the nature of aggression and how it is possible to remedy what he calls the derailment of man's aggressive drive, by inquiring impartially into its natural causes.

The concern of this book is not primarily with the fighting between species, but the aggression within members of the same group, for the author points out that the struggle between species is not dangerous in the natural state because the predator never

2. Reprinted by permission of The School in Rose Valley and the author.

goes so far as to cause extinction of the prey, but establishes an equilibrium endurable by both species. It is the inter-species aggression that has both served to preserve the family, and also, by process of selection, has caused the advanced development of fighting in many higher animals, including man.

The first chapters give observations on typical forms of aggression with discussion of its species-preserving function, and concrete examples of evolutionary changes (Lorenz calls them "inventions") by which aggression is channeled into harmless activity. The chapter entitled "Behavioral Analogies to Morality," describing these so-called inventions, and four chapters giving a conception of four very different types of social organization, make clear the natural science facts from which the author derives his belief that man can learn something useful in circumventing the dangers arising from his aggressive drives.

He describes the "pride-inspired" obstacles to human self-knowledge and declares that the long sought missing link between animals and the really humane being is ourselves! The story of man's refusal to accept the facts of evolution as pertaining to himself is discouraging, but Lorenz faces it with optimism. Why do reasonable beings behave so unreasonably? Why have people and governments never learned anything from history? These paradoxes, he says, fall into place like the pieces of a jigsaw puzzle if one assumes that human behavior is still subject to all the laws of instinctive behavior. "It is plain biology of Homo sapiens L. that ought to be considered the 'big science'. . . . Sufficient knowledge of man and his position in the universe would automatically determine the ideals for which we have to strive. Sufficient humor may make mankind blessedly intolerant of phony, fraudulent ideals."

This message from a natural scientist is confirmed by the philosopher Sir Herbert Read with his statement in *Art and Life:* "Unless we can discover a method of basing education on these primary biological processes, not only shall we fail to create a society united in love; we shall continue to sink deeper into disunity, mass neuroses and war."

As challenges to education continue to increase, we are glad to have a new book like this one by Dr. Lorenz for another guidepost.

RESEARCH THAT HELPS US UNDERSTAND HOW TO HELP GROWING youngsters develop greater emotional strength is sadly sparse.

One reason is the roadblocks put in its path. Lucy Rau, of Michigan State University, reviewing *In Pursuit of Self-Esteem*, by Pauline Sears and Vivian Sherman, for *Contemporary Psychology* in 1965, said:

Questions are often raised as to the extent to which personality testing (and the concerns with children's emotional adjustment and interpersonal relationships it reflects) is relevant or even proper to the public school as an educational institution. This volume provides a very nice demonstration of the point, which should be much more obvious than it apparently is to some segments of our society, that the child's academic learning cannot be understood or facilitated apart from the interpersonal context in which it occurs.

A happy exception to the relative invisibility of researchers in this area is Lois Murphy, who has published much of her understanding of how children learn to "cope" in *The Widening World of Childhood*, published by Basic Books, Inc., in 1962. The entire volume is recommended reading.

The problem that continually besets us is how to train teachers who will be better able to facilitate emotional growth. It means developing the teachers' sensitivity to the expression of emotion. The teacher-to-be has few models to emulate. Certainly it is the rare college course that even tries to use the emotional expression and awareness of its students to practice what is preached about "mental health."

Another problem is where to find the time in the already crowded school day. As indicated earlier, part of the time undoubtedly will come from that time now haphazardly devoted to the same, but unlabeled, area.

Part of the possible answer is suggested in a paper given by Enid Hobart Campbell, of Trenton State College, at the 1966 Annual Meeting of the Eastern Psychological Association in New York City. Teachers in training are able to ease the time and pressure burden of regular classroom teachers while learning how to deal with the psychological matters they must face one day as teachers. This partial solution has grown out of attempts to help those who fail. Perhaps it can be used before children fail. A condensed version of her paper appears here.[3]

Therapeutic tutoring is similar to tutoring in its aim of increasing the child's mastery of his academic skills, but it differs from tutoring in that it also consciously aims to develop the child's spontaneous interest in his work—to increase his self-motivation—and it is concerned about academic progress always in the context of total personality adjustment.

What the student does in the tutoring sessions is, of course, dependent upon the individual child's emotional and educational status, but there are certain general principles that apply in most cases. The tutor is first instructed to divide each session roughly into two equal time periods. One of these is reserved for the activity that the tutor has prepared for the session, while the other half is the child's own period during which he can select from a variety of play and educational materials and, within reasonable limits, do what he wants with them. To help the tutor organize her time, the remedial reading specialist tests the child and then prepares a list of suggested activities for the tutor, games, skills and so forth that would be helpful for this child. The tutor is instructed not to use materials—or to work on specific assignments—from the child's regular class.

The part of the session in which the child is free to choose his own activities is also a very important learning experience for both the child and tutor. For some children it may be one of the first occasions when an adult accepts and cares about the child's own concerns and interests; for others it serves as an opportunity to release some of the emotional tensions developed at home or during the school day; while for still others who are anxious and inhibited it presents a frightening situation where there are no guidelines or rules. This is also the part of the session when the educationally trained tutors initially feel most uncomfortable, yet many of them become able to use this time to empathize with a child in a way that they have never been able to before, to see first-hand some of the emotional and motivational pressures that intrude into the learning situation, and to discover for themselves the sense of inferiority and lack of self-confidence underlying some learning inhibitions.

The student teacher prepares a brief report describing the work accomplished during the session, the play activities of the child,

---

3. Reprinted by permission of the author.

and the effect of the child and the tutor. These reports are read and discussed during the weekly group supervisory sessions, and the students learn to develop hypotheses about things that puzzle them and develop a greater understanding and awareness of the complexity of their own emotional reactions. These sessions retain a focus on the reality aspects of the children's and tutor's reactions, and the students do not engage in any group therapy or discussions of their own emotional problems. For example, a tutor may become quite upset because her child wished to leave the session early. In the class presentation of her session, it is clear that the child wants to leave the session early shortly after he has learned that the tutor will be on vacation next week and so will not be in to see him. The general dynamic significance of the child's emotional reaction to desertion and the emotional significance of separation and loss are discussed. Then specific suggestions are made about handling the problem—such as telling the child that you are disappointed, too, and will miss him; sending him a postcard when you are away; and helping him put his own feelings into words—such as saying "perhaps you are angry with me because we cannot meet next week." But the personal significance of the tutor's reaction to the child's anger or rejection is never explored. Through this type of open discussion in group supervision sessions the student-tutors learn from each other's tutoring problems and increase their insights into all human relationships.

From the student-tutor's standpoint, one of the additional values of the course comes from their collaboration with the regular classroom teacher of the child they are tutoring. The tutors have a regular conference with the teacher every two weeks.

The future teachers who act as tutors in this program learn certain attitudes and techniques to improve their classroom functioning that they do not ordinarily acquire in their teacher training. One of the most important of these is to see the need for classroom discipline in its proper perspective; to provide a structure in which the teacher is able to teach and the student to learn, to protect the children from situations involving a high probability of physical danger, and to guide the children when their limited experience, judgment, and self-control are not adequate to the demands of the situation. Too many teachers have been taught that a punitive attitude is essential for classroom discipline, and that only when the child suffers and realizes who is "the boss" can order be maintained.

A second major discovery for some tutors is that children enjoy many of the things they learn through exploration and discovery, and that while some learning will always be arduous and difficult, the amount learned is not always proportional to the amount of suffering the child and teacher experience. Finally, the tutors discover in comparing their experiences how very different individual children are in their emotional needs and sensitivities, and how psychologically vulnerable and how psychologically resilient young children can be.

In summary, the goals of the tutoring program for the child are to help his mastery of basic reading and number skills; through his enjoyment of his work to improve his attitude towards the school, teachers, and learning; and to change his attitude towards himself as a person of competence and worth. The schools see the program as bridging an important gap between the busy classroom teacher on the one hand, and the Child Guidance Center, on the other. To the college, the program holds the hope that some of its graduates will go forth to their first teaching assignments with a greater sensitivity to the mental health needs of the children and a surer knowledge of some of the ways to meet these needs.

TEACHERS, HAVING GROWN UP IN THE ESSENTIALLY AUTHORITARIAN system of the school, tend to perpetuate that system. When in trouble we call for the "authority" or the "expert." We have had difficulty in accepting the obvious fact that there are not enough experts (or there is not sufficient authority) to help us. The teacher is faced with the dual task of developing emotional strength through classroom learning for both the normally troubled child and the child officially designated "emotionally disturbed."

For those who consider this kind of learning "therapeutic" and therefore inappropriate for the classroom, Louis Hay had an answer in "The School as a Therapeutic Community," published in 1965 in the *American Journal of Orthopsychiatry*.[4]

There is a widespread insistence that the school's therapeutic efforts should be severely limited. This is unrealistic because:

4. Copyright, The American Orthopsychiatric Association, Inc. Reproduced by permission.

1. The dividing line between learning to live effectively or destructively is probably more responsive to similar laws of learning than is ordinarily granted.

2. The perhaps 80 to 90 percent of disturbed children have no access to special agencies. Schools face the resulting critical problems now.

3. There is little likelihood that conventional therapeutic resources can be extended to meet such vast needs.

4. There is already impressive evidence that new therapeutic designs in which school resources are central can make an unprecedented therapeutic contribution.

A comprehensive program for a school as a therapeutic community should include the early identification of disordered children, cooperation with community agencies for the diagnosis and treatment of disturbed youngsters with organic disabilities, a special educational program oriented to the child's pattern of deficits and defense, casework with parents and recreational planning.

CHILDREN WHOSE EMOTIONAL STRENGTH PROVES INSUFFICIENT MAY need special help, but all children need some help. The teacher may not be able to provide special help or sufficient help directly but may be surprised to find that he is indeed the "expert" who is supervising and coordinating the efforts of others. News accounts appear with increasing frequency describing the help of college students, high school volunteers, or therapeutic "moms" who offer time to help individual students. More often than not, the classroom teacher must coordinate and direct this help offered by volunteers.

Little of the research evidence to date offers the teacher guidance in helping children develop stronger emotional resources. J. B. Edwards, in a literature review entitled "Some Studies of the Moral Development of Children," published in the English Journal, *Educational Research*, pointed out how much research effort is devoted to understanding the intellectual development of children and how little is devoted to that part of their development that will largely steer their course through life.

Why the paucity of research? Obviously a large part of the answer is that it would involve teacher-researchers who are sensitive to their own and their students' emotions. There has been an unspoken taboo on such research, and, as was pointed out earlier, teacher training programs are doing little to break it.

The general trend in this area of emotional resources seems to be away from the question of what to do with the disturbed, distraught, or ill, and toward the question of how to help growing children develop emotional strength.

Our problem is how to make the concept of "mental illness" unnecessary. School is a place where one learns to solve problems, even big ones. A child *learns* arithmetic and he *learns* to live a satisfying life. In order to do the latter he must know a great deal about himself. He must learn about his aggression and his tender feelings. He must develop his emotional assets.

How can we help him to learn about this very big part of himself that has to date been handled haphazardly in the classroom? It has been ignored, but never has been absent from the school day. It appears that we are now about to take the giant step. We are looking for a research footing. We are about to add this aspect of classroom experience to those other aspects of the classroom experience that are handled professionally by the professional teacher.

There is a lot of willing help around. The helpers, whether or not they are teachers in training, can learn from helping. Now all we need is full community approval, more research, a chance to organize our knowledge and our helpers, and a program that trains teachers to make use of all this. It seems formidable but we will do it because we must.

CHAPTER 5

Grouping

For as long as there have been textbooks of Educational Psychology most of their authors have feebly noted in passing that grouping children by chronological age seemed a curious custom of educators. The snowball rolled with lethargy into the question of "to group or not to group?"

At length this question came into focus and got reformulated. It is difficult to think of teaching without having some kind of grouping, in the educational world of the 1960s. The problem is, what kind? Do we continue the venerable custom of grouping according to age? Do we group according to ability? By the way, how do we define ability? Do we separate children with physiological handicaps from children without such handicaps? Is it true these children have more pressing psychological needs and shouldn't be burdened with the same academic requirements? What about emotionally disturbed children? Should we leave some of them in the regular classroom? Isn't it fairer to them and to the other children to group them separately?

The research evidence has been a long time in catching up with the questions but now that the answers are coming in, we still find ourselves in a dither. New questions appear. How many years should a child stay in one kind of school? Should we use a 4–4–4 system? Perhaps the 6–4–2 would be better. How about trying three years in each of four different schools? Perhaps the thing to do is to switch over entirely to ungraded classes? Perhaps team-teaching is the answer? Or maybe we could just go back to the one-room schoolhouse.

A large-scale study published by Walter R. Borg, who is Chairman of the Bureau of Educational Research in the College of Education at the Utah State University, took a long, hard empirical look at the question of ability grouping. The report of this study filled the entire Winter–1965 issue of the *Journal of Experimental Education*. The summary chapter only is reprinted here.[1]

The report is tougher sledding than most of the reading in this book. Because it is condensed information, it is suggested that the reader go through this summary slowly, diluting the condensation as best he can in order to catch the full flavor.

The general goal of this research has been to study differences in the effects upon elementary, junior high school, and high school pupils of an ability grouping system that differentiated the curriculum principally by adjusting the rate of presentation of curricular materials, and a random grouping system that differentiated the curriculum principally through the use of enrichment. Two adjacent and closely comparable school districts in Utah provided the setting in which these differences were explored. One of these districts employed random grouping with enrichment, and the other had adopted a system of ability grouping with acceleration, coincident with the start of this research.

Over 2,500 pupils from the fourth, sixth, seventh, eighth, and ninth grade levels were selected in the two districts at the beginning of the study. During the second year of the study, this sample was increased to about 4,000 pupils. Research data were collected over a four-year period in order to appraise the long term effects of the two grouping treatments. Pupils who were first tested early in grade four were followed through grade seven. As all samples were similarly followed over the period of the study, data were collected at

1. Reprinted with permission of Dembar Educational Research Services. Available in monograph form: Borg, Walter R., *Ability Grouping in the Public Schools* (Madison, Wisc.: Dembar Educational Research Services, Inc., 1966), 97 pp.

all grade levels from four through twelve. The district that employed ability grouping is referred to throughout this report as District A. The other district participating in this research, known as District R, employed random or heterogeneous grouping.

Three major types of differences were considered in analyzing most of the data. The first and most important comparisons were between comparable pupils in the two grouping treatments. These comparisons involved pupils of the same sex and ability level in the ability grouped and random grouped samples and are referred to as *between-treatment* differences. These differences provide the best evidence on the differential effects of ability grouping and random grouping upon the dependent variables. Comparisons between pupils of the same sex and in the same grouping treatment who differed in ability level are referred to as *level* or *within-treatment* differences. These comparisons tell us whether the grouping treatments had a differential effect upon pupils at different ability levels. The final classification used in the analysis was sex. Boys and girls who were in the same grouping treatment and at the same ability level were compared to provide knowledge about the sex-related differences on the dependent variables.

ACHIEVEMENT

Achievement data were collected for all samples and gains from year to year as well as gains over the entire four years were analyzed. This procedure provided a large body of data on the nature of long term achievement in the two grouping treatments. Also, because achievement data for two or more samples were available at most grade levels, extensive cross checking of the results was possible. During the first year of the study, the *California Achievement Test* was used, while in subsequent years, measures of mathematics, science, social studies and reading from the *STEP* battery were administered.

Elementary. Achievement in four subject areas as well as overall achievement were compared during the elementary school years for these samples. A total of 54 statistical comparisons based on analysis of variance and covariance were made between ability grouped and random grouped pupils. Of these 54 comparisons, 28 revealed statistically significant differences. Nineteen of these differences were favorable to District A pupils while nine favored District R pupils. Of the 19 differences favoring ability grouped pupils, 15 occurred during the first year of the study. If these first year differences had been due to a substantial superiority of ability grouping over random grouping, we would have expected the differences to grow larger each year as the cumulative effects of the better system widened the achievement gap. No such cumulative effects occurred and in fact, many of the achievement differences favoring District A disappeared by the time Sample IV pupils had completed the sixth grade. Thus, we may conclude that neither ability grouping with acceleration nor random grouping with enrichment is more effective for all ability levels of elementary-school pupils. When data for the different ability levels were considered separately, achievement advantages of the two grouping systems, though small, tended to favor ability grouping for superior pupils and random grouping for slow pupils. As was hypothesized, the achievement results for average pupils did not consistently favor either grouping treatment.

Junior High School. All five of the samples employed in this study were in junior high school at some time during the four years of the project. When we combine the achievement analyses for these five samples, we find that a total of 60 statistical comparisons were made between comparable groups in the two grouping treatments; 33 in mathematics and 27 in science. Of the differences in mathematics achievement, five were significant in favor of District A subgroups, five in favor of District R, and the remaining 23 were nonsignificant. Of the science comparisons, five differences were significant favoring District A, one favoring District R and the remaining 21 were nonsignificant.

A study of the results at each of the three ability levels indicates that there was some tendency for ability grouping to lead to greater mathematics achievement among superior pupils and greater science achievement among average pupils. Among slow pupils, the differences between the two grouping treatments were small, but tend to favor District R in both mathematics and science.

OVERACHIEVERS AND UNDERACHIEVERS

In this phase of the Utah study, samples of fourth and sixth grade pupils from random grouped and ability grouped classrooms were classified as overachievers, underachievers, and normal achievers based on the relationship between their achievement, chronological age, and mental age. The proportions of overachievers, normal achievers and underachievers among pupils of different ability levels in the two grouping systems were then compared.

There was a significant tendency for girls more frequently to be overachievers and less frequently to be underachievers than boys. This trend was present at both grade levels in both treatments.

Overall comparisons between District A and R indicated that there was a consistent trend for ability grouped pupils to be more often classified as overachievers and less often as underachievers. In comparing pupils at each of the three ability levels, we find that differences between superior pupils in the two districts were statistically significant at both fourth and sixth grades, with District A having more overachievers and a smaller percentage of underachievers than District R. No significant differences were found between the proportions of overachievers, underachievers, and normal achievers among pupils of average or low ability in the two districts.

STUDY METHODS AND ATTITUDES

Considerable evidence concerning study habits was collected over the four years of the Utah study. Pupils in Samples IV, VI, VII, and IX were administered study habits measured at grade levels ranging from seven to 12. Two measures were used, the *California Study Methods Survey* (CSMS) which yields three subtest scores, and the *Survey of Study Habits and Attitudes* (SSHA) which yield a total score only.

The Sample IV results on the CSMS showed all of the total score differences and seven of the nine subtest differences between comparable groups in Districts A and R to be statistically significant. Differences favored District R and were generally largest between pupils of superior ability. These results lead to the conclusions that pupils in a random grouping situation consistently develop better study methods during the elementary school years than pupils in an ability grouping situation.

Sample VI average pupils in District R received consistently higher scores on the CSMS than comparable District A pupils. No significant between-treatment differences were present for slow or superior pupils. Sample VIII average pupils in District R received higher SSHA scores. No significant between-treatment differences emerged from the Sample IX data. It may be concluded that if any advantage accrues from heterogeneous grouping at the secondary level, it is for average pupils, who made significantly greater gains in study habits in Samples VI and VIII.

SOCIOMETRIC CHOICE

A near-sociometric measure of the usual partial rank-order type was developed for use in this study. Three criteria were employed, each with five positive choices. Each subject was asked to indicate by placing a check mark beside names on a roster of his classmates, those whom he preferred under each criterion. The three criteria were: 1) the five children in the class who are your best friends; 2) the five children with whom you prefer to study; and 3) the five children whom you would most like to have with you if you were transferred to another classroom. Each pupil's sociometric status was obtained by summing the choices he received on the three criteria. After obtaining a sociometric choice score for each pupil, the pupils were classified as stars, regulars, neglectees, or isolates.

Sample VI pupils were administered the sociometric measure only once—in the sixth grade, and therefore, this sample was used only in the study of sociometric status patterns. Sample IV pupils were measured in the fourth, fifth, and sixth grades, and data from this sample were used to study sociometric status patterns, mobility of sociometric status, and relationships between sociometric status and other variables.

The sociometric data collected seem to provide considerable evidence relating to sociometric choice in ability grouped and random grouped classes during the intermediate grades. Analysis revealed that the overall proportions of stars, regulars, and neglectees in District A and District R were similar, thus leading to the conclusion that ability grouping did not result in a permanent leadership vacuum in groups of average and slow pupils.

Superior students were found to lose some sociometric status when placed in ability grouped classrooms. This loss was particularly evident in the star classification but was not accompanied by any increase in the neglectee-isolate classification. Data on mobility of sociometric status suggest that superior pupils regain some of this status loss after they have made an adjustment to the ability grouped situation. Average and slow pupils appear to have a far better chance of gaining social recognition in ability grouped classrooms than do comparable pupils in random grouped classrooms. For the slow pupil, ability grouping not only appears to increase the pupil's chances of being classified as a star, but also reduces his chances of being classified as a neglectee-isolate. Sociometric status mobility patterns between District A and R demonstrate a greater number of status changes in ability grouped classrooms. The trend of these changes is generally toward higher sociometric status, further supporting the conclusion that organization of pupils into ability grouped classes brings about marked changes in sociometric status patterns during the first one or two years and generally leads to permanently higher status patterns for average and slow groups.

In random grouped classrooms, the pupil's ability level appears to be an important factor in determining his sociometric status. Sociometric status patterns differ considerably for pupils of different ability levels in random grouped classrooms, with pupils of higher ability consistently obtaining more favorable mean scores. The presence of significant correlations obtained when sociometric status was related to ability and achievement for District R pupils further demonstrates the importance of ability to status in the random grouped class. On the other hand, ability does not appear to be an important factor in determining sociometric status in ability grouped classrooms. In the Utah study, sociometric status patterns for pupils of different ability levels in ability grouped classrooms were closely comparable, showing no evidence of real differences. The absence of correlations between ability and status suggest that these factors are far less important to friendship choices in ability grouped classrooms.

We were also interested in learning what happened to a pupil's social status in the two grouping systems when his ability level changed. In District A such a change meant a change in classroom assignment, while in District R the pupil would be unaware of the change. First let us consider pupils who received a lower ability level classification in a succeeding year. District A pupils in this classification experienced significantly more upward mobility than was experienced by the comparable District R pupils. Thus, the downward movement seemed to increase the ability grouped pupil's relative social status as he was recognized as having come from a higher ability group and was near the top of his new group whereas he had been near the bottom of his previous group. These data would suggest that any damage to the ability grouped pupil's self-concept that might occur because of his reclassification to a lower ability section might be compensated to some extent by gains in social status he is likely to experience in his new class.

Pupils in District A and District R who moved upward in ability level classification were also studied. Two of the three chi-square comparisons made between these pupils yielded statistically significant differences. In each instance, pupils in random grouped classrooms showed more favorable sociometric status changes than comparable pupils in District A classrooms. These findings suggest that although ability grouping might initially provide greater opportunities for social leadership for those of average and low ability, it also might make more difficult the task of maintaining or gaining social recognition if the pupil makes achievement gains sufficient to raise his ability level classification. Loss of social status that is likely to accompany his reassignment to a new classroom might outweigh any gain in status he may experience from being identified as a member of the brighter group.

The lack of any consistent significant differences between boys and girls suggests that the effects of ability grouping and random grouping on sociometric variables are about the same for the two sexes.

Low but significant correlations were found to exist between sociometric status, pupil attitude, and self-concept variables. These correlations, though low, demonstrate the presence of relationships between the pupil's social acceptance and his perception of himself, his school environment, and his peers.

PUPIL ATTITUDES

Pupils in Sample IV were administered the *USU School Inventory* during their sixth grade year. This measure contains three scales: *Attitude Toward Peers, Attitude Toward the Teacher,* and *Attitude Toward School.*

Results on the *Attitude Toward Peers* scale revealed no significant between-treatment differences. Comparison on the *Attitude Toward the Teacher* scale showed that superior girls and boys and slow boys in District A received significantly more favorable scores than comparable District A pupils. No significant differences were found between average pupils in the two districts. Thus, ability grouping appears to be associated with more favorable attitudes toward the teacher among both superior and slow pupils.

Comparisons between the two treatments on the *Attitude Toward School* scale showed one significant difference favoring slow boys in District A. Within both treatments, there were significant differences between pupils of different ability levels all indicative of more favorable attitudes for pupils of higher ability. Three of the six sex differences of the *Attitude Toward School* scale were statistically significant. These differences, all of which favored girls, were largest at the superior level.

PUPIL PROBLEMS

The instruments employed to study pupil problems were the *SRA Youth Inventory* and the *SRA Junior Inventory*. These measures are essentially check lists each of which classifies the problems listed into a number of areas. A study of the problems listed on the two inventories revealed several areas in which one of the grouping treatments employed in the Utah study might be expected to differ from the other.

The *SRA Junior Inventory, form S* was administered to Sample IV pupils in District A and R during their fifth grade year. The *SRA Youth Inventory, form A* was administered to Sample VI pupils during their seventh grade year, Sample VII pupils during their eighth grade year, and Sample VIII pupils during their ninth grade year. As the *SRA Youth Inventory* was administered to three different samples at the junior high school level, the results on this measure provide fairly reliable evidence.

In reviewing the between-treatment differences on the problem areas of the *Youth Inventory*, perhaps the most noteworthy trend is the preponderance of significant differences indicating larger mean problem scores for the District R groups. A total of 32 between-treatment differences reached or approached statistical significance for the junior high-school samples. These differences were found in all samples. Of these 32 differences, only one indicated more favorable problem scores for District R pupils while the other 31 indicated more favorable problem scores for District A.

The frequency of significant differences between the districts was also found to be related to ability level. Of the 32 aforementioned differences on the *SRA Youth Inventory*, 15 were found between superior pupils in the two districts, and in 14 of these, the District R pupils obtained higher (less favorable) scores. Eleven of the 32 differences were between average pupils in the two districts; all indicating higher problem scores for District R groups. These results, reflecting as they do a consistently high number of problems for superior and average District R groups, would suggest the presence of true treatment differences at these ability levels. This trend, although present for slow pupils, was far less pronounced, and less general from sample to sample. These data support the overall conclusion that ability grouped junior high school pupils in average or superior groups report fewer problems than do comparable pupils in random grouped classes.

SELF-CONCEPT

The principal measure of self-concept employed in this research was the *Index of Adjustment and Values*, developed by Robert E. Bills (11). Pupils in all five samples were administered the *IAV*. Samples IV and VI were each tested three times over a three year period, while Samples VII, VIII and IX were each tested twice over a two year period. In the *IAV* the pupil answers three questions about himself: he rates himself with respect to each of the traits listed (concept-of-self), tells how he feels about being this sort of a person (acceptance of self), and how he would like to be with respect to each trait (ideal-self). In addition to yielding these three scores, a fourth score, *Discrepancy*, was obtained by subtracting the *Concept of Self* scores from the *Ideal Self* score.

For each of the four *IAV* variables, 66 between-treatment comparisons were made, 22 at each ability level.

Of the 66 comparisons on the *Concept of Self* score, 23 reached or approached statistical significance. All but two of these 23 differences were in a direction favoring District R pupils. Eight were between superior pupils in the two districts, ten between average pupils, and five between slow pupils. Fifteen of these 23 differences were between girls' groups while only seven were between boys' groups. The extent and consistency of differences in the *Concept of Self* data seem to justify the conclusion that at all ability levels, pupils in random grouped classrooms have more favorable concepts of self than comparable pupils in ability grouped classrooms. With respect to concept of self, the two grouping treatments had a somewhat greater effect upon girls than boys.

Of the 66 between-treatment comparisons of the *IAV Acceptance of Self* mean scores, 15 were statistically significant and seven others approached significance. Six of the significant differences were between superior pupils, six between average pupils, and three between slow pupils in the two districts. All 15 of these significant between-treatment differences favored District R as did four of the seven differences that approached significance. Based on these data, it must be concluded that random grouping is consistently related to higher self acceptance for pupils at all ability levels and over most of the grade levels covered in this project.

The overall summary of between-treatment comparisons on the *IAV Discrepancy Score* shows 14 of the 66 differences to be statistically significant. Six were between superior pupils in the two districts. Six of these differences were between average pupils. All but one of the 14 significant differences showed higher (less favorable) *Discrepancy Score* means for District·A subgroups.

It may be concluded that the two grouping treatments have a differential effect upon the pupils' *Discrepancy Scores* with ability grouping generally associated with less favorable scores. This pattern is most pronounced in the differences between the mean scores of superior pupils in the two treatments, closely followed by average pupils. The differences between slow pupils are substantially smaller.

Of the 66 between-treatment comparisons of mean *Ideal Self* scores on the *Index of Adjustment and Values*, eight reached statistical significance. Seven of these eight differences favored District R pupils, with two occurring between superior groups, four between average groups and two between slow groups. The relatively few significant results suggests that the grouping system has little influence upon the *Ideal Self* score.

Sample IV pupils in District A who changed ability levels between the fifth and sixth grade administrations of the *IAV* were compared to determine whether changes in ability classification would be accompanied by changes in self-concept scores. The results indicated that remaining in the same ability classification in an ability grouping system appears to be less threatening to the pupil's self-concept than reclassification to either a higher or lower section. Placement of a pupil in a lower ability classification appears to bring about lower scores in *Concept of Self*, *Acceptance of Self*, and *Ideal Self*. Pupils destined to be reassigned to a lower ability classification were found to have lower scores in *Concept of Self* and *Acceptance of Self* prior to reassignment. This lower initial score may indicate that misassignment of a pupil to a higher group than his ability would justify brings about a lowering of his *Concept of Self* and *Acceptance of Self* because of his inability to perform satisfactorily in his assigned group.

Variables from four personality inventories were employed: The *California Test of Personality* (CTP); *Inventory of Factors GAMIN* (GAMIN) *Objective-Analytic Personality Tests* (OA); *and the California Psychological Inventory* (CPI). A projective measure employing cards from the *Thematic Apperception Test* (TAT) and the *Michigan Picture Test* (MPT) was also used to measure three variables that seemed particularly important.

California Test of Personality (CTP). This measure was administered to Sample IV only. It was hypothesized that superior and slow pupils in ability grouped classes would obtain higher scores on the *Feeling of Belonging* subscales. Results showed District R subgroups to be consistently higher on this score at all ability levels. These data suggest that ability grouping does not lead to a greater feeling of belonging on the part of pupils at any ability level, but instead provides a less favorable climate than random grouping.

Ability grouped pupils also received less favorable scores on *Antisocial Tendencies* in all six between-treatment comparisons, with four differences reaching statistical significance.

Inventory of Factors GAMIN. Two personality factors from this inventory, *Ascendancy and Inferiority*, were measured for pupils in Samples VI, VII, and VIII during the second year of the Utah study. Of the 18 between-treatment comparisons made on the *Ascendancy* factor, only two reached statistical significance. These results suggest that the two treatments had no differential effect upon this personality variable. No consistent between-treatment differences emerged on the *Inferiority* factor of the *GAMIN*. Our findings support the conclusion that ability grouping is no more likely to develop inferiority feelings in pupils at any ability level than is random grouping.

Objective-Analytic Personality Test Factors (OA). Tests measuring two factors from this battery were administered to Sample IV and Sample VI. No consistent pattern of between-treatment differences emerged for either of these variables. We may conclude that neither *Competent Assertiveness* nor *Anxiety to Achieve* as measured on Cattell's *OA* battery were affected differentially by the two grouping treatments.

California Psychological Inventory (CPI). The CPI was administered to pupils in Samples VI and VII. The 18 CPI variables are classified by the test author into four broad areas. Class I variables include measures of poise, ascendancy, and self-assurance. Between-treatment comparisons on the Class I variables showed no consist-ent superiority for either treatment for superior pupils and slow pupils. Average pupils received more favorable scores in random grouped classes.

Class III variables on the *CPI* include three scores aimed at meas-uring *Achievement via conformance* (Ac), *Achievement via inde-pendence* (Ai) and *Intellectual efficiency* (Ie). Between-treatment differences on these three variables for subjects in Samples VI and VII were generally nonsignificant although there was some tendency for superior pupils in District A to obtain more favorable scores.

Class IV of the *CPI* is concerned with intellectual and interest modes and is made up of three subtests: *Psychological-mindedness* (Py), *Flexibility* (Fx), and *Femininity* (Fe). No consistent between-treatment differences emerged on any of these three scores.

Projective Data. The first phase of the projective research, re-ferred to as the fifth grade study, measured aggression, depression, and inferiority feelings on an individually administered *TAT* type projective measure using a sample of 144 slow pupils taken from ability grouped and random grouped fifth-grade classes. The second phase, referred to as the sixth grade study, employed a similar group administered projective measure, using a sample of 338 slow, average, and superior pupils taken from ability grouped and random grouped sixth grade classrooms.

Between-treatment comparisons on aggression, depression, and inferiority feelings in the fifth grade study showed no statistically significant differences. Between-treatment differences on these three personality variables obtained in the sixth grade study also failed to show consistent significant differences.

The lack of significant differences in inferiority feeling support the data obtained on other samples using the inferiority subscore on the *GAMIN*. Taken together, these results present considerable evidence that ability grouping as employed in the Utah study does not cause the development of inferiority feelings among slow pupils.

OVERALL APPRAISAL OF THE GROUPING TREATMENTS

Let us now attempt to weigh the overall effects of the two group-ing treatments on superior, average, and slow pupils at the elemen-tary and junior high level. Table 20 provides a brief summary of these effects. Because of the limitations of the high school data collected in the Utah study, such an overall appraisal does not ap-

pear appropriate at that level. Any such appraisal of the two grouping treatments depends to a considerable degree upon the value
system of the person making the appraisal. In other words, different persons would assign different amounts of importance to the
various types of behavior and experience that were appraised by
the measures in the Utah study. The following evaluation, therefore, reflects the value system of the investigator. Educators having
different orientations may well draw different overall conclusions
from the findings of this research.

Elementary: Superior Pupils. The superior pupil generally showed
greater achievement gains in ability grouped classes. The differences in the Utah study were not large except for the first year, but
data for the four years reflected a significant overall advantage for
the ability grouping system. The data on overachievers supported
this finding, but as this phase of the research was carried out for
only one year, the results must be considered tentative.

The study methods data for superior pupils showed a consistent
and fairly large advantage for the random grouping treatment.
Thus, although the ability grouped bright pupil may achieve more,
he may develop less adequate study methods and be less capable
in an independent study situation than his counterpart in the heterogeneous classroom.

When we consider the non-cognitive data for superior elementary school pupils, perhaps the most noteworthy finding is the loss
in sociometric status and self-concept found for these pupils in the
ability grouped situation. Some investigators have suggested that
bright pupils have a somewhat inflated opinion of their own capabilities. If this is the case, perhaps the lower scores obtained on
these measures by superior pupils in the ability grouping situation
reflect a more healthy attitude than is found in the random grouped
classroom. In elementary school classrooms, the teacher exerts considerable influence upon the peer group situation, and it may be
that the teacher's tendency to place a very high value on achievement, results in high achieving pupils receiving a disproportionate
amount of recognition. It will be recalled that the sociometric
choice data, although indicating a reduction in the number of superior pupils of star status in the ability grouped classroom did not
show an increase in the number of neglectee-isolates for this group.
In weighing the total treatment effects for superior pupils during the
intermediate grades in the elementary school, the investigator concludes that the ability grouping treatment is slightly more desirable.

Average Pupils. In reviewing the results of the Utah study for average pupils during the fourth, fifth, and sixth grades of the elementary school, we find a complex pattern of advantages and disadvantages associated with the two grouping treatments. In terms of achievement, it seems there is nothing to choose between the two treatments for average pupils. The average pupils, however, were found to have better study methods in the random grouped treatment.

With regard to non-cognitive variables, we find that average pupils showed more favorable personality characteristics, higher self-concept scores, and fewer pupil problems in the random grouped situation. The only aspect of their experience that strongly favored the ability grouping situation was the improved sociometric status they gained in this treatment. Although this improvement in status is not to be taken lightly, it seems that the preponderance of other variables favoring the random grouped situation must lead to the conclusion that the needs of most average pupils were better met in the heterogeneous classroom.

Slow Pupils. In terms of achievement related variables, the slow pupil generally showed better performance in the heterogeneous classroom. His achievement gains were rather consistently higher in the random grouped situation as were his study habits scores.

Review of the non-cognitive variables for slow pupils does not present a clear cut advantage for either grouping treatment. The most striking result of ability grouping for slow pupils was the tremendous gains they made in sociometric status. The slow pupil's attitudes toward both the school and teacher were also somewhat more favorable in the ability grouping situation. On the other hand, the self-concept data as well as the rather limited personality data available at this level tended to favor the random grouping. The reader may recall, however, that the differences between the two treatments in self-concept scores were much smaller for slow pupils than for superior or average pupils. Thus, it is the conclusion of the investigator that the large gains in sociometric choice are the most significant single effect of the grouping treatments on slow pupils. Therefore, it is concluded that the ability grouping system provides a more favorable environment for the slow pupil than does the random grouping treatment.

Junior High School. In reviewing Table 20, the reader will note that data on overachievers and underachievers, sociometric choice, and pupil attitudes were not collected at the junior high school level. Somewhat more personality data, however, were collected at this level, and these data can be accepted with somewhat more confidence than the personality data obtained during the elementary school years.

Superior Pupils. Ability grouping led to significantly greater achievement gains for superior pupils at the junior high school level, although these differences were not large. In reviewing the non-cognitive data, superior pupils in the ability grouped classes reported fewer pupil problems and obtained more favorable scores on the *CPI* measures of poise, ascendancy and self-assurance (Class I), as well as on measures of achievement potential and intellectual efficiency (Class III). These differences on the *CPI*, however, were found in fewer than one half of the replications, and may be regarded as tentative. When all data are considered, it appears to the investigator that ability grouping is slightly more advantageous for superior pupils at the junior high-school level.

Average Pupils. The pattern is somewhat the same for average groups, with ability grouped pupils making greater achievement and more favorable study methods scores. On the non-cognitive variables, average pupils in ability grouped classrooms reported fewer problems, but obtained somewhat less favorable self-concept scores than similar groups in the random grouped classrooms. Random grouped average pupils also obtained generally more favorable scores on the *CPI* Class I variables as well as on the *Anxiety to Achieve* measures on the Cattell *OA* battery. Again there seems little to choose between the two grouping treatments although the differences in the cognitive variables seem to give ability grouping a slight advantage.

Slow Pupils. Slow pupils in random grouped classrooms at the junior high school level generally achieved more than their ability grouped counterparts. Random grouped slow pupils also received somewhat more favorable self-concept scores although they reported a greater number of problems than the ability grouped samples. The personality data for slow pupils was characterized by a complete lack of consistent differences favoring either treatment. The lack of significant differences on aggression, depression, and inferiority feelings found in the projective phase of the personality study leads us to question some of the dire consequences that have been predicted by critics of ability grouping. Although personality data at this age level are at best tentative, the inferiority feelings and other negative personality characteristics thought to be caused by ability grouping of slow pupils did not emerge in the Utah study. In considering the overall pattern of differences, however, the investigator concludes that the heterogeneous classroom pro-

Table 20—Summary of Comparisons Between the Two Grouping Treatments

Variable	Sample	ELEMENTARY			JUNIOR HIGH			Remarks
		Sup.	Aver.	Slow	Sup.	Aver.	Slow	
Achievement	All	A*	N	R	A	A	R	Achievement differences over the four years were not large.
Overachievers and Underachievers	IV, VI	A	N	N				Based on first year's data only.
Study Methods and Attitudes	IV, VI VII, IX	R	R	R	N	A		Elementary level differences largest for superior pupils.
Sociometric Choice	IV, VI	R	A	A				In ability grouped classrooms, gains of average and slow pupils are large.
Pupil Attitudes	IV							Slow boys had notably better attitudes in ability grouped classes.
Toward Peers		N	N	N				
Toward Teacher		A	N	A				
Toward School		N	N	A				
Pupil Problems	IV, VI VII, VIII	N	R	N	A	A	A	At junior high level, ability grouping was consistently related to fewer problems in all replications.
Self Concept Scores	All							Ability grouping was generally associated with less favorable self-concept scores at all levels and for all samples.
Concept of Self		R	R	R	R	R		
Acceptance of Self		R	R	R	R	R		
Ideal Self		N	R	N	N	N		
Discrepancy		R	R	R	R	R		

* A indicates results favoring ability grouping. R indicates results favoring random grouping. N indicates results favoring neither consistently.

Table 20—Summary of Comparisons Between the Two Grouping Treatments—continued

Variable	Sample	ELEMENTARY			JUNIOR HIGH			Remarks
		Sup.	Aver.	Slow	Sup.	Aver.	Slow	
Personality								
1. Feeling of Belonging	IV	R	R	R				Personality measures at elementary level of doubtful validity.
2. Anti-Social Tendencies	IV	R	R	R				
3. Ascendancy	VI, VII VIII				N	N	N	The few significant differences on 3, 4, and 5 generally favored District R, but were not consistent between replications.
4. Inferiority	VI, VII VIII				N	N	N	
5. Competent Assertiveness	IV	N	N	R				
6. Anxiety to Achieve	VI				N	R	N	
7. CPI Class 1	VI, VII				A	R	N	Differences between average were more consistent than those between superior pupils.
8. CPI Class 3	VI, VII				A	N	R	
9. Flexibility	VI, VII				N	N	N	
10. Projective test								
Aggression	IV	N	N	N				
Depression	IV	N	N	N				
Inferiority	IV	N	N	N				

* A indicates results favoring ability grouping.   R indicates results favoring random grouping.   N indicates results favoring neither consistently.

vides a slightly better environment for slow pupils at the junior high school level.

Now, WHAT ABOUT SEPARATING PHYSICALLY HANDICAPPED CHIL- dren. Are we doing that because of an assumption that their psychological needs make it too difficult for them to take academic pressure? If so, experiences similar to that of Alice Noel, who is a teacher of the multiply handicapped children in metropolitan Nashville, Tennessee public schools, should make us question our assumption. Her experience was de- scribed in the January–1966 issue of *Exceptional Children* under the title "Effectiveness of an Academically Oriented Teaching Program With Crippled Children."[2]

In the United States there appears to have developed a dichotomy between academic and social learning in special education. Many authorities and texts have stressed the importance of emphasizing personal development and social adjustment with handicapped children. Teachers frequently have interpreted this to mean that they should give priority to the mental health aspects of a program to the neglect of more formal academic learnings. For the last 15 years, I have taught crippled children. For most of these years, I patterned my teaching on the firm belief that personal and physical development should receive preference over school achievement.

About two years ago, I had a spirited discussion with a well known teacher-educator in special education, who contended that the academic standards in this area were not high enough. I decided then to make a major shift in my approach and to place greater emphasis on functional academic skills. This "revised" philosophy was based on the premise that the new approach would, in fact, provide the virtues of both the academic and the mental health approaches and thereby contribute to the children's success in school work and enhance their self-respect.

THE GROUP

The first group with whom I used this new approach consisted of six severely involved, orthopedically handicapped children. They had been under the same teacher's direction in a special class in a regular elementary school from one to ten years. Their chronologi-

2. Reprinted by permission of the Council for Exceptional Children.

cal ages ranged from 10–5 to 18–2 with a mean of 14–3, and their Peabody Picture Vocabulary Test IQ scores ranged from 71 to 119 with a mean IQ of 92.5. These data for each child, as well as academic achievement records, are shown in Table 1.

All of the children were multiply handicapped. Five of them were cerebral palsied (two athetoids, one tension athetoid, one ataxic, and one "mixed"). The sixth had spina bifida. Three had visual problems, and two had hearing problems. They lacked adequate hand use and required intensive speech therapy.

THE CLASSROOM PROGRAM

The children attended a special class in a regular elementary school. Their school day lasted five and one-half hours. Their curriculum consisted of academic subject matter, music, arts and crafts, play, rest, lunch, and physical and speech therapy. Communication and language arts received more emphasis than any other area. The children also watched science and music on educational television. They shared lunchtime, play and assembly programs with the entire school. Some children were even integrated into the regular classrooms for short periods of time.

PROCEDURES

My philosophy became "Learning Can Be Fun." I stressed the "Let's find out" approach, and the children accepted this idea for themselves. They soon requested more practical approaches to reading, such as using magazines and newspapers, and they became eager to learn to write stories and letters. They were most interested in doing academic work in the ways employed by other children in the school. A strong feeling developed among them that they should excel in some particular area. After one round table, brainstorming session, each decided he could accept responsibility, be courteous, and follow rules, even if he could not write or talk. They accomplished these goals. Discipline was not a problem, but a real asset to learning.

The children worked together in small groups both with and without me. Some tutorial teaching was necessary. Each child learned the Morse Code and finger spelling because two classmates could communicate only in these ways. Everyone studied together, including the two children without speech. The youngsters had a "chat break" in the middle of the day during which they talked in-

Table 1—Pupil's Grade Level Achievement Records
May 1963–May 1964

Pupil	Sex	Crippling Condition	CA May, 1964	IQ	Reading			Spelling			Language			Arithmetic		
					1963	1964	Gain	1963	1964	Gain	1963	1964	Gain	1963	1964	Gain
1	F	CP	18–2	94	5.0	9.7	4.7	5.3	10.0	4.7	7.5	10.0	2.5	7.6	8.1	0.5
2	F	Spina Bifida	15–0	71	5.2	7.0	1.8	4.9	6.0	2.9	6.2	7.2	1.0	3.8	5.2	1.4
3	M	CP	14–4	81	5.4	4.9	−0.5	4.6	5.0	0.4	5.0	6.1	1.1	5.9	7.5	1.6
4	M	CP	14–3	119	4.5	8.7	4.2	4.2	6.7	2.5	5.6	10.0	4.4	5.6	7.3	1.7
5	M	CP	12–8	86	3.2	3.5	0.3	2.0	2.9	0.9	3.5	4.4	0.9	3.0	3.5	0.5
6	F	CP	10–5	104	4.4	6.5	2.1	4.8	6.0	1.2	5.7	7.5	1.8	3.7	4.3	0.6

formally with each other and brought their problems to me. These problems were then discussed individually with the child or with the entire group.

After a discussion with the director of the Child Study Center at Peabody College. I decided to use the *Reader's Digest Skill Builder* and to concentrate language arts, social studies, and science around these texts. The children were highly motivated by the format and developed a high interest level in the books. They read and worked the teaching exercises eagerly. Each child was required to write a brief résumé of each story without using the book. These stories were edited by me and rewritten by the pupil. Summaries were then read aloud to the group for comment. Key vocabulary words were used for spelling, structural analysis, phonics, and definitions. Encyclopedias were consulted for further reference on pertinent subject matter. Book racks and electric typewriters were the only special equipment used. Reading tests and spelling tests were held weekly, and the rate of reading increased in every instance.

Two motivating devices in communication skills were often used —conversational French for concentration, auditory discrimination, and speech; and the writing of simple stories from nonsensical titles, such as "The Seashell and the Brick." Many of these stories were delightfully imaginative.

The four arithmetic fundamentals were first taught as skills. Teacher-made devices were used in the beginning process for counting, grouping, and so forth. A numberline and phonograph records were valuable aids. At the beginning, pupils who desired them had their own "20's" box, which contained 20 similar objects for counting. These devices were eliminated as soon as they served no useful purpose. The more mature children, who had mastered the fundamentals, delved into fractions, decimals, and the use of plane geometrical figures, which were often presented as practical problems. Banking, cooking, fund drives, record keeping, and construction of classroom devices and materials for entertainments offered worthy subjects. A book of map skills was helpful in problem solving from a printed page and in map reading. Formal spelling was taught from a standard text. The children also gave musical and square dance programs for the public.

RESULTS AND DISCUSSION

Under this new approach, the children gained in grade level scores on a standard achievement test in one academic year. The test used was the Metropolitan Achievement Test, at the elementary level first and at the intermediate level the next year. These tests were chosen primarily for content and format, and because they were used throughout the school system for all children. Many very handicapped children can read them with ease and indicate their answer choice independently.

ACHIEVEMENTS

Gains in academic achievement are shown in Table 1. In reading, the range of change during the year was from a gain of 4.7 grades to a loss of 0.5 with a median gain of 1.95 grades. In spelling, the range of change was from 4.7 grades to 0.4 with the median gain of 1.85. In language, the range of change was from 4.4 to 0.9 with a median of 1.45; and in arithmetic, the range of change was from 1.7 to 0.5 with a median of 1.4. There were no great emotional problems. It may be assumed from this that many severely involved, crippled children can learn more rapidly and retain at higher levels in a classroom situation of this kind than could be expected in a classroom primarily geared to physical development and crafts.

WHAT ABOUT HANDLING THE EMOTIONALLY DISTURBED CHILD SEParately? What would be our reasons for keeping him with the other children or separating him from the other children?

Jacob S. Kounin of Wayne State University, Wallace V. Friesen of San Fancisco State College, and A. Evangeline Norton of Wayne State University conducted a difficult study that was supported by the National Institute of Mental Health. They published their findings in an article entitled "Managing Emotionally Disturbed Children in Regular Classrooms" in the *Journal of Educational Psychology* in 1966.[3]

The *Journal* abstract stated:

This study was an attempt to delineate some dimensions of teaching style that affect the behavior of emotionally disturbed children in Grades 1–2 and 3–5 in regular classrooms. Video tapes were obtained for 1/2 day of 30 classrooms, each containing 1 or more

3. Excerpts reprinted by permission of the *Journal of Educational Psychology* © 1966 American Psychological Association.

emotionally disturbed children. Scores for deviancy and work involvement were obtained for both disturbed (E) and nondisturbed (Non E) children. Some findings are: (a) Pupils' scores vary between seatwork and recitation settings in the same classroom; (b) E children manifest less school-appropriate behavior than Non E children; (c) teachers who are successful in managing the behavior of Non E children are also relatively successful with E children; (d) techniques of handling misbehavior as such do not correlate with children's behavior; (e) teacher "With-it-ness," techniques of handling group movement, and programing for variety change in learning activities do correlate with children's behavior.

In the article the authors say:

Teachers sometimes express concern that emotionally disturbed children disrupt the behavior of others. Is this disruptive influence a consequence of the deviant behavior of emotionally disturbed children or is it generally symptomatic of unsuccessful classroom management?

After citing their evidence, they conclude that:

. . . the degree of contagion of an E child's deviant behavior is related to the degree of misbehavior occurring in the classroom. The teacher who is generally successful in managing the surface behavior of children in her classroom not only has a lower deviancy rate among emotionally disturbed children in that classroom, but also produces a classroom climate that "contains" the misbehavior of an E child and prevents it from disrupting the behavior of other children.

WE ARE IN NEED OF RESEARCH EVIDENCE THAT COMPARES LEARNING in classes with and without "emotionally disturbed" children. The assumption that "healthy" children have nothing to gain from contact with "emotionally disturbed" children may well prove faulty. Such contact may provide a concrete lesson in "being tolerant of people who are different" and "helping those less fortunate." Watching and helping a classmate gain control over his impulses can help a child learn more about how, when, and why he must control his own impulses.

What about the simple question of how often a youngster

should change grouping? Two studies were reported in the January–1966 issue of the *Journal of Educational Research*. One, by Paul Lichtman, of the Pyne Point Junior High School in Camden, New Jersey, was entitled, "They Can Succeed." He described an experiment that put youngsters in smaller classes with the same teacher for longer blocks of time. There were many indices of success, as a result. The other study, by Wallace Roby and Mahlon Hayden, of the Edwin O. Smith High School and the University of Connecticut, was entitled "An Experience with a Two-Period High School Day."

There were differences between the two studies. The latter study, for instance, apparently stretched the time but didn't shrink the classes and discovered no great improvement. Because these two studies report contrasting evidence, every difference in methodology must now be carefully investigated.

Educational research deals not only with people but with *growing* people, and the number of variables within the experimental field are awesome. This has turned out to be one of the special difficulties with studying grouping. Whenever children are grouped together on one ability or factor, we find that they are ungrouped in a thousand other ways. When reading time comes we can divide a class into redbirds, bluebirds, yellowbirds, and even chartreusebirds, but the teacher can count on having a lot of *different* birds within any one nest.

Differences can offer surprising advantages as Bernard Asbell shows in his delightful article that appeared in *Redbook Magazine* in February, 1966, under the title "Let the Children Teach."[4]

We foolish adults like to regard the education of children as a responsibility that rests solely with certified schoolteachers and sanctified parents. But the obvious fact, as any child knows, is that the most effective teachers of children are often other children.

In Oakland, California, first graders who seemed unable to learn their A B C's and 1–2–3's in regular classes are learning them

4. Reprinted by permission of *Redbook Magazine* "Copyright, McCall Corporation 1966."

eagerly in daily 45-minute sessions with sixth-grade "teachers." Especially bright sixth graders? Not always. Some of the tutors are not only backward learners themselves, but also rebellious "problem children." But they are teaching effectively. Perhaps even more important, these "teachers" are themselves becoming better learners, showing remarkable improvement in their behavior, their dress and their attitude toward learning. Having responsibility for others seems to make them more responsible about themselves.

In Michigan a child-to-child tutoring experiment that started in Ann Arbor has spread to the nearby public schools of Ypsilanti and Monroe; not only do sixth graders coach first graders but also teachers are being re-educated to supervise the tutoring to best advantage. In New York an antipoverty project, Mobilization for Youth, employs high-school students for afterschool homework help to grade schoolers; both appear to benefit. More than 100 Montessori schools, based on a system of independent study by children, have spread across America. Each child is placed in a class with a three-year age span, and he is often motivated simply by observing older children perform more sophisticated tasks.

"The idea of children's teaching other children is anything but new," says Dr. John H. Fischer, president of Columbia University's Teachers College. "Games and songs that show up in every generation have been passed down literally for centuries by boys and girls teaching them to others only slightly younger than themselves. Why shouldn't it make sense to use the same process, the same energy, to teach other things? Wherever the practice has been encouraged, the results have been at least partly good and in many instances highly successful."

Every parent has seen it happen. I have seen it in my own family. When my son Larry was 11 years old, he fell under the spell of Tim Smith, a classmate whose uncle had given him a small printing press. Larry spent long hours at Tim's house, learning to set type and print even impressions, both tasks that require great precision and patience. Then he nagged me for $40, which I finally lent him. He bought a press, solicited orders for stationery and soon afterward was able to pay me back. I don't thank myself or the collector of school taxes, but the influence and teaching skill of young Tim Smith.

Of course, these boys live in lively homes of literate parents and are surrounded by examples of accomplishment among their suburban neighbors. But how about the millions of kids spending their childhood in darkened slums, neglected by hope-bereft parents? We know that their schoolteachers are failing to teach them. But though these children fail to learn from teachers, they do succeed in learning—from each other, in the streets. They learn so well that one becomes a carbon copy of the other's alienation, hostility and aimlessness. For better or worse, this too is a kind of education—and demonstrates the power of children as learners and educators.

In Oakland, at Stonehurst School, attended mostly by children of the poor, a large number of sixth graders are excused from their classes for 45 minutes a day to work with first graders. This involves perhaps more personal attention for the little ones than they have ever had. Their teachers wisely have prescribed no curriculum; each child, out of his own sensitivity to his partner, seems to work out the right thing to do.

An 11-year-old Negro girl named Janathur, a fair student in the sixth grade, told me about the problems of Robert, her first-grade partner, whose parents speak only Spanish. It is hard to tell which of the two children was learning more.

"When we started," said Janathur, "Robert didn't know nothing. He couldn't count more than five. When I first tried giving him lessons, he'd just look at me and not say anything. For the whole first week he wouldn't tell me his name. Each day I kept asking him, but he wouldn't tell me. So I'd ask him, 'Would you like to draw a picture?' He'd shake his head—no. Then I'd say, 'Would you like me to read a story?' He'd shake his head—yes. After a whole week of that I asked him his name, and one day he said, 'Robert.' I felt so happy. I told him, 'My name is Jan and I'm your tutor.' Then I asked him what he wanted to do. He said, 'I want to learn numbers.' I was surprised because that was just what he could do least in class. Well, I began to write down numbers. He read one to five. But from six up he didn't know anything. I said, 'Six,' and wrote down the number. Then he said, 'Six' and 'Seven,' and so on. I wrote numbers on little slips of paper, mixed them up so they weren't in the right order and told him to make them right. Sometimes he got it, sometimes he didn't. But pretty soon he'd get it all the time. After he learned his numbers, he said he wanted to learn about words. We started on that and he learned them."

Janathur and Robert were not special. All the teams I saw were absorbed in their work and seemed to be having some measure of success. Janathur has a friend, Debbie Ann, who began getting notes from her little partner's mother, thanking Debbie Ann for teaching Patricia so much. But it was clear that the older girl was profiting at least as much as the younger. Debbie Ann's mother, Mrs. Barbara Perreira, who is the wife of a steadily employed sheet-metal worker, told me:

"We were thinking last year of moving to a nicer neighborhood, but I decided against it. I was afraid Debbie wouldn't get this opportunity in another school. That girl has never been so contented, and I know it's just because she has the chance of helping another person. After Debbie began tutoring, she'd come home all excited about what she'd taught that day to Patricia. Then she'd start planning the next day's lessons. She made us set up a back room in the house as her schoolwork room. My husband worried that taking time to teach someone else might make Debbie's marks go down. But they've gone up. She used to get N in arithmetic—that means 'Needs improvement.' Now she gets G, for 'Good.' "

Both Debbie and Janathur have decided to become teachers. I asked them to tell me what tutoring had taught them about education—things that adult teachers might not be aware of.

"Teachers," suggested Debbie, "most always call on the smart kids who know the right answers. When a teacher finally does call on a kid who doesn't know the answer, she just embarrasses him and makes fun of him in front of the whole class. She's always so busy with the smart ones, she has no time for the ones who need help."

"I've learned," added Janathur, "that it's best to teach somebody what he's interested in first. He really wants to learn the rest, but he may be afraid. I wanted to teach Robert the alphabet first. I kept thinking that's *supposed* to be learned first. But I'd ask him questions and he wouldn't answer. When I gave in to him and let him learn numbers, he answered. After that, I saw he *wanted* to learn the alphabet. He was just scared."

I asked the girls how tutoring had affected their own work.

"Now, after we're finished tutoring," said Debbie, "I go back to my class and think about the little kids who want to learn. If I'm ever going to teach them, I have to learn everything so I can help them learn it. That's why schoolwork is more interesting now."

"It makes my work easier," said Janathur. "Like when we get new work in arithmetic, it looks so hard. Then I tell myself I might have to explain it to somebody else. When you have to explain it, it makes you see it more clearly."

"When my teacher does something that I think is bad teaching," said Debbie, "I ask myself now how I would do it. Then I make myself my own teacher and I teach it to myself the better way."

Such statements from the mouths of children do not mean that teachers ought to be sent home and their classes turned over to the young. The importance of the teacher does not decline; his responsibility merely changes—often allowing him more time for truly creative teaching. "We should not expect," says Dr. Fischer, of Columbia, "that volunteer tutors will make the professional teacher's job easier. Their principal service is to give the teacher time to concentrate on tasks that untrained volunteers are not likely to do very well, such as introducing wholly new ideas or helping youngsters reason their way through complex problems. The teacher must also be on the lookout for misconceptions that are allowed to pass, and for gaps in systematic knowledge that need to be filled in. But the advantages of allowing young people to share in teaching and to learn from one another far outweigh the disadvantages. The practice should be widely encouraged."

Because boys are boys, young male tutors are usually gruffer than girls. But that seems to be what comes naturally, and their younger male partners take it as a form of interest and affection. I saw one young first grader in a pink sweat shirt being tutored by an older boy in a green sweat shirt who himself had been little else but trouble to his teacher—fidgety, mischievous, disdainful of study, displaying all the makings of a school dropout. Both boys were Negroes from impoverished homes. When the attention of the younger boy wandered, the older would brusquely prod him to demand attention. Yet the younger sat hunching close, nudging his shoulder into the side of his tutor, as though protecting himself from the cold. They seemed to be acting out a familial love each could understand. The older got up to go to the water cooler. The younger traipsed beside him, not wanting to miss a moment in his admiration of the older. But soon the sitting still and concentrating was too much. The younger boy went to the water cooler himself. He returned, nudged his pink sweat shirt into the green one, drilled some more, then returned to the cooler. The older boy lost patience and scolded his youngster:

"Now, you keep getting water every minute and you're going to grow up stupid and be sitting on the sidewalk. You must pay attention if you want to learn something."

This lecture on the economic consequences of ignorance was instructive not only to the first grader. The older boy, calling up memories of idle men in the street where he lived, was clarifying the consequences to himself.

Sometimes the older student learns directly from an example set by the younger. A former Stonehurst School teacher, Ruth Love, a remarkable young woman who initiated the tutoring program there, tells of a sixth grader named Rod, one of the "bad boys," whom she risked assigning as a tutor. Rod had a mother on public welfare, four sisters and no father. There were no men at home to be an example for him.

"Rod dressed like a ditch digger and never combed his hair," says Miss Love. "This wasn't because of poverty but out of his need for rebellion. But I could tell that behind his bad behavior there was an organized mind. He hated his class, so he cut up. He knew he'd be made to sit outside the principal's office. He preferred that to sitting in class. When I asked him to be a tutor he was surprised, but he said he'd try. By chance, the first grader assigned to him was an immaculate child, but one who just wouldn't open up in class. Rod got him to answer questions and study. Almost immediately Rod stopped contriving to be sent to the principal. He seemed to realize he couldn't be a cutup and a responsible teacher at the same time. Pretty soon he began washing his face and dressing more neatly. I was certain, and so was his teacher, that he was responding to the example of the younger child. He felt a sense of responsibility toward that little boy, something he previously had felt toward no one. And for the first time, instead of feeling shut out of school life he felt a part of it."

No matter how some children may make a show before adults of not caring about school, they inwardly burn to grow up to be successful. That realization was driven home to Ruth Love in the series of events that originally led her to try tutoring of children by children. A few years ago in the Stonehurst schoolyard, a 12-year-old boy named Roosevelt got into a fight for the fifth time in a week. Miss Love broke up the fight and took the boy aside.

"Now, let's analyze ourselves," she said. "What makes us teachers think you're a troublemaker? What is it that makes you fight so much?"

"Nobody cares about me at that school," the boy said sullenly. He was leaning against the school building but spoke of it as a distant place.

"I care about you," Miss Love said.

"Yeah, but you're different."

"Who told you they don't care about you?"

"They don't have to tell you. It's a feeling."

"Why don't you get into the games or the school clubs and give them a try?"

"They don't want me."

"Why not?"

" 'Cause I fight."

"So it's a circle," Miss Love said. "You fight because they don't want you, and they don't want you because you fight. Think about that and we'll talk some more in a few days."

The following Sunday, at the church Miss Love attends, a small group of her school's pupils approached her with an unusual request. They asked if they could see her on Sundays to get help with schoolwork. To her astonishment, one of the children was Roosevelt. No matter how he acted the outcast, he "wanted in."

A week later Miss Love asked the minister to invite those who wanted tutoring to stay after the service. She also asked for volunteer tutors. She was startled when 150 people showed up. Pupils seeking tutoring ranged from third grade to junior college. Volunteer tutors were not only older students, but also parents, office workers, nurses, social workers, scientists. After a few weeks, when Miss Love expected the enthusiasm to have declined, it increased. Attendance rose to 250.

Miss Love and fellow tutors visited neighboring churches to explain the tutoring program and ask people to contribute discarded books—anything interesting that might provide good practice in reading. They were deluged with storybooks as well as encyclopedias, maps and globes. Children began going to the church every night to inspect these new treasures, even though tutoring was then scheduled for only two nights a week. True, the pupils could find the same things—or better—at a public library. But they seemed to regard the library as an alien institution, just like school; librarians seemed like teachers, more concerned with kids' following strict rules than with anything else.

When the church program had been running successfully for several years, Miss Love decided to bring the experiment into her classroom. She paired good readers with slow ones within her fifth-grade class, good arithmetic students with poor ones. "The idea," she says, "was to tap the strengths of some students to help strengthen the others."

She told the tutors to prepare their own teaching lessons and during the tutoring period even avoided standing in front of the class so as not to dominate the room with her authority. The children seemed to enjoy the self-respect and self-discipline that came from being in charge. "I expected a great deal of them," she says, "and if you expect it, you get it."

Soon after that another teacher told Miss Love of her troubles with a six-year-old Mexican boy, José, who knew no English. The teacher was at a loss to know where or how she could begin teaching him. Miss Love got the bold idea of putting José in the charge of her star fifth-grade pupil, Juan, who came from a Spanish-speaking family. Juan, thrilled, asked, "Do you really think I can do it?"

Miss Love assured him he could.

Juan began inventing teaching materials. He cut up cereal boxes for flash cards. On their unprinted sides he drew pictures and labeled them with Spanish and English words. José rapidly began learning to read—in Spanish and English simultaneously. Then Juan began consulting daily with José's teacher to find out what she wanted the child to learn next. One day Miss Love asked Juan whether he thought others in his class would like to become tutors of younger people.

"Sure they would," Juan replied.

That's when Miss Love decided to try teaming sixth graders with first graders. And that's when she learned how resistant many teachers can be to a new idea. The first-grade teachers seemed willing to try but the sixth-grade teachers balked. "If they tutor every day," protested one, "they'll miss *my* teaching."

Miss Love quieted their protests by suggesting a part for sixth-grade teachers to play. As skilled professionals, she pointed out, they could be valuable in observing the tutors for changes in attitude in their own classes. The purpose, she emphasized, was not only to help the first graders but also to help the sixth graders develop responsibility and more positive feelings toward school. The teachers, pleased by this high purpose, went along.

But Miss Love's flair for devising unusual schemes had not yet been spent. She asked teachers to select half the tutors from among the school misfits—bright children who frequently got into trouble with their classmates and the school authorities. This time the first-grade teachers hit the roof. They feared exposing their little ones to the influence of older "delinquents" and "misbehavers." Miss Love persuaded them to withhold judgment.

Then she arranged for the tutors to visit classrooms and observe various teachers. Afterward the tutors talked among themselves about the best ways to teach arithmetic or discuss the structure of a story. The tutors decided it was important to refresh their memories of their own difficulties in first grade. Some recalled that they had found it hard to understand what the number 3 meant until they learned to count three circles or three pencils or three anything.

All agreed that multiplication tables were a puzzle until they understood it in terms of multiplying real things. Thus these children were confronting themselves with one of the basic philosophical problems in education not universally understood by professional educators—how to guide pupils from the realm of concrete realities to that of abstract symbols.

Occasionally Miss Love would gather the first graders together and let one of the tutors formally teach a lesson on a blackboard—acting just like a teacher. This was always a high spot for the tutor. A high spot for Miss Love was the repeated surprise of observing a tutor invent an ingenious method of teaching. One tutor, a quiet boy who apparently had a special empathy for the shyness of the first grader he was teaching, made colored cutouts of animals, equipping them with moving paws and mouths. He would talk to his first grader "through" the animal—using it as a puppet—and then give the puppet to the child so he could talk back. Later the inventor reported to his fellow tutors that he noticed the first grader was much less reticent when his puppet was doing the talking than he was when called upon to talk by himself. That afternoon in the school shop almost all the tutors began making puppets of their own. (Since then, at the University of Chicago, a psychologist with a Ph.D. has won considerable attention for independently devising a similar technique to encourage language art in verbally retarded children.)

One of the most successful teaching inventions by a tutor was simply the use of a blank piece of paper. The tutor would ask a first grader to make up his own story. The older child would write down whatever the younger one dictated, then teach the younger how to write it himself. (A New Zealand woman, Sylvia Ashton-Warner, told in her best-selling book *Teacher* of her similar idea—teaching reading and writing through a self-prescribed vocabulary.)

Another tutor had the idea of reading a storybook but stopping before it ended. The younger child would make up his own ending, as an exercise in imagination. After each of these innovations, Miss Love would call a meeting of tutors so that the inventor could demonstrate it to the others. Then they would discuss not only how to make it effective but *why* it was effective.

One evening, Miss Love had the parents of first graders come together to meet their children's tutors. The tutors demonstrated the teaching devices they had invented. When parents asked if they could make teaching aids and be coached in how to use them at home, Miss Love recruited volunteer teachers to help them.

Soon Miss Love left the Oakland schools for a job with the California State Department of Education, but not before tutoring of child by child had become part of a wide-scale experiment, supported by the Ford Foundation, to improve the Oakland schools.

Today tutoring in Oakland involves hundreds instead of dozens, in sessions scheduled in afternoons and evenings at several schools. No one is required to come but for three years they have been coming, consistently and in large numbers.

Another tutorial project is in progress at the University of Michigan's Institute for Social Research. There Mrs. Peggy Lippitt recently tried out other methods for mutual help between older and younger children.

Her experiments, supported by the United States Office of Education, were conducted in two different settings: at the University Elementary School in Ann Arbor, attended mainly by the bright offspring of university faculty members, and at Holmes School, in nearby Willow Run, with a biracial attendance of working-class and public-welfare children, many classifiable as educationally deprived. Both experiments were successful.

At first Mrs. Lippitt arranged for sixth graders in both schools to spend 45 minutes a day, three days a week, in a junior kindergarten, helping the preschoolers learn to build, paint and paste, and reading and singing to them. It worked so well that the sixth graders were permitted to become "academic assistants" in the first through the fourth grades, helping younger pupils with reading, writing, spelling and arithmetic. Two afternoons a week—also for 45 minutes—the older children met in a seminar to discuss how they could best help the younger ones, what they should expect realistically of children of a given age and how to correct errors in a manner that was encouraging instead of discouraging. Through "role playing"—the older children pretending they were younger—they tested their responses to praise, to scolding, to friendliness and to threats. Their habitual disdain for the ways of younger children turned to constructive sympathy for them.

"My kid took so long spelling a word yesterday," reported one tutor, "I wanted to hit him. But of course I didn't. I made sure I was patient."

A teacher asked one pupil what he knew now that he didn't know before about junior kindergartners four and a half years old.

"They all have troubles," the pupil replied. "You wouldn't think they had troubles. I guess everyone has. They don't like to be told what to do. They want to make up their own minds and do things without help."

Mrs. Lippitt knew that American children, particularly boys, are not naturally inclined to regard younger children with such sympathy. Before undertaking her experiments she had conducted attitude tests to determine how the children felt toward younger and older children. She found that boys generally expect younger children to be incompetent nuisances and a waste of time. Girls are more attracted to caring for them in the manner of mothers, especially if the little ones are winsome or comical. But they too lose interest when younger children tease or demand too much attention. Yet the class experiments showed these same children eager for responsibility with smaller children when the responsibility resulted in success with the youngsters and increased stature for themselves.

She found in addition that a child's attitude toward older children was one of great admiration, a desire to "be like them." In that fact lies the magnetic power of a child's eagerness to learn. When nine-year-olds were asked to identify individuals "whom they would most like to be like," they named children three to four years older than themselves.

It may come as a surprise to parents whose children are forever squabbling that half the boys with older brothers named an older brother as the ideal model. Almost half the girls with older sisters named an older sister. Yet children get little chance for deep association with older models they admire—and could learn from—in a society of school and play that emphasizes rigid grading by age.

"If a child has relationships with some who are bigger and some who are smaller," says Mrs. Lippitt, "he doesn't have to think of himself in the fixed position of being little. If he can look up as well as down at the people he lives with, he gets a more realistic picture of his place in society. He is more able to see himself as engaged in a process of evolution."

I have mentioned such concepts and programs to alumni of a disappearing American institution—the one-room, eight-grade country school. They are seldom surprised. The country school enabled younger children to observe—even envy—the older children's study. This seemed to encourage them to study by themselves in a way that modern single-grade classes often fail to help them do.

One-room country schools are now in disrepute, chiefly because their graduates enter high school less prepared than those from larger, graded schools. But many educators feel that this deficiency is the result of the inadequate training of the teachers in many one-room schools. A poorly trained, poorly equipped teacher is less likely to get good results, no matter what the system of class organization. But in eliminating the country school we also are losing the advantages of grouping children of various ages, and the influences they can have on one another.

Margaret Perkins, a highly regarded first-grade teacher in the Connecticut suburb where I live, got her elementary education in a one-room school in Vermont. It was taught by her mother.

"The children I teach," says Miss Perkins, "write better than the ones who learned with me in my mother's class. That's because I have more time to drill my pupils in first-grade subject material. But they never get an overview—nor do teachers—of the whole program, what they're progressing *toward*. What they learn seems unreal to them. When I went to school, the older children would recite history or put compositions on a bulletin board. They seemed to have important knowledge that I really wanted."

One of the ablest New York magazine editors I know attributes some of the motivation for her career to her early days in a Wisconsin one-room school.

"While we little kids sat with our little-kid readers," she says, "the big kids were reading *literature*. I wanted to be like them and couldn't wait to get there. The teacher would say to us, 'Now, don't pay attention to them; you have your own work. You have to learn this before you can have a chance to do that.' The words that stuck in our minds were 'before you can have a chance to do that.' Before I could multiply one times three I knew that eight times nine equals seventy-two. I learned the big numbers because that's what *they* were doing—the big kids."

Robert M. Hutchins, former president of the University of Chicago, recently suggested in a REDBOOK dialogue with Charlton Heston (*December*, 1965) that urban schools ought to be reorganized as one-room schools under well-trained teachers, perhaps by having a one-room school located in a store in every city block.

This suggestion is probably too radical for most city dwellers to consider seriously at present, but the development of new techniques like those in use in Oakland, California, and Michigan may show us one way to give more attention and motivation to the children who need it most, even as the supply of well-trained teachers daily diminishes.

A nation of effective teachers' helpers may be sitting in today's classrooms—among the students themselves.

AMERICAN EDUCATION HAS BEEN BUSY POURING ITS VARIED STU-dent population into a giant academic blender. The object was partly to make classroom "management" easier. At best the resulting blend has lacked spice and flavor, at worst it has produced a docile student who, during school hours, is neither fish nor fowl. We are now preparing to trade easy manage-ment for full and interesting production.

Grouping in the classroom has been arranged to minimize differences while grouping outside the classroom (on the school bus and in the street) often highlights differences. These outside-of-school groups set up a constellation of group dynamics that rolls into class each morning with heated feel-ings, confusing the educator who forgets there is life outside the school building. Perhaps now we can facilitate learning by paying open attention to differences.

We have learned a great deal from this and that kind of grouping. The general trend now seems to be to pull all our knowledge together. There is a desire to use the specialized techniques developed for teaching special children separately, while cashing in on the benefits of keeping youngsters to-gether in a way that permits or encourages them to learn naturally from one another.

It is likely that we will end up with some twenty-first cen-tury version of the one-room schoolhouse. It may not be in a store on every block because such a system seems prohibi-tively expensive. However, anyone who has taken a look at a big-city school budget recently, realizes that a few thousand autonomous schools within a large city may be cheaper than the corporate structure that we now have, and they would certainly be more likely to understand their local students.

All the grouping and ungrouping nudges us closer to a re-alization of what a human business education is. Our nation has reaped the harvest of mass production. The rewards were so great that we now almost let mass production run away with all aspects of life. We indulge in the luxury of appreciating hand-made objects. We may yet learn that when it comes to raising our young, mass-production techniques do not work. We may learn that it has been penny-wise and pound-foolish not to pay for careful individual craftsmanship in education.

One reason that team teaching and ungraded classes are in vogue is because when done well, these techniques demand more hours of work from a teacher, but they allow more rewards. The teacher knows his student, the student knows his teacher, and both know more about learning.

We must sort people into categories of one before assigning them to any larger groups.

CHAPTER 6

Learning

SHOW A TODDLER TO AN ADULT AND CHANCES ARE THE ADULT'S face will be illuminated with a bittersweet look of affection. The affection is not simply for the little human he sees before him but is partly for the self that was.

The toddler is busy going and doing, seeing and being. He is, above all, a learner and he tells us clearly that learning is a joyful experience for him. All too frequently when we meet this toddler ten years later, learning has become a burden and a bore. School is the place he has to go, and fun is found in spite of his teacher's plans to make him work at learning.

We are all agreed that school is a place to learn but what are the boundaries? Is the educator the responsible coordinator for all of a child's learning, or is one kind of learning appropriate for school and other kinds of learning appropriate elsewhere? Is it possible that some kinds of learning are simply inappropriate no matter what the setting? And how does the young human learn? What can a teacher do to facilitate the process?

Psychologists took a long, hard look at the teachers' burden several decades ago and turned immediately to their laboratories stocked with rats, pigeons, and chimpanzees. Other psychologists turned fevered attention to the college student.

It has been observed that we now know a great deal about the rat and the college student, but still very little about how a *child* learns.

Today's psychologist is asking the teacher's permission to return to the classroom that he has neglected. Jerome Bruner, who is one of today's most active psychologists in this area, has summed up his thoughts in the Introduction to his book, *On Knowing: Essays for the Left Hand*. We quote part of that introduction here.[1]

Since childhood, I have been enchanted by the fact and the symbolism of the right hand and the left—the one the doer, the other the dreamer. The right is order and lawfulness, *le droit*. Its beauties are those of geometry and taut implication. Reaching for knowledge with the right hand is science. Yet to say only that much of science is to overlook one of its excitements, for the great hypotheses of science are gifts carried in the left hand.

Of the left hand we say that it is awkward and, while it has been proposed that art students can seduce their proper hand to more expressiveness by drawing first with the left, we nonetheless suspect this function. The French speak of the illegitimate descendant as being *à main gauche*, and, though the heart is virtually at the center of the thoracic cavity, we listen for it on the left. Sentiment, intuition, bastardy. And should we say that reaching for knowledge with the left hand is art? Again it is not enough, for as surely as the recital of a daydream differs from the well-wrought tale, there is a barrier between undisciplined fantasy and art. To climb the barrier requires a right hand adept at technique and artifice.

And so I have argued in one of the essays in this volume that the scientist and the poet do not live at antipodes, and I urge in another that the artificial separation of the two modes of knowing cripples the contemporary intellectual as an effective mythmaker for his times. But it is not principally in the role of a would-be mediator between the humanist and the scientist that I have written and then rewritten the essays that comprise this book. My objective, rather, is somewhat different, perhaps more personal.

It is to explore the range of the left hand in dealing with the nature of knowing. As a right-handed psychologist, I have been diligent for fifteen years in the study of the cognitive processes:

1. Reprinted by permission of Harvard University Press.

how we acquire, retain, and transform knowledge of the world in which each of us lives—a world in part "outside" us, in part "inside." The tools I have used have been those of the scientific psychologist studying perception, memory, learning, thinking, and (like a child of my times) I have addressed my inquiries to the laboratory rat as well as to human beings. At times, indeed, I have adopted the role of the clinician and carried out therapy with children whose principal symptom presented at the clinic was a "learning block," an inability to acquire knowledge in a formal school setting, though their intelligence seemed normal or even superior. More recently, I have turned my attention to the nature of the teaching process in an effort to formulate the outlines of a "theory of instruction" and so better to understand what we seek to do when we guide another's learning either by a lecture or by that formidable thing known as a curriculum. Seeking the most beautifully simple case, I chose to study the learning and teaching of mathematics. But it was soon clear that the heart of mathematical learning was tipped well to the left. There have been times when, somewhat discouraged by the complexities of the psychology of knowing, I have sought to escape through neurophysiology, to discover that the neurophysiologist can help only in the degree to which we can ask intelligent psychological questions of him.

One thing has become increasingly clear in pursuing the nature of knowing. It is that the conventional apparatus of the psychologist—both his instruments of investigation and the conceptual tools he uses in the interpretation of his data—leaves one approach unexplored. It is an approach whose medium of exchange seems to be the metaphor paid out by the left hand. It is a way that grows happy hunches and "lucky" guesses, that is stirred into connective activity by the poet and the necromancer looking sidewise rather than directly. Their hunches and intuitions generate a grammar of their own—searching out connections, suggesting similarities, weaving ideas loosely in a trial web. Once, having come in late to dine at King's College, Cambridge, with my friend Oliver Zangwill, I found myself seated next to a delightful older man whose name I had not caught in the hurried and mumbled introductions. We agreed that the climate of debate at Cambridge might be vastly improved if some far-sighted philanthropist would establish a chair of The Black Arts and Thaumaturgy, that the effort to know had become too aseptic and constrained. My neighbor at table turned out to be E. M. Forster.

The psychologist, for all his apartness, is governed by the same constraints that shape the behavior of those whom he studies. He too searches widely and metaphorically for his hunches. He reads novels, looks at and even paints pictures, is struck by the power of myth, observes his fellow men intuitively and with wonder. In doing so, he acts only part-time like a proper psychologist, racking up cases against the criteria derived from an hypothesis. Like his fellows, he observes the human scene with such sensibility as he can muster in the hope that his insight will be deepened. If he is lucky or if he has subtle psychological intuition, he will from time to time come up with hunches, combinatorial products of his metaphoric activity. If he is not fearful of these products of his own subjectivity, he will go so far as to tame the metaphors that have produced the hunches, tame them in the sense of shifting them from the left hand to the right hand by rendering them into notions that can be tested. It is my impression from observing myself and my colleagues that the forging of metaphoric hunch into testable hypothesis goes on all the time. And I am inclined to think that this process is the more evident in psychology where the theoretical apparatus is not so well developed that it lends itself readily to generating interesting hypotheses.

Yet because our profession is young and because we feel insecure, we do not like to admit our humanity. We quite properly seek a distinctiveness that sets us apart from all those others who ponder about man and the human condition—all of which is worthy, for thereby we forge an intellectual discipline. But we are not satisfied to forge distinctive methods of our own. We must reject whoever has been successful in the task of understanding man—if he is not one of us. We place a restrictive covenant on our domain. Our articles, submitted properly to the appropriate psychological journal, have about them an aseptic quality designed to proclaim the intellectual purity of our psychological enterprise. Perhaps this is well, though it is not enough.

It is well, perhaps, because it is economical to report the products of research and not the endless process that constitutes the research itself. But it is not enough in the deeper sense that we may be concealing some of the most fruitful sources of our ideas from one another. I have felt that the self-imposed fetish of objectivity has kept us from developing a needed genre of psychological writing— call it protopsychological writing if you will—the preparatory intellectual and emotional labors on which our later, more formalized, efforts are based. The genre in its very nature is literary and metaphoric, yet it is something more than this. It inhabits a realm midway between the humanities and the sciences. It is the left hand trying to transmit to the right.

I find myself a little out of patience with the alleged split between "the two cultures," for the two are not simply external ways of life, one pursued by humanists, the other by scientists. They are ways of living with one's own experience. I recall a painfully withdrawn young physicist at the Institute for Advanced Study when I was a visiting member of that remarkable institution. His accomplishments as a flutist were magical; he could talk and live either music or physics. For all the rightness of his life, it was nonetheless a segmented one. What was lacking was not an institutionalized cultural bridge outside, but an internal transfer from the left to the right—and perhaps there was one, though my colleague could not admit it. It is a little like the amusing dialogue Louis MacNeice reports between himself and W. H. Auden on their trip to Iceland:

> And the don in me set forth
> How the landscape of the north
> Had educed the saga style
> Plodding forward mile by mile.
> And the don in you replied
> That the North begins inside,
> Our ascetic guts require
> Breathers from the Latin fire.

But the left hand is not all. For there is also in these pages much about the profound revolution that has been taking place in the sciences of man during the past decade and of the new dilemmas that have replaced the old ones. We know now, for example, that the nervous system is not the one-way street we thought it was— carrying messages from the environment to the brain, there to be organized into representations of the world. Rather, the brain has a program that is its own, and monitoring orders are sent out from the brain to the sense organs and relay stations specifying priorities for different kinds of environmental messages. Selectivity is the rule and a nervous system, in Lord Adrian's phrase, is as much an editorial hierarchy as it is a system for carrying signals.

We have learned too that the "arts" of sensing and knowing consist in honoring our highly limited capacity for taking in and processing information. We honor that capacity by learning the methods of compacting vast ranges of experience in economical symbols—concepts, language, metaphor, myth, formulae. The price of failing at this art is either to be trapped in a confined world of experience or to be the victim of an overload of information. What a society does for its members, what they could surely not achieve on their own in a lifetime, is to equip them with ready means for entering a world of enormous potential complexity. It does all this by providing the means of simplification—most notably, a language and an ordering point of view to go with the language.

This has also been the decade in which the role of activity and environmental complexity has become clear to us—both in the maintenance of normal human functioning and in the development of human capacities. The isolation experiments have made it clear that an immobilized human being in a sensorially impoverished environment soon loses control of his mental functions. The daring and brilliant experiments inspired by Donald Hebb at McGill have shown the degree to which alertness depends on a constant regimen of dealing with environmental diversity. And as if this were not enough, we also know now that the early challenges of problems to be mastered, of stresses to be overcome, are the preconditions of attaining some measure of our full potentiality as human beings. The child is father to the man in a manner that may be irreversibly one-directional, for to make up for a bland impoverishment of experience early in life may be too great an obstacle for most organisms. Indeed, recent work indicates that for at least one species, the utilitarian rat, too much gray homogeneity in infancy may produce chemical changes in the brain that seem to be associated with dullness. One wonders, then, about the issue of the appropriate exercise of mind early in life as a condition for fullness later.

Perhaps, too, and for the first time, we have come to a sense of the nature of early mental life, indeed early intellectual life. My generation of psychologists has been fortunate in its exploration of early intellectual development—massively so in the flow of work that has come from Piaget at Geneva, and especially so in the quantitatively meager but brilliant work of the too-early dead Vygotsky at Moscow. Piaget has given us a respectful sense of the manner in which an intrinsic and self-contained logic characterizes mental operations at any stage of development, however primitive it may be. Vygotsky has given us a vision of the role of internalized dialogue as the basis of thought, a guarantor of social patterning in that most lonely sphere, the exercise of mind.

The decade in psychology and its allied fields has been energizing: the lock step of "learning theory" in this country has been broken, though it is still the standard village dance. It is apparent to many of us that the so-called associative connecting of physical stimuli and muscular responses cannot provide the major part of the explanation for how men learn to generate sentences never before spoken, or how they learn to obey the laws of the sonnet while producing lines never before imagined. Indeed, all behavior has its grammatical consistency; all of it has its consistency of style.

Perhaps the moment is uniquely propitious for the left hand, for a left hand that might tempt the right to draw freshly again, as in art school when the task is to find a means of imparting new life to a hand that has become too stiff with technique, too far from the scanning eye.

THE NEA Journal, IN ITS MARCH–1966 ISSUE RAN A SPECIAL FEA-ture section on learning. Mary Alice White (now at Teachers College, Columbia University, and formerly a public school psychologist) is one of the more articulate writers in this field. Her article, which was entitled "Speculations on the Child's World of Learning" is reprinted here in its entirety. She points out that we have been obsessed with the idea that children must understand underlying principles and generalizations that hold various pieces of knowledge together. She goes on to suggest that we may well have been barking up the wrong learning tree.[2]

Following a curriculum carefully designed by experts, teachers know what to teach, in what order, and to some degree, how. As they teach, they can verify some things that the children have learned. For example, if they have taught about the associative property in the new mathematics, they can ask a fourth grader to define associative property and to work examples. In this way, they can determine how well he has learned what they have taught about the associative property.

What they generally don't find out is what children have learned in the classroom that teachers have not predetermined is important for them to learn but which is important in the minds of the *pupils.* One way to determine this kind of learning is to ask a fourth grader to tell a third grader in his own words what third graders need to know in order to enter fourth grade. This is what an investigator heard when a fourth grade girl and a fourth grade boy under-

2. Reprinted by permission of National Education Association and the author.

took to teach a third grade boy in what we call "teaching exchanges":

Fourth grade boy (4B): You have to know math. You should know your tables, multiplication and dividing. We have 10 × 20 or 90. . . .

Fourth grade girl (4G): And the unit on fractions—know your combinations.

4B: Like $^1/_2$ and $^1/_4$ and $^1/_8$.

4G: And the 3 properties—commutative, associative, and distributive.

4B: Math is more important. Spelling is pretty easy, but the tests are hard.

The fourth graders gave 3B typical homework examples to see if he could perform the *precise* techniques that they were currently using. No rules or principles were discussed.

4B: Take 3 × 40. That equals what × 10 × 3?

Investigator (Iv): What's the distributive property? I don't think I know.

4B: I don't know. (pause) It's breaking it down so you can add it easier.

4B and 4G went on to give 3B several examples reconstructed from their workbook involving the distributive property, but at no time was the property mentioned or connected with the examples.

Iv: What's the associative property?

4B: It's not as important as the commutative.

4G: One number changes the grouping. Is that associative? We wrote papers about them.

4B: We do averages. We'll do the score thing we had. Like 4 people get scores—and you add them and get 107. You divide 4 into 107. (He tries to divide.) No, that's wrong. Say 108.

Iv: Why don't you use 107? What do you do when it doesn't go in?

4B: We don't get examples where it doesn't go in. It would be a mistake and I'd check it.

One can dismiss the above teaching exchange as invalid on any number of grounds. If, however, one accepts the interview as having some validity, either the teaching or the pupils appear to be at fault. The teaching, in my opinion, was certainly as good as that found in an average suburban school. The pupils in this school have an average IQ of 110, and come largely from middle and upper management, professional, and retail business backgrounds.

If we accept the substance of this teaching exchange between the pupils as partially representing a child's view of the world of learning, we conjecture that *broad principles and relationships perceived by the teacher and the text are not perceived by these children.*

Perhaps they are not taught effectively, perhaps the children are not ready to grasp them, or perhaps these relationships seem much less important to the child than the ability to perform those specific skills required to survive daily in the classroom. If the latter, we speculate: The more specific, the more ritualistic, the more detailed the procedures of the classroom, the more important these will seem to the children. *Procedure may precede principle* in the children's world, or procedure may *be* principle.

What happens when the principle itself is the prime object of a teaching unit? Let us dip into an experimental science program, that of *Science—A Process Approach* by the American Association for the Advancement of Science Commission on Science Education. The purpose of this new science curriculum is to introduce children to scientific skills basic to further learning. By the end of third grade, it is hoped that the child will have learned "some important fundamental process skills, a good many basic scientific concepts, and some organized knowledge about the natural world."

The third grade children in the following teaching exchange had just completed a week's unit on classification, in which they had classified certain materials into sets, and had termed these sets "gas, liquid, and solid." They had watched ice cubes go from solid to liquid, and, when heated, to vapor. The children had been enthusiastic, and both teacher and principal felt that appropriate learning had taken place about classification as a scientific process.

The teacher selected 3B, the brightest boy in science, and 3G, an average girl in science, to teach this unit to two second graders, 2B and 2G. The two third graders selected materials for the lessons including paper, crayon, chalk, an empty beaker, a magnifying glass, and a beaker with water.

As 3B and 3G arranged on the table an empty beaker, chalk, and a beaker containing some water, the two second graders seemed fascinated as though a magic trick were about to be performed. 3B and 3G talked at the same time, excitedly and enthusiastically, explaining this arrangement to the two second graders:

3B and 3G: Here is an air set, a gas set, and this is a solid set [the chalk]—it has particles—and this is a liquid set because it doesn't have particles and it pours.

3B: The container doesn't matter. (To 2B and 2G) *You* put the crayon in a set.

2B looks puzzled; 2G looks bewildered.

3B explains: You can't pour a crayon, so it's not liquid. A gas? No. So it must be solid.

2B and 2G remain puzzled. 3B and 3G go on to classify the materials they have brought with them.

Third grade teacher: What do we call what we are doing? What name do we use for it?

3B and 3G don't respond. Teacher is disappointed; 3B and 3G aren't apparently concerned, and return immediately to their teaching.

3B and 3G: What's this? (table)

2B and 2G: Solid.

3B and 3G: And paper?

2B: A solid? (confused) No, not a solid because you can tear it.

3G: It's a solid because it has little particles.

2G tries to see the "particles" by putting the magnifying glass close to the paper. She still looks bewildered as she puts the magnifying glass down.

Up to now, the children had used only the materials they had brought with them or that had been used in the classroom unit. The investigator wanted to know if they could classify other materials.

Iv: How about grass?

3B and 3G: Soft.

(Is soft a different set from solid, or is there a soft-solid and a hard-solid?)

What does this teaching exchange illustrate? To what extent were these third graders able to demonstrate scientific process, concepts, and organized knowledge? The teacher was extremely disappointed that her pupils did not connect the term "classification" with their demonstration or attempt to show that a basic process was available for categorizing other types of information.

What was the children's perception of this science learning? We speculate that to them the sorting of certain objects according to three labels was a novel guessing game. They apparently concluded that if something didn't fit one of the three categories, it wasn't especially important.

The *important* thing from their point of view appeared to be to perform the game as it had been taught, much the way children of this age teach each other a card game. The rules are rules. Ambiguity is irrelevant and wastes time. This game is *not* like other games; it is *this* game. You play it with *these* materials.

It seemed to the investigator that the children had not learned the meaning of particles, solids, gas; of classification as a process for doing something useful; of classification apart from the particular things on the table; or of classification as a scientific tool.

In a unit devoted primarily to the teaching of a principle, it seemed that these children missed the important goal as seen from the teacher's point of view. A poor unit? Possibly. Poor teaching? Possibly. A poor sample of children? Possibly. A poor investigative procedure? Possibly.

It may well be that the explorations reported here, and others involving different school subjects and different combinations of children, indicate nothing more than random errors in learning and teaching. Perhaps each child's world is so unique, so personal, that it can never be described. On the other hand, perhaps the explorations do present evidence for certain consistent dimensions of what we term the child's worth of learning and can at least provide the basis for some speculations.

On the basis of these observations I speculate that the child's school learning begins upon a sea of chaotic information, with various particles floating around, unconnected and undifferentiated. What does stand out for him are the precise behavioral ways of the classroom. For a first grader and a kindergartner, the important things about school are one's cubbyhole, one's place in line, having two crackers and not three, and having singing after juice. The excitements are losing something, a substitute teacher, and having a birthday party.

A gradual discrimination between behaving and what adults call learning develops somewhere between the first grade and the sixth. Initially, what most children learn is to behave as teacher asks. These *behavioral* procedures develop into *learning* procedures for doing something, such as reading. Doing this something emerges into a skill, which eventually is a source—as well as a result—of learning.

I speculate that from the child's point of view this transition from behaving to learning is dominated by concrete procedures, not by concepts. Why the procedures are to be followed is not the focus of their learning attention. (To many a child, what to write about is somehow less important than putting a certain heading on every paper.)

The implication of these speculations leads to a major theoretical conflict. On the one hand, scholars have stressed the importance of teaching the structure of a field of knowledge, the basic processes upon which further learning can be built. They emphasize relationships and principles, rather than scattered and rote information. It is a highly intelligent way for an *adult* to learn.

The explorations reported here lead to quite a different notion about how children perceive learning. They indicate that children may be procedural learners, not process learners. If this is relatively accurate, then we may need to study the development of *procedures* in children, rather than processes. If we ask for processes, basic concepts—the relationships which adults prefer—we may think children ignorant. But if we asked pupils for their repertoire of procedures, what would they tell us? In short, perhaps we have been asking children the wrong questions about what they learn in school.

Ultimately, if these sketchy notions outlined here prove to be of some validity, then we would have to explore how we can teach process through procedure, assuming this is both possible and desirable.

IN THAT SAME ISSUE OF THE *NEA Journal*, FRANK RIESSMAN, WHOM the reader has met earlier in this book, if not before, published an article entitled "Styles of Learning." His words are, as usual, a refreshing reminder to us. Here he reminds us that children are individuals with individual styles of learning we would do well to respect.[3]

In any classroom, probably no two pupils learn the same things in the same way at the same pace. Some learn most easily through reading; others through listening; still others through doing things physically. Some prefer to work under the pressure of deadlines and tests; others like a more leisurely pace. Some learn by being challenged by people ahead of them; others learn best by helping people behind them.

Everyone has a distinct style of learning, as individual as his personality. These styles may be categorized principally as visual (reading), aural (listening), or physical (doing things), although

3. Reprinted with permission of the National Education Association and the author.

any one person may use more than one. Some persons, for example, find it much easier to pace the floor while reading an assignment than to sit perfectly still at a desk. Their style may be more physical.

A common characteristic of the disadvantaged child is his physical approach to learning. He has been exposed to very little reading because his parents rarely have the time to read to him. For this reason, it may be easier for him to learn to read by acting out the words than by hearing them spoken by his teacher. This is borne out by the fact that children at a school in one of New York City's poorest neighborhoods are learning to read effectively by singing and dancing to the words. Since songs and physical movement have been incorporated into the teaching of reading, the percentage of retarded readers in the school has reportedly been cut in half.

For a long time now, teachers and guidance workers have tended to ignore the concept of different styles of learning. They have, instead, focused their attention on emotion, motivation, and personality as causes for learning or failure to learn. When confronted with an intellectually able student whose learning fails to measure up to his learning potential, they have tended to attribute this failure to an emotional block or personality conflict. Little attention has been given to how a pupil's learning could be improved simply by concentrating on the way he works and learns.

I believe that a careful analysis of the way a child works and learns is of greater value than speculation about his emotional state. He may indeed feel sibling rivalry or certain irrational fears, but these conditions may not affect his learning as much as the methods his teacher uses to teach him. The important consideration, in my opinion, is whether the methods of learning imposed by the teacher utilize sufficiently the strengths in a child's style of learning.

Most teachers, unfortunately, have been trained to look upon learning in a general way. Their preparation, which may include no more than a few survey courses in educational psychology, neglects the idiosyncracies involved in learning.

For example, most teachers probably assume that the best way to study a reading assignment is first to survey the chapter. This is what they have been taught from the early grades through college because it is the way most people learn best. Some students, however, become so anxious and disturbed at being told to take an overall view of a chapter that they cannot function. Their style calls for reading a chapter slowly, section by section. Requiring such a person to skim the entire chapter first makes no more sense than telling a person who can't resist peeking at the last chapter of a mystery that he must read the book straight through.

The general recommendation that one must have a quiet place to study may be equally lacking in validity. Strangely enough, some people do their best studying in a noisy place, or with certain sounds such as music or even traffic in the background. The textbooks do not talk about this because, for the "average" person, peace and quiet are more conducive to learning.

Style is also very much involved in taking tests. For some individuals, the prospect of a test operates as a prod that stimulates them to absorb a great deal of material they need to master. On the other hand, being faced with a test causes many people to become disorganized, overanxious, and unable to work. After a test, some pupils are so upset over their mistakes that they develop an emotional block about remembering the correct answers to the questions on which they erred. Consequently, they repeatedly miss the same questions. For others, finding out that they gave wrong answers aids recall and challenges them to master the problems.

Each classroom is likely to include students whose styles of learning vary widely. Although the teacher cannot cater completely to each student's particular style, he can attempt to utilize the strengths and reduce or modify the weaknesses of those in his classes.

An individual's basic style of learning is probably laid down early in life and is not subject to fundamental change. For example, a pupil who likes to learn by listening and speaking (aural style) is unlikely to change completely and become an outstanding reader. I am not suggesting that such a pupil will not learn to read and write fluently but rather that his best, most permanent learning is likely to continue to come from listening and speaking.

Since the student is the person most vitally concerned, the first step is to help him discover his particular style of learning and recognize its strengths and limitations.

In identifying a style, it is extremely important to ascertain the person's work habits as precisely as possible. If a youngster is in despair because he cannot get any work done during the study time allowed in class or in the study hall, teachers should question him carefully about his routine. What does he do first when study time is announced? How does he try to make himself concentrate? What disturbs him?

Perhaps his answer will be: "At first I'm glad we have time to do the work at school so that I will be free when school is out. I open my book to the assignment, but it's noisy because kids are asking the teacher questions or flipping through their books or whispering. I go sharpen my pencils while I'm waiting for it to get quiet.

"By the time things settle down, I know I don't have too much time left and that I have to hurry or I won't get done. I try to read fast, but the words all run together and mean nothing. Some of the smart kids are already through, and I haven't even started. I usually give up and decide I may as well do it all at home like all the other dumb bunnies do."

A number of things may be involved in this boy's problem. Possibly he is a physical learner (sharpening the pencils may show some need for movement) who has difficulty with visual learning. Apparently he warms up slowly and works slowly, for when he tries to hurry, he finds he can do nothing.

The physical learner generally gets his muscles into his work, and this takes time. Such a student must realize that attempts to rush himself are of no avail, but that this does not make him a "dumb bunny." Once he gets past his warm-up point and begins to concentrate on his work, he may work very well for long periods of time.

If this student is made aware of the way he learns, he can schedule any work requiring concentration for longer periods of time, and use short periods for something less demanding, perhaps a review of the day's schoolwork. Probably his warm-up period will gradually decrease as he becomes less anxious about failing to keep pace with his fellow students.

A pupil can take advantage of the strengths inherent in his style of learning to balance his weaknesses. For example, consider the pupil who has to learn to read, although his learning style is physical rather than visual.

In order to teach reading to a youngster for whom reading is stylistically uncongenial, the teacher may want to try role playing, which is related to a physical style of learning. The pupil is more likely to be able to read about something that he just role played.

By teaching reading in this way, the teacher is not helping the pupil develop a reading style; he is helping the pupil develop a reading skill.

In a sense, the teacher is overcoming the pupil's difficulty with reading by making use of the pupil's strength, whether it be physical, aural, or whatever.

The challenge to every teacher is first how to identify the learning strengths in his pupils and then how to utilize them to overcome weaknesses. This is the central problem in the strategy of style.

THE PSYCHOLOGISTS ARE NOT COMING BACK TO THE CLASSROOM empty-handed. They are bringing with them souvenirs of their travels. "Reinforcement" and "conditioning" are becoming increasingly respectable words in the vocabulary of an educational psychologist. This is not simply a matter of things having gone full circle. We are not quite back where we once were; rather than a circle we have a spiral.

The words are being used in slightly different context and on a slightly different level. Few psychologists dare talk to teachers about rats. They know they must talk about the learning problems of real children even when using words like "conditioning" and "reinforcement." One reason these words are again so prominent is the panacea of teaching machines.

Sophisticates know that it is not the machine that counts but the program it contains. They also know that flashy machines are easier to find than soundly constructed programs.

Programmed learning is not a new idea. Pressey spoke of it softly some years back. Skinner threw a new floodlight on it in this decade and the "hardware boys" jumped on the bandwagon. The hardware boys are the publishers who saw that there was a mountain of nickels to be made by selling machines that would help Johnny get better grades in school.

The panacea is paling now because so many people are becoming sophisticated. It takes a long time to write a program and it takes a longer time to learn how to write an educationally sound and theoretically correct program. Programmed learning and even its flashy outerwear, the teaching machine, is undoubtedly here to stay. The hard task before us is to learn how to use it.

We have the Madison Avenue brothers of the publishing

industry to thank for making "teaching machine" a household word and "programmed learning" a classroom word. They unwittingly helped to roll out the carpet for the return of the behaviorist whom we now find working everywhere.

The News and Trends Section of the April–1966 issue of the *NEA Journal* reports:

Delinquent teen-agers are paid points for correct answers to tests and in programmed classes at the National Training School for Boys in Washington, D.C. The students—aged 14 to 17—are learning at a rapid rate according to Harold L. Cohen, who is director of the experimental project funded by the Office on Juvenile Delinquency and Youth Development; the U.S. Department of Health, Education and Welfare; and the Federal Bureau of Prisons. The youths are paid in negotiable points. Although the points may be exchanged for such things as pinball-machine plays and lounge time, the experimenters have noticed an increase in the number of youths who trade their points for library time and for taking more study courses.

DONALD L. AVILA AND WILLIAM WATSON PURKEY, OF THE UNIversity of Florida, believe that the behaviorist should be heartily welcomed back into the classroom fold. Their article entitled "Intrinsic and Extrinsic Motivation—A Regrettable Distinction," published in the July–1966 issue of *Psychology in the Schools*, is reprinted here.[4]

In educational circles a distinction is usually made between two kinds of motivation. First there is intrinsic motivation, which is an internal, autonomous, energy source, inherent in the organism. Second, there is extrinsic motivation, which is an external energy source, apparently perceived as being similar in structure and function to the intrinsic source, that the teacher is able to draw on through his training and skill.

Little is done about intrinsic motivation aside from defining it. It is something that the student brings to class and is either directed towards the goals of the teacher or is not. The teacher can do little or nothing to tap this source if it is not already predisposed to func-

4. Reprinted by permission of *Psychology in the Schools*.

tion in his favor. Therefore, the majority of the educators' time is spent with the second kind of motivation; with discussing and defining ways in which the teacher can *extrinsically* motivate his students.

This form of categorization is perpetrated by the educator because motivation is perceived as being free from the processes of control or manipulation. Since these terms have singularly negative connotations, the teacher feels a need to engage in processes when teaching that have little or no "control" in them. He fears being accused of controlling or manipulating his students, and therefore claims not to control or manipulate, but to extrinsically motivate his students. It is the contention of the writers that this is an unjustifiable fear, that the intrinsic-extrinsic distinction leads to a tremendous amount of waste and failure, and that those individuals who persist in making the distinction are engaging in self-delusion. There is a distinction to be made, but the intrinsic—extrinsic distinction obscures the true nature of motivation, and prevents the teacher from becoming highly skilled in the process that is truly the essence of all human interaction, that is, controlled manipulation.

Let us first examine the nature of motivation. There is only one kind of motivation, and that is the personal, internal motivation that each and every human being has at all times, in all places, and when engaged in any activity. As Combs (1962) has stated, ". . . people are always motivated; in fact, they are never unmotivated. They may not be motivated to do what we would prefer they do, but it can never be truly said that they are unmotivated." Again turning to Combs (1965) we find a succinct statement of the nature of this motivation, which is, ". . . an insatiable need for the maintenance and enhancement of the self; not the physical self—but the phenomenal self, of which the individual is aware, his self concept." For the teacher, this is a given, a basic drive toward self-fulfillment. It may be inherent, or learned, but in either case, it is present by the time the child enters school; it is a built-in advantage, a force that comes from within the individual that, by school age, cannot be appreciably altered. No human being can ever motivate another, no matter what the situation or how strong the desire.

To conjure up an external force that is similar to basic internal motivation is to create figments of the imagination, to confuse issues, and to distract from the real value of the teacher. The teacher is the external force, and a strong force, yet not as a motivator, but as a manipulator of his charges. He does not motivate, but he controls an environment in which he manipulates himself and other classroom variables in such a way that what he is trying to teach appears to be self-enhancing to his students. He casts the situation and himself in such a way that the information and knowledge he is presenting is personally meaningful and enhancing to the student.

All human relationships are controlled and manipulated. None are without these two processes. Human relationships differ only in the degree to which and the manner in which manipulation and control are administered. Each day we give to and withhold from our children love and material goods. In our classrooms we reward and punish our students by sending them first one place and then another, by praising or blaming, by giving good grades and bad. Each day we greet our friends in an accepting or rejecting manner, bring them into or force them out of our confidence. All of these activities are examples of how we manipulate ourselves and control the objects in our environment in an attempt to get others to do what we want, in an attempt to make our personal interactions satisfying to both ourselves and those with whom we interact. It is on the basis of one degree or another of manipulation and control that all human relationships are established, conducted, and maintained.

Acceptance of this position does not mean that one must give up his basic humanistic philosophy. Even the most student-centered teacher or client-centered counselor is engaging in a process of controlled manipulation when he sets up conditions in such a way, and conducts himself in such a manner that he creates a warm, friendly, accepting atmosphere. One can only be free if he is in a system in which those persons in control allow him to behave freely. Freedom for growth is a basic humanistic principle, yet it is actually not a great deal different, nor less controlling than the rule of the benevolent dictator.

However, unwarranted fear, and failure to accept the reality of control and manipulation have often caused teachers to reject useful ideas and techniques and engage in labored discussions that result in no concrete classroom applications; and schools to encourage slovenly educational practices. The fate that has so often been accorded the ideas of the more behavioristically oriented social scientists offers a perfect example of what can result from this unwillingness to accept the inevitability of manipulation and the responsibility of control.

The behaviorist has sincerely devoted the lion's share of his time to studying the nature of human interaction generally, and the learning process specifically. He has been conscientious and scientific in his explorations, and although his efforts have fallen far short of being a hundred per cent fruitful, he has generated many concepts and techniques that are immediately applicable to classroom use. Yet, many teachers have been unwilling to even listen to these principles, let alone attempt to apply them in practice. The typical teacher responds to behavioristic principles with statements such as "Those tricks are only good for cats and dogs. They are too mechanical. I want to motivate my students, not raise pets!" Or, if accepting their applicability to human behavior, responding with "Conditioning may be all right for some things, but it just involves too much control for me. It takes too much of the humanness out of learning." The teacher is suggesting that control and manipulation are processes apart from human interaction, and that he can have nothing in common with the behaviorist because the behaviorist is so frankly attempting to control human behavior. The teacher, being a humanist, has no use for control. And, therein, as this paper attempts to point out, lies the fallacy. B. R. Bugelski (1964) has recently published a textbook that could well serve as a tremendously practical handbook for the teacher, and help to make him much more efficient at his teaching task if he were to make daily use of the principles it enumerates. Yet, few teachers will probably ever read this little book because behavioristic psychology and humanistic education have little in common in the eyes of the teacher educator as well as the practicing teacher. It is hoped that the present discussion has helped to clarify the wastefulness and futility of perceiving such a cleavage, such a difference in purpose between behavioristic and humanistic philosophies. Such perceptions can prevail simply through a failure to distinguish between motivation and manipulation, and a failure to accept the reality of what is truly involved in the process of human interaction.

Humanistic psychologies, such as phenomenology and self-theory, have defined for the teacher the nature of the organism's motivation, namely self-enhancement, and the conditions that are most likely to result in the greatest amount of learning: a warm, friendly, accepting atmosphere that gives each student an opportunity to invest himself into the learning situation. Behavioristic psychologies, such as operant conditioning, suggest many techniques whereby the teacher can control and manipulate the learner and the learning situation so that the learner will perceive both the material being taught and the learning situation as being self-enhancing. Thus, humanism, behaviorism, the student, and the teacher can and should act as a well organized, cooperative, team that is playing the game for the common purpose of making the learning process as meaningful, useful, and successful as possible.

REFERENCES

Bugelski, B. R. *The psychology of learning applied to teaching.* New York: Bobbs-Merrill, 1964.

Combs, A. W. (Ed.) Perceiving, behaving, becoming. *Yearbook of the Association for Supervision and Curriculum Development,* 1962.

Combs, A. W. Some basic concepts in perceptual psychology. Paper read at Amer. Personnel Guid. Ass., Minneapolis, April, 1965.

WHILE WE ARE THINKING ABOUT REINFORCEMENT AND THE MANIPU-lation of human behavior it is wise to remember that these are not simply matters between teacher and student, even in the classroom. Peers have a tremendous influence on a child's learning but we still know little about how that influence operates. Susan Tiktin and Willard W. Hartup, of the University of Minnesota, published an article entitled "Sociometric Status and the Reinforcing Effectiveness of Children's Peers" in the *Journal of Experimental Child Psychology* in 1965. It describes some of the pioneering investigation in this area. The Journal summary states:[5]

Changes in response rate on a marble-dropping task of 84 elementary school children were studied in relation to the sociometric status of the peer who dispensed verbal reinforcement during the task. One-third of the Ss from each of two grade levels, second and fifth, were reinforced by popular peers, one-third by unpopular peers, and one-third by socially isolated peers. Response rate increased significantly during the testing session when S was reinforced by an unpopular peer, did not change when the reinforcing agent was an isolate, and tended to decrease when the reinforcing peer was popular. Also, the response rate of second graders increased during the session while the performance of fifth graders

5. Reprinted by permission of the *Journal of Experimental Child Psychology.*

decreased. The present findings, in conjunction with earlier results, demonstrate the enhancing effect of verbal reinforcement dispensed by unpopular peers relative to popular or socially isolated peers on performance in a simple task.

The "Discussion" section of the article reads as follows:

Peers differentially affected children's performance in this experiment according to the sociometric status of the reinforcing agent. The difference scores of children reinforced by unpopular peers increased significantly over time; the difference scores of Ss reinforced by popular peers tended to decrease (although not significantly); and the difference scores of Ss reinforced by isolated peers remained approximately at the initial level. Since these changes were noted in the analysis of the difference scores, it would appear that the approval, rather than the sheer presence, of the reinforcing agent was operative in generating the sociometric effects. Confirmation of this interpretation, however, awaits a study of children's performance when the total task is completed in the presence of a passive, nonreinforcing peer.

The performance differences associated with sociometric status of the reinforcing agent are reminiscent of earlier findings. It was previously reported that, for nursery school Ss, the main effect on performance of the reinforcing agent's friendship status was significant while the interaction between friendship status and minutes in the session only approached significance (Hartup, 1964). The borderline interaction, however, was quite similar to the significant interaction obtained in the present study. Reinforcement by a disliked peer better maintained performance over the six-minute session than reinforcement by a liked peer. Taken together, then, two studies now indicate that when children are reinforced by peers, performance on a simple task holds up better when approval is dispensed by a child who is unpopular or disliked than by a child who is popular or liked.

A significant second-order interaction was obtained in the present study between Sociometric Status of the reinforcing agent, Sex of S, and Grade Level. This interaction is of interest chiefly because it suggests that the foregoing conclusion may require some qualification for older children. The data analysis showed that the effects of reinforcement by an unpopular peer depended on the age and sex of the child. Specifically, the performance of fifth-grade boys was poorer over the session as a whole than during the baseline period when source of the reinforcement was an unpopular peer. Complex changes in peer interactions occur just prior to adolescence and these may prevent generalizing the results obtained with young Ss to samples of preadolescent children. Quite possibly the second-order interaction obtained in the present study is a function of these changes but further research, with older children and adolescents as Ss, is indicated on this point.

Verbalization and glances by S during the experimental session were believed to be pertinent to the hypothesis that differences in performance associated with the reinforcing agent's sociometric status stem from differential capacity of popular, unpopular, and isolated peers to elicit interfering attention-seeking responses. The analyses of variance based on the tangential responses, however, did not parallel the performance results. Further, only one of 12 correlation coefficients between the measures of tangential behavior and response rate was significant and in the expected direction. Previous investigators (Patterson and Anderson, 1964; Hartup, 1964) have reported evidence suggesting that attention-seeking accounts for a small, but significant, portion of the variance in peer-reinforced performance. Considering the present results, however, the evidence is equivocal concerning the possibility that differential task performance with popular, unpopular, and isolated peers results from differential elicitation of competing dependency responses.

A significant interaction between Grade Level and Minutes was also obtained in the present study. Peer reinforcement appeared to have a cumulative enhancing effect on the performance of second graders but an increasingly interfering effect for fifth graders. This finding is probably related to the fact that fifth-grade Ss responded at a significantly higher rate than second-graders during the baseline period. Whether the older Ss were physically unable to sustain an initially high level of performance or whether they became particularly bored with the simple task is not known. In any case, the age difference is difficult to interpret because age of S was confounded with age of reinforcing agent (i.e., second graders were reinforced by second graders while fifth graders were reinforced by fifth graders). The present results demonstrate that the sociometric status of the reinforcing agent has similar effects on children's performance across quite disparate age groups. The data also indicate, however, that there are sources of variance in peer reinforced performance associated with chronological age that require further study.

REFERENCES

Hartrup, W. W. Friendship status and the effectiveness of peers as reinforcing agents. *J. exp. child Psychol.*, 1964, 1, 154–162.

Patterson, G. R., and Anderson, D. Peers as social reinforcers. *Child Develpm.*, 1964, 35, 951–960.

THE READER CAN SEE THAT RESEARCH IN THIS PARTICULAR AREA IS promising but of little immediate use to the classroom teacher. It is useful in stimulating our thinking, however. It should generate hunches or their more respectable relatives, "hypotheses."

Teachers talk of classroom learning ranging from the simplest unit (which has something to do with conditioning) to the biggest kind of learning (which has to do with identification or patterning one's self after the teacher). An interesting paper by Frank M. Hewett, entitled "Teaching Speech to an Autistic Child Through Operant Conditioning," was presented at the 1965 Annual Meeting of The American Orthopsychiatric Association in New York City. It was reprinted in the *American Journal of Orthopsychiatry* later in 1965. It is particularly interesting because the idea of learning by identification was drawn largely from psychological evidence based on experiences in psychoanalytically oriented psychotherapy. This paper shows the new-wave behaviorist standing at today's crossroads of psychotherapy and education.[6]

The autistic child is a socialization failure. One of the major characteristics of autism which both illustrates and perpetuates this failure is defective speech development. The nature of speech peculiarities in autistic children has been described by Kanner, (6) and according to Rimland (12) lack of speech is found in almost one-half of all such children. The follow-up studies of Kanner and Eisenberg (7) indicate that presence or absence of speech by age five has important prognostic implications. Almost without exception the autistic child who reached his fifth birthday without developing speech failed to improve his level of socialization in later years. Even with psychotherapy, autistic, atypical children who had no speech by age three were found by Brown (1) to remain severely withdrawn and generally unimproved.

While intensification of speech training efforts with younger autistic children would seem a logical therapeutic maneuver, such children are characteristically poor pupils. Conventional teaching techniques are seldom successful because of the autistic child's profound withdrawal and preference for self rather than other-directed activities.

BACKGROUND

The staff of the Neuropsychiatric Institute School at the University of California, Los Angeles, has been exploring operant conditioning techniques for teaching communication skills to autistic children. Reading and writing have been taught to a twelve-year-old autistic boy who had never developed speech. (4) Recently a four-and-a-half-year-old, nonverbal autistic boy was the focus for a speech-training program.

In operant conditioning, the pupil learns to produce a given response (e.g., vocalization) following presentation of a cue or discriminative stimulus (e.g., teacher's prompt) in order to obtain a desired reward or positive reinforcement (e.g., candy). In a similar manner he learns to avoid responses which lead to an undesirable consequence or negative reinforcement (e.g., isolation).

Operant conditioning techniques have been successful in increasing the frequency of vocalizations in normal infants (11) and reinstating speech in nonverbal schizophrenics. (5) An attempt to initiate speech in an autistic child is described by Weiland (13) who withheld a desired object (e.g., ball) until the child produced the word, "ball."

Speech training with animals has long involved conditioning procedures. Hayes (3) established a three-word vocabulary in his famous chimpanzee, Vicki, by making receipt of food contingent on vocalization. These vocalizations were later shaped into words by manipulating the lips of the chimp until closer and closer approximations of the desired words were obtained.

Mowrer (9) has written extensively on teaching birds to talk. According to Mowrer it is essential that the trainer's appearance become associated with positive reinforcement. He draws a parallel between this and the mother-child relationship during infancy. The mother's voice acquires secondary reinforcement value and is imitated because of its close association with food gratification and removal of pain. In a like manner presentation of food and water to birds becomes the basis for teaching speech as these positive reinforcements are paired with the trainer's presence and his verbal cues.

THE SUBJECT

Peter is a four-and-a-half-year-old Caucasian boy diagnosed as autistic at age 2. He failed to develop speech although he said "Da-da" and "Ma-ma" during his first year. All attempts at speech ceased at one-and-one-half years and Peter was nonverbal when admitted to the Children's Service of the Neuropsychiatric Institute (NPI). Peter preferred to be left alone during infancy and became upset when picked up or cuddled. He was described as "too good," a young child who sought repetitive, mechanical activities rather than social interaction. At about age two Peter began to develop marked oppositional tendencies and became hyperactive, aggressive and uncontrollable in his behavior. His mother was constantly chasing him out of the street and away from danger. Peter's interest in mechanical gadgets increased and he developed an unusual degree of fine motor coordination. Recent neurological and laboratory tests were negative, and Peter's medical history has been uneventful. His hearing has also been judged as unimpaired. Peter has an older brother and sister who are normal.

PROCEDURE

In planning the program of speech training, provision had to be made for gratifying and controlling Peter. Gratification and control are basic ingredients in all effective learning situations. Children learn those tasks which prove rewarding and which are taught in a systematic and structured manner. Autistic children, left to their own devices, are highly selective learners who obtain gratification by bizarre, inappropriate means; set their own limits, and consequently learn a restricted number of socialization skills. Before such children can be trained, the teacher must discover ways of providing gratification and establishing control. With respect to the latter, Phillips (10) has emphasized the importance of consistent and direct intervention of the autistic child's demands if behavioral changes are to be effected.

Food and candy are generally effective positive reinforcers, although autistic children may be quite variable in their preference. Peter was apathetic about food but displayed a consistent desire for candy as well as other positive inforcers to be described later.

Candy, however, would not control Peter's behavior. He was highly distractable, and his attention could only be engaged for brief periods with the promise of a candy reward. In an effort to reduce extraneous stimuli to a minimum and to introduce negative reinforcement as a lever for establishment of control, a special teaching booth was constructed for Peter.* The booth was divided into two sections, joined by a movable shutter (2 x 2½ feet) which could be raised and lowered by the teacher. The teacher occupied one half of the booth and Peter the other half. Each section of the booth was four feet wide, three and one-half feet in length and seven feet high. The only source of light came from the teacher's side and was provided by two spotlights which were directed on the teacher's face. When the shutter was down, Peter's side of the booth was dark. When it was raised, light from the teacher's side flooded through the opening and illuminated a shelf in front of Peter. To the left of the shelf was a ball-drop device with a dim light directly above it. This device consisted of a box into which a small wooden ball could be dropped. The ball rang a bell as it dropped into the box and was held inside the box until released by the teacher. When released, the ball rolled out into a cup at the bottom of the box where it could be picked up. This ball-drop device was Peter's "key" for opening the shutter. When the ball was released into the cup, he picked it up and dropped it into the box. At the sound of the bell, the teacher raised the shutter and initiated contact between the two of them.

In this setting the teacher not only provided candy and light as positive reinforcers but also used music, a ride on a revolving chair, color cartoon movies and a Bingo number-matching game which Peter liked. Isolation and darkness served as negative reinforcers and were administered when Peter failed to respond appropriately within a five-second period. Pilot trials with Peter and four other autistic children revealed the positive reinforcers to be effective in varying degrees and that all subjects would "work" to avoid isolation and darkness.

---

* The author wishes to acknowledge the contribution of Mr. Frank M. Langdon, vice principal of the NPI School, in the design and construction of this booth.

The training program with Peter can be divided into four phases: introduction, social imitation, speech training and transfer.

PHASE ONE—INTRODUCTION

When Peter was brought by his parents for admission there was a noticeable lack of separation awareness on his part. Despite the fact that he never had been away from home before, he walked away from his parents and into the ward without any visible reaction. Peter immediately was isolated in a room with an individual nurse where he remained for the first week of hospitalization. He was only taken from this room at mealtimes, when he accompanied the teacher to the teaching booth where he was fed. Peter quickly learned the mechanics of the booth. During this introductory phase he obtained each mouthful of food or drink of liquid by using the ball-drop "key." The shutter would be open when Peter was placed in the booth. The teacher fed him a portion of food and then lowered the shutter, releasing the ball into the cup. Peter picked the ball up and dropped it into the opening. At the sound of the bell, the shutter opened bringing the teacher's lighted countenance into view and providing another mouthful of food for Peter. This process was repeated mouthful by mouthful and sip by sip for one week.

By the third day of this first phase the teacher held food or liquid out for Peter but did not deliver it until eye contact was established. This first task of looking the teacher directly in the eye before getting food and drink was learned quickly, and immediate eye contact upon presentation of food was established 83 per cent of the time by the twentieth feeding.

The initial phase served not only to introduce Peter to the booth environment in which speech training would later be attempted, but also to acquaint him with the teacher. At first the teacher often would encounter resistance as he attempted to lead Peter from his ward room because of the change in activity involved. But by the fourth day of this phase Peter responded to the teacher's verbal command and walked to the door to meet him. During the course of his feeding sessions Peter remained in his chair directly in front of the teacher 57 per cent of the total time on the first day to 90 per cent on the day of the final feeding.

Throughout this paper, references are made to various positive reinforcers such as candy and food as providing necessary gratification for Peter. The teacher-child relationship which began at this early stage is not discussed. It is definitely felt, however, that the teacher acquired secondary reinforcement properties through constant association with primary reinforcers as described by Mowrer. While no attempt was made to control the teacher's facial expressions, physical contact with Peter and verbalization, these undoubtedly played an increasing role in motivating and controlling him as the training process progressed.

PHASE TWO—SOCIAL IMITATION

Once Peter had been introduced to the booth, he was removed from isolation on the ward and allowed to participate in activities with the other children. Twenty-minute social imitation training sessions (in the booth) were held both morning and afternoon. During these sessions Peter learned to follow simple verbal directions and to imitate the teacher's hand movements. A variety of positive reinforcers was used at the beginning of this phase so that candy, the most potent reward, could be used during the speech-training phase.

Peter learned to place his hand on the teacher's face in order to obtain a segment of childrens' music. The music would continue so long as Peter kept his hand on the teacher's head. Peter appeared to enjoy testing this routine by quickly withdrawing his hand and replacing it to see if he could change the pattern.

The next task given Peter was that of clapping his hands in imitation of the teacher. Such a response would be rewarded by a single rotation of a motorized chair on which Peter sat. The handclap imitation proved a difficult task for him, and the shutter frequently was lowered because he was inattentive or failed to respond within the five-second limit. Once Peter learned the imitative handclap, another response was introduced. This required him to place both of his hands on his face in order to see a sequence of a color cartoon movie shown on a small screen to his right. This response was learned in one day. Additional social imitation training was done with the revolving chair as a reward. Peter readily learned to touch any part of his head (e.g., ear, nose) in imitation of the teacher. Each correct response within a five-second time limit earned a single rotation of the chair.

This phase was accomplished during the first month of the training program. Only those responses which Peter gave in direct imitation of the teacher were rewarded, and random responses were ignored. The main goal of this phase was to develop a reciprocal imitative relationship as a basis for speech training.

PHASE THREE—SPEECH TRAINING

Peter had begun to vocalize spontaneously during phases one and two. He emitted 23 random spontaneous vocalizations on the first day of the booth feeding, and 79 random vocalizations during the final feeding day. In addition, music appealed to Peter, as it does to many autistic children, and he had been heard humming parts of familiar childrens' songs. He also had spontaneously hummed a few bars of the tune used as music reinforcement during phase two. The teacher selected the first three notes of this tune as the initial response in the speech-training phase, and candy was introduced as a positive reinforcer. A small lighted window was placed on Peter's side of the booth. A piece of candy could be dropped behind the glass where it remained in view until the teacher flipped it out to Peter.

The speech-training phase began with the teacher's placing a piece of candy behind the window and flipping it out. Peter was immediately drawn to this source of candy. Another piece of candy then was placed behind the window where it remained in view while the teacher hummed the first notes as an imitative cue. Peter was resistant to responding and only after several shutter drops did he imitate on cue and receive his candy reinforcement.

Once this response was established, the teacher began work on the first word. Peter had randomly made a shrill, undifferentiated vowel sound (e-oö) during his spontaneous vocalizations in phases one and two. The teacher produced this vocalization and expected Peter to imitate it on cue for a candy reward. This was quickly established and actual speech training was under way.

Shaping this undifferentiated vowel sound into a word was the task at hand. The method of *successive approximation* described by Isaacs was used. The word "go" was selected for shaping because it denoted action and would lend itself to meaningful transfer in phase four. The teacher began by providing an imitative cue slightly in the direction of "go-o-o-o-o." Peter willingly approximated it. On successive trials, the teacher's cue moved more and more toward the word "go." The shaping of this word was accomplished dramatically in two days, and Peter consistently produced a well-articulated "go" on cue in order to obtain candy.

Overoptimism in such cases is inevitable but seldom warranted. Establishing the first conditioned word may be deceivingly simple, but retaining it is another matter. For five days, Peter readily responded with an imitative "go" to receive candy and quickly transferred this response to make the revolving chair "go." On the sixth day, however, he refused to respond appropriately. Instead of "go" he produced the vocalization, dä-dē. For the next seven days he refused to say "go."

Peter would be given five seconds to respond. If an inaccurate response was given, the shutter was dropped and a five-second penalty of isolation and darkness was administered. If the next trial produced the same response, an additional five-second increment was added and a penalty of ten seconds ensued. This increase was cumulative, and longer and longer periods were spent with Peter and the teacher separated. At the close of the penalty period, the ball was released, Peter dropped it into the box, rang the bell, and contact with the teacher resumed.

A power struggle had begun. In an effort to resolve it, the teacher went back to providing the undifferentiated vowel sound (ē-oö) as a cue. But Peter did not respond. The major concern at this time was that the teacher would become an aversive reinforcer and that the positive relationship previously established would be negated. It was decided to wait out this resistance and to handle each inaccurate response in the prescribed manner. Finally, on the eighth day Peter began to imitate the undifferentiated vowel sound. This was quickly shaped back into the word "go," and at no time in the program did Peter display this marked resistance again.

In our previous pilot speech conditioning with autistic children, introduction of the second word often eliminated the initially learned word from the child's repertoire. It was, therefore, with some concern that the second word "my" was introduced in connection with a Bingo number-matching game which Peter liked. In order to obtain a Bingo marker, Peter was held for successive approximations of the word "my." This word was selected for its usefulness in denoting possession in the later transfer phase. During training on the new word, careful attention was given to systematically reviewing the previously learned word "go," and Peter discriminated well between the two words. The giving of an alternate reinforcer for the new word (e.g., Bingo marker) instead of candy appeared important in aiding discrimination.

The speech-training phase lasted six months during which time Peter acquired a 32-word vocabulary: go, my, see, candy, shoe, key,

I, want, hi, bye-bye, mama, daddy, water, toilet, food, eye, ear, nose, mouth, hair, Peter, fine, please, juice, cracker, cookie, milk, Johnny, Marguerite, yes, no, school.

Once the first two words "go" and "my" were learned, Peter's speech became echolalic and he readily attempted to imitate all words the teacher said. However, improvement of his articulation of the 32-word vocabulary was emphasized rather than the building of a larger vocabulary.

Following the acquisition of "my," candy reinforcement was provided on a periodic basis for all new words learned.

Photographs were taken of Peter, his mother, father, brother and sister and he learned the name for each picture. In addition, pictures of Peter eating ("food"), drinking ("water") and going to the bathroom ("toilet") were used as cues. An attempt was made to break the echolalic pattern of Peter's speech, and he learned to answer the direct questions: "How are you? What's your name?" The technique used to teach Peter the appropriate responses to these questions (e.g., "Fine" and "Peter") was developed by Lovaas. (8) First, Peter was given both question and answer for imitation (e.g., "How are you fine"). Gradually the teacher faded the question portion by saying it softly and quickly while emphasizing the answer (e.g., "How are you, FINE!"). Peter soon made a clear imitation of "fine" while paying less and less attention to the question. In a single training session, he learned to respond appropriately to these two direct questions.

The speech-training and transfer phases overlapped as Peter was required to use his conditioned words in a meaningful social context from the beginning of phase three.

PHASE FOUR—TRANSFER

As soon as Peter had learned the word "go," transfer from the teaching booth to the hospital ward was emphasized. Each day when the teacher arrived Peter was required to say "go" as the teacher turned the key in the ward door lock to take him out for a training session.

A ward nurse later was brought into the teaching booth with the teacher. She immediately gained Peter's cooperation for social imitation tasks and the word "go." After working several sessions the nurse held Peter for the word before he was taken through the dining room door and out of the ward on walks. Peter was enrolled in the preschool program with another teacher, and she also participated in several booth-training sessions. Later Peter was required to say "go" in order to enter the schoolroom door. He also was held for "my" before he could obtain a desired object during school periods.

As Peter's vocabulary began to increase, he was required to ask for water, the toilet and food by preceding these words with the phrase, "I want." Also receipt of each periodic candy reinforcement was contingent on "I want candy." Such items as juice and crackers served in the preschool also were given to Peter only when he asked for them. These words were not introduced in the booth. Verbal imitation generalized from the teacher and the booth to other adults and even children in the ward environment.

The children in the preschool became very interested in Peter's attempts at speech and provided constant reinforcement of his words by prompting him. One older boy would hold a toy car at the top of a slanting block runway and let it "go" only when Peter directed him verbally. Peter proved a willing participant in such games.

The major effort during the transfer phase was undertaken with Peter's family. When Peter was permitted six-hour visits twice a week during the seven months of the program, he was not allowed to go home overnight. His parents knew that speech training was being attempted with Peter but not the exact nature of the program. On one occasion, however, while he was on a walk and his parents were moving more slowly than he desired, Peter spontaneously said, "go."

Once he had mastered the 32-word vocabulary Peter's parents were allowed to observe a training session through a one-way vision screen. Most of Peter's training sessions at this point were held outside the booth since he no longer needed the controlled teaching environment. Later both parents were brought into the room and directly observed the training session. Peter performed well with his parents at his side.

When the teacher pointed to Peter's mother and asked "Who's this?" Peter immediately said, "Mama," and took the photograph of his mother and placed it on her lap. He responded in a like manner for "Daddy." His parents then took the place of the teacher and evoked Peter's verbal repertoire using the photographs, Bingo game, candy and water. The transfer from teacher to parents was uneventful.

After this introduction to the speech program, Peter's parents (and occasionally his brother and sister) joined the teacher for weekly training sessions. Peter also was sent home on weekend visits, and the parents were advised regarding ways in which his newly acquired speech could be used at home. The entire family became involved in reinforcing his speech.

From this point on, Peter had great difficulty separating from his parents and often cried and clung to them as he was to report back into the hospital. Once the parents had left, Peter was given to long periods of crying on the ward. These reactions were in marked contrast to the detachment and apathy he exhibited upon separation following visits during early stages of the program.

A notable event occurred when Peter spontaneously imitated his mother's saying "money" and subsequently added, "I want money," in order to get coins to operate a vending machine. Shortly thereafter he approached the ward nurse saying, "I want toilet," or, "I want school," at the appropriate time, and his conditioned speech began to take on properties of meaningful language.

Peter remained in the speech-training program for eight months following phase three. For most of that period he participated as an outpatient, living at home, and attending the NPI School three times weekly for a two-hour preschool program and 40-minute, speech-training sessions. His speaking vocabulary grew to 150 words, and he demonstrated an insatiable desire to learn new words and phrases. Reading lessons also were introduced at this time as a means of enlarging his vocabulary. At the time of discharge, Peter was returned to the care of the referring psychiatrist, enrolled in a private nursery-kindergarten, and placed with a speech therapist who had observed the speech-training procedures in the NPI School.

DISCUSSION

In reviewing the significance of the conditioned speech which Peter acquired during the program it is important to consider the difference between speech and meaningful language.

Speech can be defined as articulated vocal utterances which may be the basis for communication, but meaningful language implies expression of thought and emotion in an appropriate and integrated manner. Birds may acquire speech but not true language skills.

Peter's rapid acquisition of words in association with visual and auditory cues is viewed as an important stage in the development of language. Although he did not systematically acquire the readiness for speech as does the normal child whose socialization experiences from early infancy are intimately involved with words, Peter learned to value and use word symbols. He also generalized an experimentally acquired vocabulary to the larger environment and used it to verbally express his needs (e.g., "I want toilet," or, "I want water").

How successful Peter will be in expanding his speech and converting it to truly meaningful language remains to be seen. That a sizeable communication breakthrough has occurred between an isolated, autistic boy and the social environment, however, cannot be denied.

Not only did this breakthrough make Peter more aware of his social environment, but it also altered the reaction of others toward him. This was clearly seen when nursing staff sought him out for verbal interaction, providing cues for imitation and holding him for speech before granting requests. Although many problems exist between Peter and his family, his newly acquired speech seems to hold promise for improving their relationship and facilitating limit-setting at home.

Goldfarb (2) has suggested that the response of others to the speech defects of schizophrenic children actually may reinforce such defects. Thus, the nature of the relationship between a nonverbal schizophrenic child and the environment may not be conducive to improved socialization. Meeting the needs of such a child by responding to his primitive and often bizarre attempts at communication may merely make an unsocialized existence more rewarding. In addition, the nonverbal schizophrenic child may be perceived as so atypical and difficult to reach that others develop less personal and involved means of relating with him.

The speech-training program described in this paper represents an intensive effort to establish the vital link of speech and language between a nonverbal, autistic boy and his environment during the critical period of early childhood. Peter's success in acquiring the beginnings of spoken language appears to warrant further investigation of operant techniques for establishing communication skills in autistic children.

REFERENCES

1. Brown, J. 1960. Prognosis from presenting symptoms of preschool children with atypical development. Amer. J. Orthopsychiat. 30: 382–390.

2. Goldfarb, W., P. Braunstein and I. Lorge. 1956. A study of speech patterns in a group of schizophrenic children. Amer. J. Orthopsychiat. 26: 544–555.

3. Hayes, C. 1951. The Ape in Our House. Harper and Co., New York.

4. Hewett, F. 1964. Teaching reading to an autistic boy through operant conditioning. The Reading Teacher. 17: 613–618.

5. Isaacs, W., J. Thomas and I. Goldiamond. 1960. Application of operant conditioning to reinstating verbal behavior in psychotics. J. Spch and Hring Dis. 25: 8–12.

6. Kanner, L. 1948. Child Psychiatry (Second edition). Charles C. Thomas Co., Springfield, Illinois.

7. ——— and L. Eisenberg. 1955. Notes on the Follow-up Studies of Autistic Children in Psychopathology of Childhood. Hoch and Zubrin, eds. Grune and Stratton, New York.

8. Lovaas, O. 1965. Teaching intellectual skills to schizophrenic children. (Unpublished manuscript.)

9. Mowrer, O. 1950. Learning Theory and Personality Dynamics, Ronald Press, New York.

10. Phillips, E. 1957. Contribution to a learning theory account of childhood autism. J. Psychology. 43: 117–124.

11. Rheingold, H., J. Gewirtz and H. Ross. 1959. Social conditioning of vocalization in the infant. J. Comp. and Physio. Psych. 52: 68–73.

12. Rimland, B. 1964. Infantile Autism. Appleton-Century-Crofts, New York.

13. Weiland, H., and R. Rudnick. 1961. Considerations of the development and treatment of autistic children. The Psychoanalytic Study of the Child. International Universities Press, New York. 16: 549–563.

AND SO THE TREND IN LEARNING, AS IN OTHER AREAS, SEEMS TO BE to blend several old ideas into a "new" idea and to test the synthesis in the fire of today's pressing educational needs. We are now agreed that learning is not of one kind, it is a many splendored thing. There is left-handed, indirect learning and right-handed, direct learning. Sometimes learning one thing at a time gets us to a rich, broad understanding, but sometimes we must see what's "behind" a piece of learning before it is sufficiently worthwhile to stick.

The procedure of learning, the form, may have greater value to a child than the process, or how he learns. Perhaps we communicate too much joy when a child catches on to a "correct procedure" though we believe we are interested in teaching the learning process.

People can be prodded to learn but the process is private. Different individuals learn differently and one's *style* is important. Teacher style and learner style are both partly a product of early cultural learning and are bound to conflict at times. A girl who stands very close to the teacher and talks very loud may be trying to share her moment of learning joy but the teacher may see only a child who is "fresh" and lacking in respect.

Should children be grouped according to learning style? Should they be matched with a teacher whose style is complementary or similar? It may well be that boys learn differently or develop their learning abilities more slowly than girls. If so, how can this difference best be handled in the classroom? Peers may provide a stimulus or a distraction in the classroom, and most times they provide both.

The teacher, as the somewhat controlling coordinator of classroom learning, is forced to juggle all these factors. We are determined to educate the children of the United States. We are determined to help them learn. If someone has an idea about how one child learns or all children learn, we are receptive and ready to test the idea. Somehow we must permit children to grow beyond the stage of the inquisitive toddler without losing the joy of learning.

CHAPTER 7

Reading

SOME FEW ISSUES IN THE PSYCHOLOGY OF EDUCATION BLOOM ONCE, demand enormous attention, and then disappear, never to be seen again. They are an unusual species. Most ideas bloom every other year or every other generation. Another variety, the perennial, is always with us. An excellent example of the perennial is reading.

The reasons why we're concerned about reading vary from year to year but we are always concerned about reading. The ability to read is, after all, the key to civilization. If one cannot read it is fantastically difficult to learn the lessons of the past and to share many other people's thoughts about the present and future.

One subissue typical of our constant concern is the question of when a child should learn to read. Picture magazines have recently shown parents frantically requesting their infants' attention, as they wear enormous signs that say "mama" or "dada." The family dog is usually less cooperative about wearing his sign, but bottle or toy must have its appropriate label.

These pictures and articles have sent thousands of parents into a panic. Are they cheating their children? Is it true that John, Jr. will not be admitted to Yale because he learned to read his first word at age three instead of at age two?

An interesting article by Robert and Marguerite Krebs appeared in the April, 1966 issue of *Parents Magazine*. It was appropriately entitled "When Should a Child Learn to Read?" The entire article is reprinted here.[1]

"Judy won't enter kindergarten until Fall but already she's bored with first grade books."

"Billy's the same. I'm afraid he'll be too far ahead when he goes to school, but what can I do?"

"Oh dear, I try to teach Mark to read but he just doesn't seem to want to learn."

More and more often when parents talk about their young children, the subject of learning to read is raised. The earlier the child reads, the prouder his parents are. Yet the value of teaching preschool-age children to read is questionable.

The advocates of early reading argue that because there is so much more to learn today than ever before, it is important to start teaching children basic academic skills before they go to school. It has been claimed that the years before six are wasted in nursery school or kindergarten if youngsters get no reading instruction there. If a child can be taught to read, why wait?

Actually, educators have long been aware that children can be taught to read before they go to school. Lewis Terman's well-known study of intellectually gifted children, started more than forty years ago, showed that "Nearly half of the children learned to read before they went to school; at least twenty per cent before the age of five, six per cent before the age of four and slightly more than one per cent before three." Through the years there have been other studies of early readers which show that reading—in some sense of the word—can be taught to many preschool children.

In general, however, the public has been unaware of such findings. But recently much publicity has been given to various systems of teaching very young children to read. One method makes use of electric typewriters; another method, it is claimed, will enable babies as young as ten months of age to learn to read at home.

But most educators and psychologists regard such training as a waste of time because the children are not really learning to read, and the instruction keeps them sitting still when they should be running and jumping and playing.

When three-year-old Timmy is urged to show his grandparents

1. Reprinted with permission of *Parents Magazine* and Robert E. Krebs, Ed.D., and Marguerite C. Krebs, Ph.D.

he can read, he opens his book at a page illustrated by a hat with the word printed under it and "reads" "hat." On the next page is a picture of a ball, similarly labeled. Again Timmy says the word. But this kind of reading is no more than what J. C. Gagg of the *London Times* calls "word barking." Unless a child can bring some background of knowledge and experience to his reading he will get little from it. This is one of the chief arguments for waiting to teach the mechanics of reading. At six or seven a child can form concepts and express them. Consequently, he can read more widely and with more understanding than all but a very few younger children. For these sound reasons, nursery schools and kindergartens prefer to ready a child for reading by adding to his experiences rather than by beginning formal instruction.

Reading readiness is a phrase educators use to indicate the time when a child is sufficiently advanced, mentally, socially, emotionally, and physically to learn to read. Of course, reading readiness varies from child to child, and since most children have many opportunities to pick up some words when they want to, many youngsters begin to learn to read before first grade. This kind of natural learning is prompted by the child's desire to know what it says on the sign, or the cereal box, or the storefront. As Olga Adams, former kindergarten teacher at the University of Chicago Lab School recently wrote, "Even in . . . kindergarten, reading plays a considerable part because it is almost impossible to envision a classroom that has no reading in it." It can be seen that exposure to printed matter is different from formal instruction.

To answer the claim that early formal teaching is desirable because there is so much more to learn than before, and therefore the earlier children begin the better, educators point out that for average children there is apparently no lasting advantage to early reading.

B. V. Keister, an elementary school teacher in Nebraska, made one of the first studies of early readers. He found that the children who began reading about a year younger than the typical first-grader learned reading skills appropriate to first-graders but the skills were not permanent.

Much the same thing was found by Professor Vernon of London University who compared the reading ability of Scottish and English children. Scottish children are taught to read at age five and English children at six. By eight there were no significant differences between them in reading comprehension.

Although such studies cannot be considered definite, the fact that early instruction in mathematics appears to be equally impermanent seems significant. In a project nearing completion at the University of Chicago, the mathematical knowledge and skills of thirteen-year-olds in twelve different countries are being compared. A preliminary finding is that by thirteen there is no difference in their mathematical skills even though in some countries formal instruction in math was begun at five, in some at six, and in others at seven.

In addition to the various studies already under way, still another kind of research is needed. We know that many learning difficulties are the result of emotional problems. What becomes of the child whose parents or teachers try unsuccessfully to teach him to read at three, four, or five? Will early failure affect his later achievement? Make him unsure of himself in other ways? Create tension between a child and his parents?

Young Mrs. Grey is typical of the mother who pushes her son too hard and too early. She is determined that Benjy learn to read before he starts school, so they spend fifteen minutes a day reading. Occasionally it is fun for them both, but many sessions end with Benjy sulking and his mother frustrated. Part of Mrs. Grey's trouble is that, like most parents, she has had no training or experience as a reading teacher. Yet reading is not only the most important tool of learning, it is one of the most complicated subjects a child has to master.

John Gardner, now Secretary of Health, Education, and Welfare, in a report to the President's Commission on National Goals in Education wrote, "Reading is the most important of all (subjects). The first step to improve the teaching of reading is to improve the teachers. . . . It is a mistake to suppose that reading can be taught by an untrained person." And even a parent who has had experience teaching usually has little patience with his own child when he is slow to learn.

This doesn't mean that parents should not help children who want to learn. A child's questions should be answered and he should certainly be encouraged to look at and "read" picture books. In this way the youngster who has a genuine drive to learn to read before school will have the chance to do so. As a rule, such children are above average in intelligence, and come from homes in which someone has read to them regularly from the time they were very little. Most of the natural early readers have above average memories, considerable ability to amuse themselves, and spend fewer hours watching television than do average children.

Even though a child has many of these characteristics he still may not be a prime candidate to be an early reader. For example, our son, Michael, now four, was an early and avid talker. We began reading to him before he was a year old. He listened attentively and loved to be read to. We were sure he would be eager to read by himself before he started school. We were even more certain of this when he began to learn the alphabet before his second birthday. However, he has stopped there for the time being. At four, he shows only slight interest in reading by himself. Michael still likes books, and enjoys being read to. If he asks a question about a word we answer it but we are not trying to force him to read to himself.

What can we conclude from the studies and articles on early reading? First, it is clear that there is no single answer applicable to all children. A young child who has the intellectual, social, and emotional maturity to read should not be prevented from learning if he wants to. However, most children will get more benefit from being prepared to read rather than from actual teaching during their preschool years.

A child shows it clearly when he feels the joy of accomplishment. It isn't always so easy to detect feelings of humiliation and shame that accompany failure, but the effects can be profoundly disturbing. Reading is a fundamental discipline of learning. It provides pleasure and companionship. It stimulates the imagination. It is altogether too important to rush a child into before he is ready to absorb all it has to give.

FOR YEARS TEACHERS HAVE LAUGHED AT THE WHITE PICKET WORLD in which Dick and Jane watch Spot run. They have laughed because they know this type of world has meaning to relatively few children. They have laughed and they have continued to use the "Dick and Jane" books to teach reading.

Suddenly today's teachers are interested in a new kind of book. The children who live inside the pages of this new book have skin that is yellow, white, brown, red, or black.

We have remembered that people like to read about people they know. Children are interested in the real world they see around them. It is interesting because it is genuine. It offers affection, humor, and horror. It is also a world that changes rapidly.

We have caught on to this fact where adults are concerned, and now offer much text material in paperback. But we still think of children's readers as something permanent, in hard cover, that must be preserved for years. Throw-away newspapers or paperbacks that permit crossword puzzles, number tracing, and coloring can be geared to a child's current neighborhood experiences but just don't seem "right" somehow.

Dick and Jane are alive and safe but in hiding. They will surely live on forever. They have brought joy to children who, while not necessarily entranced with the stories, were entranced with a new-found ability to read. Mostly they will live on because we adults need them. We need to believe that their happy world does exist.

Some schools are now trying out throw-away paperbacks and local interest newspapers, some with photographs of the neighborhood, but it has hardly become acceptable practice. Some books, such as the Bank Street Readers, present interesting and appropriate reading material for a probable majority of children. Some publishers, in haste to jump on a probably profitable bandwagon, have colored Dick and Jane brown or purple, however, and gone on about their same old business. We are now guaranteed a great outpouring of good and bad books about children who not only have different skin colors but different worlds in which to grow. It will take us a few years to learn how to sort these.

The larger problem is how to use them in teaching and a nagging question is whether the trend will continue from the lower grades through the upper grades.

Benetta B. Washington, who has been a classroom teacher and principal and is now Director of the Women's Centers of the Job Corps, faced some of these questions in her article entitled "Books To Make Them Proud" that appeared in the May–1966 issue of the *NEA Journal*. The entire article is reprinted here.[2]

The goal of public education should go beyond giving the individual an opportunity to fulfill his basic material needs. It should also give him a chance to acquire a feeling of dignity and worth. The self-concept, after all, is learned. Individuals develop their concept of self from the kinds of experiences they have in life, at home, on the street corner, in school. They discover that they are liked, wanted, and accepted from having been wanted and accepted and having experienced success. The child, in particular, learns that he is understood and loved, not from being told, but from the ways in which he is treated.

Many of our youth have been told for too long by too many voices in our society that they are failures, that they are inferior, that they have no future ahead of them. These youngsters do not know who they are, what they can be, or even what they want to be. They are afraid, but they do not know of what. They are angry, but they do not know at whom. They are rejected, but they do not know why.

The schools, unfortunately, reinforce this attitude by neglecting to make a conscious effort to give these children any kind of self-concept.

I believe that many youngsters from minority groups fail in school because the materials in the classroom do not correspond to anything they experience in life. How is life depicted in common basic classroom readers? How is the family described? In what Nancy Larrick has aptly called "The All-White World of Children's Books," the family is generally intact, loving, rarely with more than four in the family, and includes daddy with a briefcase. The most severe crisis, in readers for young people, arises when the family terrier gets lost.

A small Negro boy put the problem more simply when he complained to his teacher that he didn't like the stories in his readers because "I don't know any people like that."

One means of attacking the problem is through the utilization of books which stress the inherent worth of all people, as well as books and other learning materials which describe the kinds of urban, multiracial society in which the students live.

In the Cardozo High School Project in Washington, D.C., the books used for literature classes are those in which the characters and situations are immediately recognizable to the students, nearly all of whom are Negro.

Works that have been the most popular and effective with these students include Salinger's *Catcher in the Rye*, Sillitoe's *Loneliness of the Long-Distance Runner*, Hansberry's *Raisin in the Sun*, Baldwin's *Blues for Mister Charlie,* and *Inherit the Wind* by Lawrence and Lee. Only two of these works are concerned with Negro life, but all of them seem to have some relevance to Negro youth living in an urban society.

Once the students see the relevance of contemporary literature to their own lives, they have little difficulty making the transition to literature of the past.

For example, students who responded to Holden Caulfield's dilemma in *Catcher in the Rye* were able to perceive a similar dilemma in the struggle of Oedipus. Through these two works, one contemporary and one classical, they discovered that other persons, like themselves, can be caught in a web of events and that others also become frustrated in their inability to cope with these situations. In gouging out his eyes, Oedipus represented their own sometimes violent reaction to frustration.

One teacher at Cardozo used the quarrel between Agamemnon and Achilles in the *Iliad* to teach a lesson about anger. After reading some parts of the story to her class, she asked one of the boys to read the rest of it aloud. As the boy read, he began to stumble over some of the more difficult words. Finally in anger at himself, the boy threw his book at the boy in front of him. This immediately started a fight between the two boys.

The teacher quickly calmed the two by pointing out that the student who had thrown the book was angry with himself, rather than with the boy in front of him. "You can't take it out on other people because you fail at something," she told the boy who had thrown the book. "You know you can do better, but it takes time. Your present feelings are precisely what this story is about."

The book-throwing incident led to a discussion of why Achilles and Agamemnon had argued and of which one was justified in his anger. The students also discussed how each of them would have reacted had he been in the place of either of the two Greek heroes.

Social studies, as well as literature, offers an opportunity for moving from an understanding of the world of today to that of the past. Books and pamphlets, such as Martin Luther King's *Letter from a Birmingham Jail* and Harper Lee's *To Kill a Mockingbird* can assist the student in understanding the contemporary struggle in civil rights, as well as provide a basis upon which to search the past. This approach can lead to Gandhi's concept of nonviolence, to Thoreau's *Walden,* or to reading John Hope Franklin's *The Militant South: 1800–1861* with fresh insights.

The student may use his awareness of the contemporary scene

to comprehend struggles and events of the past, such as those depicted in Upton Sinclair's *The Jungle*, which dealt with the deplorable conditions under which workers labored in the stockyards, or those described in Markham's poem, "Man with the Hoe," which portrayed the plight of the farmer in the late nineteenth century.

In all of this kind of teaching is the implicit need for the student to realize that the Negro has been an integral part of this nation's history, not outside of it. Durham and Jones' recent book, *The Negro Cowboys*, is an example of how modern scholarship has provided a new perspective on the role of Negroes in American history.

Books which contain illustrations showing members of minority groups are also useful. Photographs are superior to drawings; the former are realistic, while the latter remain impressionistic.

Thus far, it seems, most school books that treat members of minority groups with dignity are those written for the primary grades. There is an urgent need for such books for older students if the schools are to bridge the gap between the world of school books and the real world of the disadvantaged youngster.

WHEN WE THINK WE HAVE A NEW ANSWER TO WHY SOME CHILDREN can't read, experienced reading teachers hold their breath and wait and see. Some of the "answers" are labeled by history as fads. Most add their small contribution to our understanding of reading and then shrink to life-size significance. It is rare for several years to pass without one "big" possible answer making its appearance. Though few of these answers remain big, it is crucial that we give our full attention to each in order to do a proper job of sorting. A current answer was described in the May 13, 1966 issue of *Time Magazine* under the heading "Some Johnnies Just Can't."[3] The article follows.

When Johnny can't read—and 15% of the 36 million U.S. elementary-school children are at least two years behind in reading capability—Johnny's parents usually blame the teachers or their techniques. Teachers often snap back that Johnny just won't try. In perhaps 2,000,000 of these cases, researchers are now discovering, neither school nor student is at fault: Johnny can't read because of a neurophysiological disorder, most often called dyslexia. But he can be helped.

3. Reprinted by permission from *Time, The Weekly Newsmagazine;* © Time, Inc. 1966.

The Symptoms. While precise definitions of dyslexia vary, most experts agree that it appears to be inherited in many cases, but may also be the result of early brain injury, and that it leads to reading difficulties in children who otherwise show normal intelligence in mental tests. Dyslexics display a whole syndrome of symptoms (some of which are no cause for concern in preschool-age children, but may indicate dyslexia if they persist beyond this age). Usually they confuse spatial relationships. Horizontally, this leads, for example, to spelling *first* as *frist*, *very* as *vrey*. Vertically, it may cause mixups between *u* and *n*, *b* and *p*, *R* and *B*. Their sense of time may be confused, so that even if they hear well, they tend to transpose sounds, get sentences mixed up.

Dyslexics jumble left and right, lack the fine coordination needed in such activities as writing. Their balance is shaky; their sense of rhythm is faulty. They generally reason well but falter in shifting reasoning to symbols such as letters and numbers. Detecting the dyslexic is complicated by the fact that he is also likely to suffer from emotional problems. Although he is as bright as other kids, he becomes frustrated and angry over his poor reading, turns rebellious, seems not to care.

The Solutions. If pinpointed before his emotional problems become overwhelming, the dyslexic can readily be taught to overcome his reading problems. Techniques vary, but effective reading instruction is being given in many reading centers, including New York University's Reading Institute and the Orton Reading Center in Winston-Salem, N.C. Tutorial instruction at Columbia Teachers College clearly shows, says the college's Mrs. Marvin Sleisenger, that such children can learn if "we teach in slow motion." But Frances McGlannan, whose own son's dyslexia led her to found the Language Arts Center in Miami to help such children, puts through 70 students at a time under 18 teachers, takes about a year to enable second-graders to rejoin their public-school classmates at the proper reading level. Older children take longer to catch up.

Since the dyslexic child has faulty visual and auditory perception, Mrs. McGlannan tries to reinforce these senses by stressing touch techniques. Children make human and animal figures out of clay to get a clearer conception of spatial relationships, work with big Masonite squares and circles to get a grip on geometric symbols. They stand on one foot and hold out their arms to comprehend the ideas of leftness and rightness. They manipulate letters that have been fashioned from pipe cleaners, feel the shapes with their eyes closed as the teacher pronounces the letter's sound. The aim, says Mrs. McGlannan, is to blend sight, sound and touch in order to straighten out jumbled perceptions by "involving all the sensory pathways."

In today's specialized research, medical experts have not been aware of the educator's problems with dyslexia and educators have not been aware of the medical knowledge about it. A big step was taken two weeks ago with the formation of a national committee on dyslexia. Headed by Psychiatrist Archie A. Silver of N.Y.U.'s School of Medicine and Hospital Administrator Robert R. Roberts of Redding, Calif., it consists of physicians, psychologists and educators, who by working together can more effectively analyze and attack what promises to be a solvable medical-educational problem.

AN ARTICLE ABOUT TEACHING THE DYSLEXIC CHILD APPEARED IN THE April 16, 1966 issue of *Saturday Review*, under the title "Teaching the Dyslexic Child: New Hope for Non-Readers," by Careth Ellingson and James Cass. It is reprinted here in full.[4]

In modern society, dependent as it is on the printed word, those who cannot read are cut off irrevocably from most of the normal channels of learning and communication. Our lives are dominated by instructions, directional signs, and the many sources of information and pleasure—all written—that provide the key to the complexities of modern living. The non-reader finds it impossible to function in this world, either personally or professionally, except at a very elementary level.

Firm figures on the number of children in the country who encounter serious difficulty in learning to read are hard to come by. The experts differ in their estimates—not least because they are sometimes focusing on slightly different groups of children. For instance, Dr. Richard L. Carner, director of the University of Miami Reading Clinic, estimates conservatively that "20 per cent of all children of normal intelligence or above suffer from reading difficulties severe enough to impede learning substantially." Some estimates run much higher. Dr. Katrina de Hirsch, director of the Pediatric Language Disorder Clinic at the Columbia-Presbyterian Medical Center in New York, on the other hand, has written that "most people agree that from 10 to 14 per cent of all school children . . . have difficulties in mastering the printed word."

4. Reprinted by permission of *Saturday Review*.

Estimates of the number of children who suffer from dyslexia—or "specific language disability" (SLD), as it is often called—vary even more. However, a widely quoted estimate of 10 per cent of all children of normal intelligence or above appears to be safely conservative. And for about two-thirds of these children—an estimated 2,000,000 to 3,000,000—the disability ranges from moderate to very severe.

But the *exact* figures are not important. What *is* important is the fact that large numbers of intellectually able children are barred from living normal lives by a remediable disability that makes it impossible for them to learn.

Medical knowledge of dyslexia dates back to the late nineteenth century when the term "word blindness" was first used to describe individuals with normal sight who, nevertheless, were unable to read words or even letters. Since that time a great many studies have identified aspects of the disorder more exactly, but its specific cause remains elusive. Considerable confusion has persisted, too, in the definition and use of the term dyslexia. Some authorities have included within its meaning various kinds of minimal brain damage, and other neurological and developmental disorders. But in 1961, the Johns Hopkins Conference on Dyslexia defined the term as a genetic, neurological dysfunction, uncomplicated by other factors. (It is this latter definition that is assumed here.)

Despite the advance in medical knowledge in recent years, however, little awareness of the problem has penetrated the world of classroom education, and most children suffering from dyslexia have received little or no help. The resulting cost in human waste and suffering has been high.

Consider the child. During his early years he is an average, healthy, happy human being. He has seemingly developed normally, and often displays above-average intelligence. Then he enters school. Suddenly he is faced with an environment in which learning to perceive written symbols has become his most important task. It rapidly becomes clear to him that success, both now and in the future, is dependent upon this one complicated—and for him, impossible—skill. The circuits in his personal computer, for some reason, don't receive and process the symbolic data channelled to them from his eyes and ears with the accuracy and consistency of his fellows. He is lost. While the other children are gradually "learning their letters" and one by one are taking off on the high road to learning, he is mired on the low road—going nowhere. What has happened?

No one knows exactly why the dyslexic child is unable to perceive the world of symbols through his senses and record what he sees and hears without distortion. But there is general agreement on the various forms that this distortion may take.

It is common, for instance, for the dyslexic child to have imperfect directional sense—to confuse left and right and up and down. As a result he is likely to reverse letters and words, or syllables within words: "b" becomes "d," "p" becomes "q;" "saw" may be written as "was," "left" as "felt," "on" as "no," and "sorrow" as "sowro;" and numbers may be similarly reversed with "42" substituted for "24." Up and down confusion leads him to write "M" for "W," and "d" for "p." All children, up to about age six, have difficulties of this kind, but the dyslexic child's reversals are far more numerous and persist much longer.

The perceptually impaired child is likely to have difficulty in seeing a word or a complex form as a whole—his attention is attracted by details and he fails to see their relationship to the whole. He may also have trouble in differentiating a figure from its background—he has to work consciously to identify the figure or word that he is supposed to see, as other children hunt for the hidden figures in a visual puzzle that conceals figures in masses of foliage. Many times he also has difficulty in recognizing the same word or object when it appears in a different context, or in a different size or color. "When," for instance, is the same word whether it appears alone on a flash card or as one of several hundred words on a printed page; it is the same whether it is printed in six-point type or in three-inch letters, whether it is printed in black or yellow or red. But for the child with specific language disability, it may be recognized easily in one context or form or color, but appear totally strange in another. He lives, therefore, in an unreliable world in which he is constantly deceived by his senses as the symbols he is required to master elude him.

The dyslexic child's auditory perception, also, is almost certain to be imperfect and to result in similar distortions. In spite of normal hearing he is likely to have difficulty in distinguishing between close gradations of sound and he may scramble even the simplest messages. He may be able to pronounce the sounds of p, a, and t in "pat," but when he blends them together, they come out "tap." If he is asked to write the sentence, "The first bat in the pile is broken," for instance, it is likely to come out, "The frist tab in the pill is brokn."

There are, of course, many other manifestations of the SLD

child's problem that are apparent to the trained observer, but there are also simple clues to the condition that can be identified easily by the parent or teacher. Very often, for example, the first hint of any disability appears when reading instruction starts in school. Although up to that time his progress has appeared perfectly normal, suddenly he is in trouble. His performance in reading does not match that in other areas of learning, nor does it come up to expectations based on intelligence tests that do not require reading. He is likely also to be experiencing difficulty in other language areas such as spelling and writing.

His family history may also provide clues since many specific dyslexics come from families in which left-handedness or ambidexterity is common. He himself may display no clear preference for the right or the left hand. And in many cases other members of the family also have a history of language difficulties. Interestingly enough, an unusually high number of cases are children of eminent surgeons whose ambidexterity has added a crucial dimension to their surgical skill.

Perhaps the most difficult cases to identify, however, are those of exceptionally bright children who are suffering from only a mild disability. Despite the fact that their academic progress is substantially impeded, the problem is concealed by their capacity to achieve despite the disability.

But the problem of the dyslexic child is not one that affects only the child—his family and teachers are almost equally involved. To be sure, the emotional disorganization that such a child faces is almost overwhelming. He is confronted with parents, teachers, and friends, in fact, a whole world that seems to feel that he is deliberately malingering. Because of his demonstrated intelligence, his teachers do not understand why he will not learn, and wonder where they have failed. His parents, too, wonder what they have done that should make him seem to want to misbehave. And his friends do not understand his apparent unhappiness with life—a state of mind that, at times, manifests itself in extremely aggressive behavior.

Look at the problem from a child's vantage point. Danny, age nine, in excellent physical health, with a high average I.Q., is one of four children. After three years in public school his world was in ruins. During the first two grades he was always behind in his class work, at the bottom of his reading group. By the third grade he began to feel that it wasn't even worth trying any more. Danny's parents tried to be understanding and helpful, but his increasing irritability and his emotional outbursts over minor incidents, his growing rejection of parental control, and his continued lack of academic progress, triggered problems within the family circle. The family began to function *around* Danny, avoiding whenever possible a direct confrontation with him. But this line of action was not the answer; it just confirmed Danny's opinion of himself as unloved, stupid—a failure.

One day Danny and his mother were shopping in the downtown area of their community, with which he was not familiar, when they became separated. Danny wandered about for more than two hours, becoming more and more confused and frightened. Finally, he was found by a policeman. But even when found, he could not give his correct address or telephone number—he kept reversing the digits—and he could not write the information for the police. Nor did he particularly want to. He had decided that his mother had lost him deliberately because she no longer wanted him around. The police had to wait for Danny's mother to appear.

That evening Danny's parents decided that he should go to a psychologist for help with his "emotional problems." In many ways it was a relief to his parents when the psychologist, after extensive testing, diagnosed his problem as specific dyslexia, with an emotional overlay which he was sure would completely disappear if the child received the proper, specialized scholastic help his condition required.

Danny is one of the lucky ones. Today, two years later, he is a bright-eyed, carefree boy who is achieving in school, is secure in his family's love, and is ready to compete with other boys of his age. His parents are aware that with each new phase of his development they will have new problems to face (to date there is no *cure* for dyslexia). For example, when Danny is old enough to drive a car, he will need special help with directional problems—to make sure that he won't turn left when he should turn right. But these are solvable problems. Danny has it made.

Hundreds of thousands of other Dannys don't. Yet the prospect for them is brighter than ever before. A substantial body of medical and educational research already exists on dyslexia, and a number of well-known medical scholars, both in the U.S. and in Europe, are actively exploring the problem. A limited number of reading clinics, such as Dr. Carner's at the University of Miami, have the knowledge and facilities to work with dyslexic children, and we may hope that their number will increase.

But most hopeful, perhaps, is the work being carried on at the

McGlannan School, a small research language arts center in Miami. With an enrollment of sixty-five and a staff of twenty, the school is dedicated to the unusual objective of putting itself out of business. Its purpose is to develop methods of identifying and teaching the dyslexic child that can be taken over by the public schools.

The school's founder and director, Frances K. McGlannan, became interested in dyslexia while doing graduate work in the field of clinical reading. During seven years of teaching and research she became convinced that reading clinics, despite their excellent work with dyslexic children, were limited by the clinical necessity of teaching on a tutorial, or one-to-one, basis. A successful effort to help an estimated 2,000,000 to 3,000,000 school-age children, she decided, would require the development of methods and techniques that could be employed in regular classrooms by trained classroom teachers. The McGlannan School is the result.

Today, the school, in its second year of operation, offers a full, ungraded curriculum for grades one through six, and works with a carefully selected "pure sample" of children with genetic language disability. It is a teeming center of ordered chaos, boasting a well appointed clinic, an extensive testing program, a pilot teacher-training project, and an exciting atmosphere of constant experiment and discovery. Once the requirements of the students are met, primary efforts are directed toward practical research into improved techniques. Typical of its many efforts in this direction is a project in which statistically paired students are being given different kinds of training in areas of perceptual constancy and horizontal spatial relations to determine which exercises have the most carry-over value to the printed page. And in another area, the staff, working with the school psychometrist, Mrs. Isabel Wills, is correlating statistics from professionally administered psychological tests with classroom testing that may be performed by a trained teacher in order to develop a screening instrument for identifying dyslexic children.

Early identification of a child's disability is the key to effective treatment. Delay in diagnosis increases the problems enormously. Frequently the first grader with the neurological development of a four-year-old is forced into the same classroom mold as his classmates with the advanced perceptual skills of seven-year-olds. The large numbers of children troubled with SLD fall into this category.

The McGlannan School's basic approach to teaching a dyslexic child does not differ materially from that employed generally by reading clinics and specialists in this country and abroad. Where the school does differ is in its successful effort to carry over into group teaching tested clinical methods by which children are taught individually, thus accomplishing in a classroom what has previously been achieved only in tutoring sessions. This requires detailed interpretation of the test patterns of each child's learning strengths and weaknesses, which, in turn, determines the specific teaching methods to be employed and the way in which students are grouped in the classroom.

Another contribution is its continuing staff effort to refine these techniques and to develop specific adaptations of them to "unlock" the special problems of individual children. Mrs. McGlannan's clinical assistants, Mrs. Clara Leonard and Mrs. Norma Banas, classify and edit these special methods so that they are available to the entire staff immediately.

Learning in the schools is usually approached through the eyes and the ears—the visual and auditory senses. But since the dyslexic child cannot receive symbolic data through these senses without distortion, they must be supplemented by other channels of communication. For him, then, touch and movement—the tactile-kinesthetic avenue to learning—add a "third dimension" to the teaching-learning process. He becomes increasingly familiar with the symbols that he finds so elusive visually through a wide range of activities that allow him to feel them, trace them, arrange them in various sequences, and associate their shape and sound with familiar objects. Starting with simple geometric forms and directionality training, he gradually works through to the letters of the alphabet, and finally to complete words. In this process, his whole being has become involved.

The same approach proves useful in the later grades. Social studies is built upon time lines and sequences that cannot be "seen" and upon geographic locations that are lines on a map. When a dyslexic child looks at a map of the continents, it may appear to him to be a mere collection of symbolic designs. "Looking," therefore, does not necessarily mean that the child "sees" that Africa is larger than Australia, or that England has a jagged coast line while Florida's is smooth. But if he traces the continents, colors them, cuts them out, and then pastes them in proper position on a styrofoam globe, he *is* able to see them and their relationship to each other.

There is, obviously, no real barrier to teaching a dyslexic child. The basic prerequisite is a teacher with knowledge of the problem and its treatment, patience, and ingenuity in adapting techniques to the individual child. A second necessity is parents who understand the problem and are willing to learn along with the child. A third, and most important, is early identification. Given these three necessities, a year or two of intensive treatment—depending upon the severity of the disability—will prepare most children to enter regular school classrooms. But these children will continue to need special help and understanding from their families and teachers.

What, then, are the chances for the hundreds of thousands of boys and girls whose disability has not been discovered? Today, though better than ever before, they are far from encouraging. A very few public schools are attempting to help dyslexics—along with other nonreaders—in their remedial programs. A limited number of university-based reading clinics are equipped to identify and treat the problem. Yet even in these cases the child is likely to spend an hour in the afternoon being tutored at a clinic—after spending a frustrating five or six hours in a classroom where there is little or no understanding of his problem.

Yet it need not be so. The knowledge that is necessary to institute full-scale programs for dyslexics in the schools is already available. When asked whether the clinical teaching techniques could be introduced into a public school system, Mrs. McGlannan said, "With properly trained personnel in each school, it could be done virtually overnight. But until the public and the profession understand the human cost of failure to act, the future holds little promise for these children. They will continue to be as handicapped by the public and professional ignorance surrounding their problem as they are by the problem itself."

ADULTS COMPLAIN ABOUT THE CONTEMPORARY "RAT RACE" WHILE urging their children to jump into the race at an early age. The years of childhood build a foundation for life. If we are more interested in hustling children into early reading than in helping them find fun in reading, it is possible that we will build a generation of people who hate the printed word.

Benetta Washington mentioned Harper Lee's book, *To Kill a Mockingbird*. The reader may remember that the heroine of that book did not know how or when she learned to read. She just found herself happily reading. She would sit on her father's lap while he read the newspaper and one day the black marks on the white paper represented words.

Reading is rewarding if it holds pleasant associations or seems worthwhile in other ways. If your skin is white, you have the usual number of problems, and you live in the United States, but all written stories are about yellow-skinned people who live in a constantly joyous, foreign-sounding place, coincidentally called the United States, you will probably lose interest in reading. If the stories offer a chance to learn about yourself, to solve your problems, and to explore your own world, you begin to see the value of reading skill.

Reading *can be* a pleasure. It *is* a necessity in our culture. Many children have special difficulties in learning to read. We must continually refine our understanding of their difficulties and search for effective help. The current attack on dyslexia represents one such effort.

The trend today is still toward taking apart the act of reading in order to better understand it. The chances are that we will kill the joy connected with it, just as we have done in many areas of learning.

But one day the trend will reverse itself, or move in a circle that is really a spiral, and we will find ourselves putting together what we have learned from the dissecting. We will rediscover the old-fashioned pleasure that can come from reading. That particular turn of the spiral is not, however, in sight at the moment.

CHAPTER 8

Teaching

WHEN SOMEONE ASKS YOU TO THINK OF A GOOD TEACHER YOU MAY think of Socrates or Annie Sullivan, but chances are you would think first of one or two teachers who have had a special influence in your own life. You would be willing to testify that these human beings did something for you or to you that has made a difference. You are fairly sure that if the path of your life had not crossed theirs, you would now be living differently. Why? What made the difference?

Why are some teachers superior? What is teaching? Is it an art? Is it true that some people are just "natural teachers"? Is it true that we can train people in methodology but we cannot do anything to insure that they will be superior teachers? Can more teachers be that "special person" to more students?

One of the most widely read and influential psychologists of our century is B. F. Skinner, of Harvard University. His article, "Why Teachers Fail," was published in the October 16, 1965 issue of *Saturday Review*. He convincingly states our need to take a closer look at what happens between student and teacher. His article is reprinted here in full.[1]

1. Reprinted with permission of *Saturday Review* and the author.

The most widely publicized efforts to improve education show an extraordinary neglect of method. Learning and teaching are not analyzed, and almost no effort is made to improve teaching as such. The aid which education is to receive usually means money, and the proposals for spending it follow a few, familiar lines. We should build more and better schools. We should recruit more and better teachers. We should search for better students and make sure that all competent students can go to school or college. We should multiply teacher-student contacts with films and television. We should design new curricula. All this can be done without looking at teaching itself. We need not ask how those better teachers are to teach those better students in those better schools, what kinds of contact are to be multiplied through mass media, or how new curricula are to be made effective.

Perhaps we should not expect questions of this sort to be asked in what is essentially a consumer's revolt. Earlier educational reforms were proposed by teachers—a Comenius, a Rousseau, a John Dewey—who were familiar with teaching methods, knew their shortcomings, and thought they saw a chance to improve them. Today the disaffected are the parents, employers, and others who are unhappy about the products of education. When teachers complain, it is as consumers of education at lower levels—graduate school authorities want better college teaching, college teachers work to improve high-school curricula, and so on. It is perhaps natural that consumers should turn to the conspicuous shortcomings of plant, personnel, and equipment rather than to method.

It is also true that educational method has not been brought to their attention in a favorable light. Pedagogy is not a prestigious word. Its low estate may be traced in part to the fact that under the blandishments of statistical methods, which promised a new kind of rigor, educational psychologists spent half a century measuring the results of teaching while neglecting teaching itself. They compared different methods of teaching in matched groups and could often say that one method was clearly better than another, but the methods they compared were usually not drawn from their own research or even their own theories, and their results seldom generated new methods. Psychological studies of learning were equally sterile—concentrating on relatively unimportant details of a few typical learning situations such as the memory drum, the maze, the discrimination box, and verbal "problems." The learning and forgetting curves that emerged from these studies were never useful in the classroom and came to occupy a less and less important place

in textbooks on educational psychology. Even today many distinguished learning theorists insist that their work has no practical
relevance.

For these and doubtless other reasons, what has been taught as
pedagogy has not been a true technology of teaching. College
teaching, indeed, has not been taught at all. The beginning teacher
receives no professional preparation. He usually begins to teach
simply as he himself has been taught, and if he improves, it is only
in the light of his own unaided experience. High-school and grade-
school teaching is taught primarily through apprenticeships, in
which students receive the advice and counsel of experienced
teachers. Certain trade skills and rules of thumb are passed along,
but the young teacher's own experience is to be the major source
of improvement. Even this modest venture in teacher training is
under attack. It is argued that a good teacher is simply one who
knows his subject matter and is interested in it. Any special knowledge of pedagogy as a basic science of teaching is felt to be unnecessary.

The attitude is regrettable. No enterprise can improve itself to
the fullest extent without examining its basic processes. A really
effective educational system cannot be set up until we understand
the processes of learning and teaching. Human behavior is far too
complex to be left to casual experience, or even to organized experience in the restricted environment of the classroom. Teachers need
help. In particular they need the kind of help offered by a scientific
analysis of behavior.

Fortunately such an analysis is now available. Principles derived
from it have already contributed to the design of schools, equipment, texts, and classroom practices. Programmed instruction is,
perhaps, its best known achievement. Some acquaintance with its
basic formulation is beginning to be regarded as important in the
training of teachers and administrators. These positive contributions, however, are no more important than the light which the
analysis throws on current practices. There is something wrong
with teaching. From the point of view of an experimental analysis
of behavior, what is it?

Corporal punishment, which has always played an important
role in education, provides one clue. As H. I. Marrou says in *A History of Education in Antiquity*: "Education and corporal punishment
appeared as inseparable to a Hellenistic Greek as they had to a
Jewish or an Egyptian scribe in the time of the Pharaohs. . . . When

the men of antiquity thought back to their schooldays they immediately remembered the beatings." The cane is still with us, and efforts to abolish it are vigorously opposed. In Great Britain a split leather strap for whipping students called a taws can be obtained from suppliers who advertise in educational journals, one of whom is said to sell 3,000 annually. (The taws has the advantage, shared by the rubber truncheon, of leaving no incriminating marks.)

The brutality of corporal punishment and the viciousness it breeds in both teacher and student have, of course, led to reform. Usually this has meant little more than shifting to noncorporal measures, of which education can boast an astonishing list. Ridicule (now largely verbalized, but once symbolized by the dunce cap or by forcing the student to sit facing a wall), scolding, sarcasm, criticism, incarceration (being "kept after school"), extra school or home work, the withdrawal of privileges, forced labor, ostracism, being put on silence, and fines—these are some of the devices that have permitted the teacher to spare the rod without spoiling the child. In some respects they are less objectionable than corporal punishment, but the pattern remains: the student spends a great part of his day doing things he does not want to do. If a teacher is in any doubt about his own methods, he should ask himself a few questions. Do my students stop work immediately when I dismiss the class? (If so, dismissal is obviously a release from a threat.) Do they welcome rather than regret vacations and unscheduled days of no school? Do I reward them for good behavior by excusing them from other assignments? Do I punish them by giving them additional assignments? Do I frequently say, "Pay attention," "Now remember," or otherwise gently "admonish" them? Do I find it necessary from time to time to "get tough" and threaten some form of punishment?

The teacher can use aversive control because he is either bigger and stronger than his students or able to invoke the authority of parents or police who are. He can coerce students into reading texts, listening to lectures, taking part in discussions, recalling as much as possible of what they have read or heard, writing papers, and so on. This is perhaps an achievement, but it is offset by an extraordinary list of unwanted by-products traceable to the basic practice.

The student who works mainly to escape aversive stimulation discovers other ways of escaping. He is tardy—"creeping like snail unwilling to school." He stays away from school altogether. Education has its own word for this—"truancy"—from an old Celt word meaning wretched. A special policeman, the truant officer, deals with offenders by threatening still more aversive consequences. The dropout is a legal truant. Children who commit suicide are often found to have had trouble in school.

There are subtler forms of escape. Though physically present and looking at teacher or text, the student does not pay attention. He is hysterically deaf. His mind wanders. He daydreams. "Mental fatigue" is usually not a state of exhaustion but an uncontrollable disposition to escape, and schools deal with it by permitting escape to other activities that, it is hoped, will also be profitable. The periods into which the school day is broken measure the limits of successful aversive control rather than the capacity for sustained attention. A child will spend hours absorbed in play or in watching movies or television who cannot sit still in school for more than a few minutes before escape becomes too strong to be denied. One of the easiest forms of escape is simply to forget all one has learned, and no one has discovered a form of control to prevent this ultimate break for freedom.

An equally serious result which an experimental analysis of behavior leads us to expect is that students counterattack. If the teacher is weak, the student may attack openly. Physical attacks on teachers are now common. Verbal attacks in the teacher's absence are legendary. When the teacher is present, attacks may take the form of annoyance, and students escape punishment by annoying surreptitiously—by groaning, shuffling the feet, or snapping the fingers. A "tormenter" was a surreptitious noise maker especially designed for classroom use.

Counterattack escalates. Slightly aversive action by the teacher evokes reactions that demand severer measures, to which in turn the student reacts still more violently. Escalation may continue until one party withdraws (the student leaves school or the teacher resigns) or dominates completely (the students establish anarchy or the teacher imposes a despotic discipline).

Vandalism is another form of counterattack that is growing steadily more serious. Many cities maintain special police forces to guard school buildings on weekends. Schools are now being designed so that windows cannot be easily broken from the street. A more sweeping counterattack comes later when, as taxpayers or alumni, former students refuse to support educational institutions. Anti-intellectualism is often a general attack on all that education represents.

A much less obvious but equally serious effect of aversive control is plain inaction. The student is sullen and unresponsive. He "blocks." Inaction is sometimes a form of escape. Rather than carry out an assignment, the student simply takes punishment as the lesser evil. It is sometimes a form of attack, the object of which is to enrage the teacher. But it is also in its own right a predictable effect of aversive control.

All these reactions have emotional accompaniments. Fear and anxiety are characteristic of escape and avoidance, anger of counterattack, and resentment of sullen inaction. These are the classical features of juvenile delinquency, of psychosomatic illness, and of other maladjustments familiar to the administrations and health services of educational institutions.

In college and graduate schools the aversive pattern survives in the now almost universal system of "assign and test." The teacher does not teach, he simply holds the student responsible for learning. The student must read books, study texts, perform experiments, and attend lectures, and he is responsible for doing so in the sense that, if he does not correctly report what he has seen, heard, or read, he will suffer aversive consequences. Questions and answers are so staple a feature of education that their connection with teaching almost never occasions surprise. As a demand for a response that will meet certain specifications, a question is almost always slightly aversive. An examination, as a collection of questions, characteristically generates the anxiety and panic appropriate to avoidance and escape. Reading a student's paper is still likely to be called "correcting" it. Examinations are designed to show principally what the student does *not* know. A test that proves to be too easy is made harder before being given again, ostensibly because an easy test does not discriminate, but more probably because the teacher is afraid of weakening the threat under which his students are working. A teacher is judged by his employers and colleagues by the severity of the threat he imposes: he is a good teacher if he makes his students work hard, regardless of how he does so or of how much he teaches them by doing so. He eventually evaluates himself in the same way; if he tries to shift to nonaversive methods, he may discover that he resists making things easy as if this necessarily meant teaching less.

Proposals to add requirements and raise standards are usually part of an aversive pattern. A well known educator has written: "We must stiffen the work of our schools . . . we have every reason to concentrate on [certain subjects] and be unflagging in our insistence that they be really learned . . . Senior year [in high school] ought to be the hardest . . . [We should give] students work that is both difficult and important, and [insist] that it be well done. . . . We should demand more of our students." These expressions were probably intended to be synonymous with "students should learn more" or possibly "teachers should teach more." There may be good reasons why students should take more mathematics or learn a modern language more thoroughly or be better prepared for college or graduate school, but they are not reasons for intensifying aversive pressures. A standard is a level of achievement; only under a particular philosophy of education is it a criterion upon which some form of punishment is contingent.

Most teachers are humane and well disposed. They do not want to threaten their students, yet they find themselves doing so. They want to help, but their offers to help are often declined. Most students are well disposed. They want an education, yet they cannot force themselves to study, and they know they are wasting time. For reasons which they have probably not correctly identified, many are in revolt. Why should education continue to use the aversive techniques to which all this is so obviously due? Evidently because effective alternatives have not been found. It is not enough simply to abandon aversive measures. A Summerhill is therapeutic, not educational. By withholding punishment teachers may help students who have been badly treated elsewhere and prepare them to be taught, but something else is needed if they are to teach. What is that something else, and why has it not yet solved the problem?

A child sees things and talks about them accurately afterward. He listens to news and gossip and passes it along. He recounts in great detail the plot of a movie he has seen or a book he has read. He seems to have a "natural curiosity," a "love of knowledge," an "inherent wish to learn." Why not take advantage of these natural endowments and simply bring the student into contact with the world he is to learn about? There are practical problems, of course. Only a small part of the real world can be brought into the classroom even with the aid of films, tape recorders, and television, and only a small part of what remains can be visited outside. Words are easily imported, but the verbal excesses of classical education have shown how easily this fact may lead to a dangerous overemphasis. Within reasonable limits, however, is it not possible to teach simply by giving the student an opportunity to learn in a natural way?

Unfortunately, a student does not learn simply when he is shown or told. Something essential to his natural curiosity or wish to learn is missing from the classroom. What is missing, technically speaking, is "positive reinforcement." In daily life the student looks, listens, and remembers because certain consequences then follow. He learns to look and listen in those special ways that encourage remembering because he is reinforced for recalling what he has seen and heard, just as a newspaper reporter notes and remembers things he sees because he is paid for reporting them. Consequences of this sort are lacking when a teacher simply shows a student something or tells him something.

Rousseau was the great advocate of natural learning. Emile was to be taught by the world of things. His teacher was to draw his attention to that world; but otherwise his education was to be negative. There were to be no arranged consequences. But Emile was an imaginary student with imaginary learning processes. When Rousseau's disciple, Pestalozzi, tried the methods on his own flesh-and-blood son, he ran into trouble. His diary is one of the most pathetic documents in the history of education. As he walked with his young son beside a stream, Pestalozzi would repeat several times, "Water flows downhill." He would show the boy that "wood swims in water and . . . stones sink." Whether the child was learning anything or not, he was not unhappy, and Pestalozzi could believe that at least he was using the right method. But when the world of things had to be left behind, failure could no longer be concealed. "I could only get him to read with difficulty; he has a thousand ways of getting out of it, and never loses an opportunity of doing something else." He could make the boy sit still at his lessons by first making him "run and play out of doors in the cold," but Pestalozzi himself was then exhausted. Inevitably, of course, he returned to aversive measures: "He was soon tired of learning to read, but as I had decided that he should work at it regularly every day, whether he liked it or not, I determined to make him feel the necessity of doing so, from the very first, by showing him there was no choice between this work and my displeasure, which I made him feel by keeping him in."

The failure of "showing and telling" is sometimes attributed to lack of attention. We are often aware that we ourselves are not listening or looking carefully. If we are not to punish the student for not looking and not listening, how can we make him concentrate? One possibility is to make sure that there is nothing else to be seen or heard. The schoolroom is isolated and freed of distractions. Silence is often the rule. Physical constraints are helpful. Earphones reassure the teacher that only what is to be heard is going into the student's ears. The TV screen is praised for its isolation and hypnotic effect. A piece of equipment has been proposed that achieves concentration in the following desperate way: the student faces a brightly lighted text, framed by walls which operate on the principle of the blinders once worn by carriage horses. His ears are between earphones. He reads part of the text aloud and then listens to his recorded voice as he reads it again. If he does not learn what he reads, it is certainly not because he has not seen it!

A less coercive practice is to make what is to be seen or heard attractive and attention-compelling. The advertiser faces the same problem as the teacher, and his techniques have been widely copied in the design of textbooks, films, and classroom practices. Bright colors, variety, sudden change, big type, animated sequences—all these have at least a temporary effect in inducing the student to look and listen. They do not, however, *teach* the student to look and listen, because they occur at the wrong time. A similar weakness is seen in making school itself pleasant. Attractive architecture, colorful interiors, comfortable furniture, congenial social arrangements, naturally interesting subjects—these are all reinforcing, but they reinforce only the behaviors they are contingent upon. An attractive school building reinforces the behavior of coming in sight of it. A colorful and comfortable classroom reinforces the behavior of entering it. Roughly speaking, these things could be said to strengthen a positive attitude toward school. But they provide merely the setting for instruction. They do not teach what students are in school to learn.

In the same way audiovisual aids usually come at the wrong time to strengthen the forms of behavior that are the principal concern of the teacher. An interesting page printed in four colors reinforces the student simply for opening the book and looking at it. It does not reinforce reading the page or even examining it closely; certainly it does not reinforce those activities that result in effective recall of what is seen. An interesting lecturer holds his listeners in the sense that they look at and listen to him, just as an interesting demonstration film reinforces the behavior of watching it, but neither the lecture nor the film necessarily reinforces listening or listening in those special ways that further recall. In good instruction interesting things should happen *after* the student has read a page or listened or looked with care. The four-color picture should *become* interesting when the text that accompanies it has been read. One stage in a lecture or film should be interesting only if earlier stages have been carefully examined and remembered. In general, naturally attractive and interesting things further the primary goals of education only when they enter into much more subtle contingencies of reinforcement than are usually represented by audiovisual aids.

It is possible that students may be induced to learn by making material not only attractive but memorable. An obvious example is making material easy. The child first learns to write in manuscript because it resembles the text he is learning to read; he may learn to read material printed in a phonetic alphabet; he may learn to spell only words he will actually use; and so on. This sort of simplification shows a lack of confidence in methods of teaching and often merely postpones the teacher's task, but it is sometimes a useful strategy. Material which is well organized is also, of course, easier to learn.

Some current psychological theories suggest that material may be made memorable in another way. Various laws of perception imply that an observer "cannot help" seeing things in certain ways. The stimulus seems to force itself upon the organism. Optical illusions are often cited as examples. These laws suggest the possibility that material may be presented in the form in which it is irresistibly learned. Material is to be so "structured" that it is readily—and almost necessarily—"grasped." Instructional examples are, however, far less persuasive than the demonstration offered in support of them. In trying to assign an important function to the material to be learned, it is particularly easy to overlook other conditions under which learning actually occurs.

No matter how attractive, interesting, and well structured material may be, the discouraging fact is that it is often not learned. Rather than continue to ask why, many educational theorists have concluded that the teacher cannot really teach at all but can only help the student learn. The dominant metaphor goes back to Plato. As Emile Bréhier states it in *The Hellenic Age*, "Socrates . . . possessed no other art but maieutics, his mother Phaenarete's art of delivering; he drew out from souls what they have in them . . ." The student already knows the truth; the teacher simply shows him that he knows. The archetype is the famous episode in the *Meno* in which Socrates takes an uneducated slave boy through Pythagoras's theorem for doubling the square. In spite of the fact that this scene is still widely regarded as an educational triumph, there is no evidence that the child learned anything. He timidly agrees with various suggestions, and he answers leading questions, but it is inconceivable that he could have reconstructed the theorem by himself when

Socrates had finished. Socrates says as much later in the dialogue: "If someone will keep asking him these same questions often and in various forms, you can be sure that in the end he will know about them as accurately as anybody." (Socrates was a frequency theorist!)

It must be admitted that the assignment was difficult. The boy was starting from scratch. In his little book, *How to Solve It*, Polya uses the same technique in presiding at the birth of the formula for the diagonal of a parallelepiped. His students make a more positive contribution because they have already had some geometry. But any success due to previous teaching weakens the claim for maieutics. And Polya's promptings and questionings give more help than he wants to admit.

It is only because mathematical proofs seem to arise from the nature of things that they can be said in some sense to be "known by everyone" and simply waiting to be drawn out. Even Socrates could not argue that the soul knows the facts of history or a second language. Impregnation must precede parturition. But is it not possible that a presentation that has not seemed to be learned is the seed from which knowledge grows to be delivered by the teacher? Perhaps the intellectual midwife is to show the student that he remembers what he has already been shown or told. In *The Idea of a University* Cardinal Newman gave an example of the maieutic method applied to acquired knowledge. It will stir painful memories in many teachers. A tutor is talking with a candidate about a bit of history—a bit of history, in fact, in which Plato's Menon lost his life.

"What is the meaning of the word *Anabasis*?" says the Tutor. The Candidate is silent. "You know very well; take your time, and don't be alarmed, *Anabasis* means . . ."

"An ascent," says the Candidate.

"*Who* ascended?"

"The Greeks, Xenophon."

"Very well: Xenophon and the Greeks ascended. To what did they ascend?"

"Against the Persian king: they ascended to fight the Persian king."

"That is right . . . an ascent; but I thought we called it a *descent* when a foreign army carried war into a country? . . . "Don't we talk of a descent of barbarians?"

"Yes."

"Why then are the Greeks said to go up?"
"They went up to fight the Persian king."
"Yes; but why *up* . . . why not *down*?"
"They came down afterwards, when they retreated back to Greece."
"Perfectly right; they did . . . but could you give no reason why they are said to go *up* to Persia, not *down*?"
"They went *up* to Persia."
"Why do you not say they went *down*?"
"They went *down* to Persia."
"You have misunderstood me. . . ."

Newman warned his reader that the Candidate is "deficient to a great extent . . . not such as it is likely that a respectable school would turn out." He recognized a poor student, but not a poor method. Thousands of teachers have wasted years of their lives in exchanges which have been no more profitable—and all to the greater glory of maieutics and out of a conviction that telling and showing are not only inadequate but wrong.

Although the soul has perhaps not always known the truth nor ever been confronted with it in a half-forgotten experience, it may still *seek* it. If the student can be taught to learn from the world of things, nothing else will ever have to be taught. This is the method of discovery. It is designed to absolve the teacher from a sense of failure by making instruction unnecessary. The teacher arranges the environment in which discovery is to take place, he suggests lines of inquiry, he keeps the student within bounds, and so on. The important thing is that he should tell him nothing.

The human organism does, of course, learn without being taught. It is a good thing that this is so, and it would no doubt be a good thing if more could be learned in that way. Students are naturally interested in what they learn by themselves because they would not learn if they were not, and for the same reason they are more likely to remember what they learn in that way. There are reinforcing elements of surprise and accomplishment in personal discovery that are welcome alternatives to traditional aversive consequences. But discovery is no solution to the problems of education. The individual cannot be expected to rediscover more than a very small part of the facts and principles that have already been discovered by others. To stop teaching in order that the student may learn for himself is to abandon education as a medium for the transmission of the accumulated knowledge and wisdom of a culture.

There are other difficulties. The position of the teacher who encourages discovery is ambiguous. Is he to pretend that he himself does not know? (Socrates said Yes. In Socratic irony those who know enjoy a laugh at the expense of those who do not.) Or, for the sake of encouraging a joint venture in discovery, is the teacher to choose to teach only those things that he himself has not yet learned? Or is he frankly to say, "I know, but you must find out" and accept the consequences for his relations with his students?

Still another difficulty arises when it is necessary to teach a whole class. How are a few good students to be prevented from making all the discoveries? When that happens, other members of the class not only miss the excitement of discovery but are left to learn material presented in a slow and particularly confusing way. Students should, of course, be encouraged to explore, to ask questions, to study by themselves, to be "creative." When properly analyzed, the kinds of behavior referred to in such expressions can be taught. It does not follow, however, that they must be taught by the method of discovery.

Effective instructional practices threaten the conception of teaching as a form of maieutics. If we suppose that the student is to "exercise his rational powers," to "develop his mind," to learn through "intuition or insight," and so on, then it may indeed be true that the teacher cannot teach but can only help the student learn. But these goals can be restated in terms of explicit changes in behavior, and effective methods of instruction can then be designed.

In his famous four idols, Francis Bacon formulated some of the reasons why men arrive at false ideas. He might have added two special Idols of the School that affect those who want to improve teaching. The Idol of the Good Teacher is the belief that what a good teacher can do, any teacher can do. Some teachers are, of course, unusually effective. They are naturally interesting people, who make things interesting to their students. They are skilful in handling students, as they are skilful in handling people in general. They can formulate facts and principles and communicate them to others in effective ways. Possibly their skills and talents will someday be better understood and successfully imparted to new teachers. At the moment, however, they are true exceptions. The fact that a method proves successful in their hands does not mean that it will solve important problems in education.

The Idol of the Good Student is the belief that what a good student can learn, any student can learn. Because they have superior ability or have been exposed to fortunate early environments, some students learn without being taught. It is quite possible that they learn more effectively when they are not taught. Possibly we shall someday produce more of them. At the moment, however, the fact that a method works with good students does not mean that it will work with all. It is possible that we shall progress more rapidly toward effective education by leaving the good teacher and the good student out of account altogether. They will not suffer, because they do not need our help. We may then devote ourselves to the discovery of practices which are appropriate to the remaining—what?—ninety-five percent of teachers and students.

The Idols of the School explain some of the breathless excitement with which educational theorists return again and again to a few standard solutions. Perhaps we should regard them as merely two special cases of a more general source of error, the belief that personal experience in the classroom is the primary source of pedagogical wisdom. It is actually very difficult for teachers to profit from experience. They almost never learn about their long-term successes or failures, and their short-term effects are not easily traced to the practices from which they presumably arose. Few teachers have time to reflect on such matters, and traditional educational research has given them little help. A much more effective kind of research is now becoming possible. Teaching may be defined as an arrangement of contingencies of reinforcement under which behavior changes. Relevant contingencies can be most successfully analyzed in studying the behavior of one student at a time under carefully controlled conditions. Few educators are aware of the extent to which human behavior is being examined in arrangements of this sort, but a true technology of teaching is imminent. It is beginning to suggest effective alternatives to the average practices that have caused so much trouble.

INVESTIGATION OF THE MYSTERIOUS INTERACTION BETWEEN TEACHER and student is difficult. However, we no longer view it as impossible. A chapter published by Edmund Amidon and Anita Simon, "Teacher-Pupil Interaction," in *Review of Educational Research* in 1965 summarizes our research status in this area.[2]

Since the early 1950's, a number of researchers have focused their attention on teacher-pupil interaction in the classroom. Bales

2. Reprinted by permission of *Review of Educational Research* and the authors.

(1950), an early observer of small-group interaction, described interaction as resulting when two or more persons behave overtly toward one another so that each receives some impression or perception of the other distinct enough to incur reaction. The studies reviewed in this chapter utilized observational data to measure the overt behavior of pupils and teachers as they interact. This chapter will present a brief description of some systems currently used to collect and categorize observational data involving teacher-pupil interaction and then will summarize research related to the following areas: teaching patterns; achievement; climate, perception, and personality; and teacher education.

SYSTEMS FOR OBSERVING TEACHER-PUPIL INTERACTION

Some of the systems that attempt to categorize teacher-pupil interaction are concerned primarily with intellectual activity in the classroom, some focus upon social-emotional behavior, and others are multidimensional. The systems described below are grouped in these three divisions: cognitive, affective, and multidimensional.

These systems—those briefly described and those listed as additional references—are the major systems currently in use to categorize teacher-pupil behavior directly or from taped classroom conversation. Some of these systems have been used only in secondary school classrooms.

Cognitive Systems. The system developed by Bellack and others (1963) contains three major categories: (a) pedagogical moves, which are classified as structuring, soliciting, responding, and reacting; (b) content analysis, which contains subcategories of substantive, substantive-logical, instructional, and instructional-logical meanings; and (c) emotional meanings, defined in terms of valence, potency, and activity. Gallagher and Aschner (1963) and Aschner (1963) used a system containing four major categories for classifying thought processes: cognitive memory, convergent thinking, divergent thinking, and evaluative thinking. An additional category is called routine. Taba and others (1964) developed a system that has two basic categories: One deals with the pedagogical function of a thought unit, which can be either psychological or strategic; the other concerns levels of thought, which include grouping and labeling, interpreting and making inferences, and predicting consequences. Each of these has subheadings.

Affective Systems. Withall (1949) developed a system which contains seven categories for teacher statements: learner-supportive, acceptant, problem-structuring, neutral, direction, reproving, and self-supporting. Flanders (Amidon and Flanders, 1963) developed a system containing seven categories for teacher talk: accepts feelings, praises, accepts ideas, questions, lectures, gives direction, and criticizes. In addition, it contains two categories for pupil talk: student talk-responding and student talk-initiation. Another category notes silence or confusion. A system developed by Hughes (1963) divided teacher behavior into these seven functions: controlling, imposition, facilitating, developing content, response, positive affectivity, and negative affectivity.

Multidimensional Systems. The Observation Schedule and Record (OScAR) developed by Medley and Mitzel (1958, 1963) is a comprehensive system for cataloguing teacher-pupil interaction, class structure, and classroom activities and materials. The three major dimensions of the system are emotional climate, verbal emphasis, and social organization.

TEACHING PATTERNS

Bellack and others (1963) presented a creative description of how teachers and students interact, characterizing the rules of the "classroom game." For example, a rule for teachers is that "the teacher will be the single most active person playing the game." A rule for pupils is "the pupil's primary task in the game is to respond to the teacher's solicitations." Bellack and his associates, using their category system, found in their study of 15 high school social studies teachers that the two most common patterns of classroom discourse, making up nearly 50 percent of the interaction, were (a) teacher solicitation—student response and (b) teacher solicitation—student response—teacher reaction. Although the study was done on the secondary level, it is relevant for elementary schools. Their system is extremely sophisticated, and the classification of verbal interaction requires that observers study and classify a typescript made from a tape recording. Classifying emotional qualities from a printed typescript is difficult because there is little opportunity to take account of the effect of intonation and other cues on the affective climate of the classroom. Therefore, in order to classify emotional tone, Bellack found it necessary to play the tape recordings collected in the study to a separate group of high school students whose reaction was then used to rate the emotional tone of the tape-recorded classes.

Giammatteo (1963), using Flanders' system, studied 150 elementary school teachers during language arts periods. He found that teachers accounted for more than 50 percent of the talk in the classroom and that most student talk was in response to teachers' questions. Although a large number of teachers were included, each teacher was observed for only 45 minutes. Using supervisory ratings as a criterion of teaching excellence, Amidon and Giammatteo (1965) compared the interaction patterns of 30 "superior" teachers with 150 randomly selected teachers in 11 elementary school districts. Using Flanders' categories, they found that superior teachers talked less, accepted more student ideas, encouraged more pupil-initiated participation, and gave fewer directions than did average teachers. The lack of reliability of supervisory ratings calls into question their criteria for superior teaching.

Using her own system of categorization, Hughes (1959) found in a study of 41 elementary school teachers that the median proportion of "controlling" acts was 46 percent. She also concluded that over 80 percent of the teachers studied were dominative in over half of the acts they performed. Control was the major function used, and simple memory-recall was the most common mental activity solicited by teachers. The teachers evaluated their students positively more often than negatively, but gave students criteria for evaluations less than half of the time. There appears to be opportunity for error in Hughes's study because the observers attempted to write down everything that happened in the classroom and to classify this later, using typescripts made from their notes. While Hughes stated that her intention was to describe teacher functions, she appeared to have built into her description "good" and "bad" values. Categories such as controlling, imposing, and negative affectivity, for instance, were discussed as if they were bad.

Much of the work on teacher-pupil interaction patterns has been done by Flanders (1960) and his associates (Amidon and Flanders, 1963; Flanders and Amidon, 1962). Although the major portion of the data was collected in the seventh and eighth grades, the results are relevant for elementary schools and are consistent with those reported by Giammatteo, Hughes, and Bellack. Perhaps these results are best summarized by Flanders' rule of two-thirds: in the average classroom someone is talking two-thirds of the time; two-thirds of this is teacher talk; and two-thirds of teacher talk consists of direct influence (lecture, direction giving, or criticism). Perhaps the greatest limitation found in research using Flanders' system was the lack of emphasis upon specific cognitive aspects of classroom interaction.

The studies reviewed in this section are significant because they describe what Bellack referred to as "the rules of the game." Apparently teachers and pupils follow common patterns in their class-rooms which can be described and classified and which seem to indicate generally that classrooms are predominantly controlled by dominative teacher behavior.

ACHIEVEMENT

Amidon and Flanders (1961), using the Flanders system, con-ducted a study in which 54 eighth grade classes were taught geom-etry in a two-hour period by a teacher using either direct influence (lecture, direction giving, or criticism) or indirect influence (accept student ideas and feelings, praise, or question). They found that dependent-prone students learned significantly more from indirect teaching. In a more extensive study, Flanders (1960) found that seventh and eighth grade students in social studies and geometry learned significantly more when their teachers were indirect rather than direct. Above-average student participation, above-average acceptance of student ideas, and below-average teacher talk were associated with higher achievement. Schantz (1963), using Flanders' categories, tested the effect of indirect and direct teaching on high and low ability children in fourth grade science lessons. She found that the high ability group exposed to indirect teacher influence scored significantly higher on a science test at the end of the experi-ment than did the high ability group exposed to direct teacher influence.

Spaulding (1963) tested a hypothesis suggested by Bush (1954) which theorized that content-oriented teachers would produce above-average achievement in reading and arithmetic. Using his own sys-tem, Spaulding observed 21 elementary school teachers, but his data did not support the Bush hypothesis. Taba (1964) trained 20 elementary teachers to raise the level of thought processes used by their pupils. Using her own category system, she found that some children of low IQ performed on the same high level of abstraction with the same frequency of participation as did some children of high IQ when their teachers used appropriate strategies. Taba also found that children whose teachers were trained to use appropriate strategies gained significantly in ability to make inferences. She reported low correlations between level of thought used by pupils and any of the variables traditionally thought to influence the ability to abstract: intelligence, reading comprehension, achieve-ment in social studies, and social status.

In a study of 12 intellectually superior classes, Gallagher and Aschner (1963) attempted to relate the type of teacher questions to the production of divergent thinking on the part of pupils. Five consecutive classroom sessions were tape recorded. Using her categories for classifying thinking, Aschner found, in general, that when the percentage of divergent questions from the teacher was high, the percentage of divergent thinking production from children was also high. Conversely, when the percentage of divergent questions was low, divergent thinking produced by the children was also low. Boys tended to do more divergent thinking than girls.

CLIMATE, PERCEPTION, AND PERSONALITY

Morse, Bloom, and Dunn (1961) attempted to determine the relationships among pupil perception, teacher perception, and the perception of trained outside observers of four dimensions of classroom activity: development, mental health, group processes, and achievement. The observers used a rating scale developed by Morse to describe interaction in 30 classrooms in grades 5, 8, and 9. In general, if pupils rated one dimension high, they tended to rate all dimensions high; if they rated one dimension low, they rated all low. This was likewise true for the trained observers, who also saw the four areas as compatible. On the other hand, teachers tended to rate the dimensions on an either-or basis. If teachers rated their classes high in achievement, they tended to rate them low in the other three dimensions. The authors also found that observers and pupils tended to agree on their ratings of the achievement dimension, while the teachers' perceptions correlated negatively with both.

Ryans (1960), in a study involving a large number of elementary and secondary schools, found that his three dimensions of teacher behavior (friendly versus aloof, businesslike versus slipshod, and stimulating versus dull) yielded high intercorrelations in elementary school teaching but low intercorrelations in secondary school teaching. Ryans' observers used rating scales that were similar to those used by Morse. His findings in the elementary school tended to support those of Morse, that an observer perceives certain teaching dimensions as interrelated; however, his secondary school findings did not support those of Morse. Flanders (1959), in a series of studies spanning 10 years, attempted to relate pupil attitudes as measured by a climate index to teacher influence patterns as identified by trained observers using the Flanders system. The studies, carried out in elementary and secondary schools in the United States and New Zealand, indicated that a positive social-emotional climate tended to be associated with indirect teacher influence.

Travers and others (1961), utilizing two large samples of elementary school teachers, attempted to relate teacher needs to teacher behavior. The four dimensions of needs (achievement, affiliation, recognition, and control), as identified by a projective instrument, appeared to be unrelated to the overt behavior of teachers as recorded by observers using the Withall categories. However, teachers' "need" to control, as measured by a paper-and-pencil test, the *Teacher Preference Schedule*, was significantly related to teacher controlling behavior in the classroom. Bowers and Soar (1961), using the *Minnesota Multiphasic Personality Inventory* (*MMPI*) as a measure of teacher personality, attempted to relate patterns of teacher personality to patterns of observed teacher behavior as indicated by the *OScAR*. They found the highest relationships between the psychopathic deviate (Pd), schizophrenic (Sc) and hysteria (Hy) scales of the *MMPI* and the *OScAR* dimensions of emotional climate, verbal emphasis, and social structure. Bowers and Soar concluded that teachers who (a) lacked maturity, depth of affect, and ability to feel personal loyalties (high Pd) and (b) were constrained, cold, remote, and inaccessible (high Sc) were less likely to have supportive emotional climates, extensive pupil-pupil interaction, or any great amount of pupil group work in their classrooms. Medley (1961), in a study in which he used the *MMPI*, found that teachers who had positive pupil-teacher rapport as indicated by high *Minnesota Teacher Attitude Inventory* (*MTAI*) scores tended to score high on the Hy and Pd scales, while low *MTAI* scorers were highest most frequently on the hypochondriasis (Hs) and depression (D) scales. There appears to be no consistent pattern of relationships in these three studies between the variables of teacher personality and teacher behavior. Lewin's (1951) theoretical analysis of the relationship between personality and behavior would lead one to expect a rather predictable relationship between these two variables. A theoretical analysis combined with an empirical investigation may be necessary to account for apparent contradictions.

TEACHER EDUCATION

Schueler, Gold, and Mitzel (1962) pointed out that the variable of emotional climate could be categorized and identified by a trained observer. Using the *OScAR*, they observed three groups of elementary school student teachers and found that the variable most clearly related to the overt teaching behavior of student teachers was that of the classroom, which apparently is made up of components of classroom culture and cooperating teacher. They found that the variable of college supervisor of student teachers had little identifiable effect on student teaching behavior. Wilk and Edson (1962, 1963), in an attempt to relate predictor variables, such as scores on the *MTAI, MMPI,* and *Miller Analogies Test,* and counselors' judgments based on interviews with 30 prospective elementary education students, found high relationships between high *MTAI* scores and integrative teaching behavior as measured by the Flanders system and the *OScAR.* They did not find a high relationship between low *MTAI* scores and dominative student teacher influence. Wilk and Edson found that counselors were not able to identify students who later exhibited integrative student teaching behavior on the basis of an interview and admissions data.

Kirk (1964) found that the teaching patterns of elementary school student teachers who had been taught the Flanders system could be changed. These student teachers encouraged more pupil-initiated talk, reduced the amount of patterning involving teacher question and pupil response, and resisted the normal trend to increase the number of directions given to a significantly greater extent than did student teachers not taught the system. Kirk concluded that this difference was accounted for by the objective feedback which the Flanders system provided. Gage (1963) studied the effect of feedback on teachers and indicated that feedback may be the crucial element in an in-service training program designed to change teachers' classroom behavior. Taba and others (1964) suggested that as teachers begin to receive feedback about their teaching strategies, they will have the opportunity to modify their teaching habits.

CONCLUSIONS AND NEEDED RESEARCH

Within school classrooms there appeared to be definite patterns of teacher-pupil interaction which could be objectively observed and categorized. These patterns were apparently related to achievement, perception, and classroom climate. While there also appeared to be a relationship between teacher personality and teacher-pupil interaction patterns, there seemed to be uncertainties about the exact nature of this relationship. Perhaps additional theoretically oriented research on teacher behavior and teacher personality would help to clarify some of the relationships between teacher characteristics and teaching outcomes.

The application of teacher-pupil interaction research in teacher education programs appears to hold great promise for the improvement of education. The feedback provided by these observational systems seems to have significant influence on the behavior and attitudes of teachers. However, much additional research is needed to determine the ultimate place of observational systems in the field of teacher education.

REFERENCES

Amidon, Edmund, and Flanders, Ned A. "The Effects of Direct and Indirect Teacher Influence on Dependent-Prone Students Learning Geometry." *Journal of Educational Psychology* 52: 286–91; December 1961.

Amidon, Edmund J., and Flanders, Ned A. *The Role of the Teacher in the Classroom: A Manual for Understanding and Improving Teachers' Classroom Behavior.* Minneapolis, Minn.: Paul S. Amidon & Associates, 1963. 68 pp.

Amidon, Edmund J., and Giammatteo, Michael M. "The Verbal Behavior of Superior Teachers." *Elementary School Journal* 65: 283–85; February 1965.

Aschner, Mary Jane McCue. "The Analysis of Verbal Interaction in the Classroom." *Theory and Research in Teaching.* (Edited by Arno A. Bellack.) New York: Bureau of Publications, Teachers College, Columbia University, 1963. pp. 53–78.

Bales, Robert F. *Interaction Process Analysis.* Cambridge, Mass.: Addison-Wesley Publishing Co., 1950. 203 pp.

Bellack, Arno A., and others. *The Language of the Classroom: Meanings Communicated in High School Teaching.* U.S. Department of Health, Education, and Welfare, Office of Education, Cooperative Research Project No. 1497. New York: Institute of Psychological Research, Columbia University, 1963. 200 pp.

Bowers, Norman D., and Soar, Robert S. *Studies of Human Relations in the Teaching-Learning Process. V. Final Report: Evaluation of Laboratory Human Relations Training for Classroom Teachers.* U.S. Department of Health, Education, and Welfare, Office of Education, Cooperative Research Project No. 469. Chapel Hill: University of North Carolina, 1961. 210 pp.

Bush, Robert N. *The Teacher-Pupil Relationship.* Englewood Cliffs, N.J.: Prentice-Hall, 1954. 252 pp.

Flanders, Ned A. "Teacher-Pupil Contacts and Mental Hygiene." *Journal of Social Issues* 15: 30–39; February 1959.

Flanders, Ned A. *Teacher Influence, Pupil Attitudes, and Achievement.* U.S. Department of Health, Education, and Welfare, Office of Education, Cooperative Research Project No. 397. Minneapolis: University of Minnesota, 1960. 121 pp.

Flanders, Ned A., and Amidon, Edmund J. "Two Approaches to the Teaching Process." *NEA Journal* 51: 43–45; May 1962.

Gage, N. L. "A Method for 'Improving' Teacher Behavior." *Journal of Teacher Education* 14: 261–66; September 1963.

Gallagher, James J., and Aschner, Mary Jane M. "A Preliminary Report: Analyses of Classroom Interaction." *Merrill-Palmer Quarterly of Behavior and Development* 9: 183–94; July 1963.

Giammatteo, Michael C. *Interaction Patterns of Elementary Teachers Using the Minnesota Categories for Interaction Analyses.* Doctor's thesis. Pittsburgh: University of Pittsburgh, 1963. 144 pp. Abstract: *Dissertation Abstracts* 25: 2365; No. 4, 1964.

Hughes, Marie M. *Helping Students Understand Teaching.* Salt Lake City: University of Utah, 1959. 157 pp.

Hughes, Marie M. "Utah Study of the Assessment of Teaching." *Theory and Research in Teaching.* (Edited by Arno A. Bellack.) New York: Bureau of Publications, Teachers College, Columbia University, 1963. pp. 25–36.

Kirk, Jeffery. *Effects of Teaching the Minnesota System of Interaction Analysis to Intermediate Grade Student Teachers.* Doctor's thesis. Philadelphia: Temple University, 1964. 268 pp. Abstract: *Dissertation Abstracts* 25: 1031; No. 2, 1964.

Lewin, Kurt. *Field Theory in Social Science.* New York: Harper & Brothers, 1951. 346 pp.

Medley, Donald M. "Teacher Personality and Teacher-Pupil Rapport." *Journal of Teacher Education* 12: 152–56; June 1961.

Medley, Donald M., and Mitzel, Harold E. "A Technique for Measuring Classroom Behavior." *Journal of Educational Psychology* 49: 86–92; April 1958.

Medley, Donald M., and Mitzel, Harold E. "Measuring Classroom Behavior by Systematic Observation." *Handbook of Research on Teaching.* (Edited by N. L. Gage.) Chicago: Rand McNally & Co., 1963. Chapter 6, pp. 247–328.

Morse, William C.; Bloom, Richard; and Dunn, James. *A Study of School Classroom Behavior from Diverse Evaluative Frameworks: Developmental, Mental Health, Substantive Learning, and Group Process.* U.S. Department of Health, Education, and Welfare, Office of Education, Cooperative Research Project No. 753. Ann Arbor: School of Education, University of Michigan, 1961. 114 pp.

Ryans, David G. *Characteristics of Teachers: Their Description, Comparison and Appraisal.* Washington, D.C.: American Council on Education, 1960. 416 pp.

Schantz, Betty Marie Baird. *An Experimental Study Comparing the Effects of Verbal Recall by Children in Direct and Indirect Teaching Methods as a Tool of Measurement.* Doctor's thesis. University Park: Pennsylvania State University, 1963. 96 pp. Abstract: *Dissertation Abstracts* 25: 1054; No. 2, 1964.

Schueler, Herbert; Gold, Milton J.; and Mitzel, Harold E. *The Use of Television for Improving Teacher Training and for Improving Measures of Student-Teaching Performance. Phase I: Improvement of Student Teaching.* U.S. Department of Health, Education, and Welfare, Office of Education, Grant No. 730035. New York: Hunter College, City University of New York, 1962. 127 pp.

Spaulding, Robert L. *Achievement, Creativity, and Self-Concept Correlates of Teacher-Pupil Transactions in Elementary Schools.* U.S. Department of Health, Education, and Welfare, Office of Education, Cooperative Research Project No. 1352. Urbana: College of Education, University of Illinois, 1963. 126 pp.

Taba, Hilda, and others. *Thinking in Elementary School Children*. U.S. Department of Health, Education, and Welfare, Office of Education, Cooperative Research Project No. 1574. San Francisco: San Francisco State College, 1964. 207 pp.

Travers, Robert M., and others. *Measured Needs of Teachers and Their Behavior in the Classroom*. U.S. Department of Health, Education, and Welfare, Office of Education, Cooperative Research Project No. 444. Salt Lake City: University of Utah, 1961. 190 pp.

Wilk, Roger E., and Edson, William H. *A Study of the Relationship Between Observed Classroom Behaviors of Elementary Student Teachers, Predictors of Those Behaviors, and Ratings by Supervisors*. U.S. Department of Health, Education, and Welfare, Office of Education, Cooperative Research Project No. 473. Minneapolis: College of Education, University of Minnesota, 1962. 78 pp.

Wilk, Roger E., and Edson, William H. "Predictions and Performance: An Experimental Study of Student Teachers." *Journal of Teacher Education* 14: 308–17; September 1963.

Withall, John. "The Development of a Technique for the Measurement of Social-Emotional Climate in Classrooms." *Journal of Experimental Education* 17: 347–61; March 1949.

WE SEE THAT THE TEACHER'S PERSONALITY AND BEHAVIOR INFLUence the classroom experience in a variety of ways. No one is surprised at this. But evidence to substantiate our casual observation now permits us to dig in to an understanding of *how* the influence actually works.

A study of classroom climate was reported by Richard Schmuck in *Psychology in the Schools* in 1966. In his article, entitled "Some Aspects of Classroom Social Climate," he describes the study of peer-group friendship and influence choices in twenty-seven classrooms that covered a broad socioeconomic range. Positive classroom climate ("diffuse liking structure" rather than clumps of good guys and bad guys) was found related to positive attitude toward peers, teachers, and academic work. Some special attention was paid to the teachers. A part of the report is reprinted here.[3]

The 27 teachers studied were similar in many ways. Their social backgrounds were much less diverse than those of their pupils. For the most part, they grew up in lower-middle class homes, in small

3. Reprinted with the permission of *Psychology in the Schools*.

towns or suburbs, and in small families. All except three were married. Each had had more than three years of teaching experience and was regarded by his principal as doing a sound teaching job. All of them had sought more professional education by volunteering for an in-service training program in interpersonal relations in the classroom.

Although these teachers were quite similar they did differ significantly in ways basic to their teaching. Interviews indicated that clear differences existed among the teachers in their conceptions of classroom roles. The teachers with more positive social climates compared with others, spoke about mental health concepts and psychological principles more. They had more detailed ideas about personality dynamics and were more vigilant of new ideas in teaching which would help them build more constructive classroom relationships. For instance, they saw their pupils in terms of anxieties, motives, self-esteem, attitudes toward school, and peer group relations. They saw the teaching mission, moreover, as including both academic learning and personality growth and development.

Another questionnaire measured the teachers' cognitive structures concerning mental health and academic learning. Each teacher was asked to write about his ideas of good mental health practices and conditions in the classroom as well as his notions of classroom practices and conditions conducive to effective learning. Each was given 25 small index cards and these directions:

> Let us suppose that the following situation occurs. A visiting teacher from Russia engages you in conversation about school practices in this country. Assume that your visitor knows very little about American teaching practice. He wants to know what you consider to be good mental health practices and conditions in the classroom. What sorts of things would you include in a list which he could refer to as he tries to learn about classroom mental health?
>
> Using the cards which have been provided, write one item on each card (word, phrase, or sentence) which describes good classroom mental health practices or conditions. Use as many of the cards as you need. A total of 25 cards is supplied.
>
> In order to ensure that the Russian visitor has understood you, try to organize the items you listed on the cards. Do this in the following way: Lay out in front of you all the cards you used in listing mental health practices and conditions. Look them over carefully and see if they fall into some broad, natu-

ral groupings. If they do, arrange them into such groups. Now look at your groups and see if these can be broken into sub-groups. If they can, separate the cards accordingly. It is also possible that these sub-groups can be broken down still further.

The teachers were asked next to rank order the mental health concepts according to their importance and to give their groups and sub-groups names or titles. Then, these same procedures were repeated with 25 other index cards; this time each teacher wrote on classroom practices and conditions conducive to academic learning. Finally, the teachers were presented with their two sets of cards on mental health and learning and asked to indicate any linkage between the two.

The results showed that the teachers did not differ significantly on the kind and number of academic learning concepts which they listed; however, the teachers with more positive social climates did tend to mention cooperative classroom work more and grading less than other teachers. The teachers did differ significantly on the number and kind of mental health concepts written out. Teachers with more positive social climates mentioned almost twice as many mental health conditions important to their teaching as the other teachers. They also showed more sophistication in the detail with which they sub-grouped these. Teachers with less positive climates, for instance, emphasized physical conditions of the classroom much more than other teachers. One such teacher gave four physical conditions top priority for mental health, "bright colors in the room," "good lighting," "fresh air," and "cleanliness of the room." Teachers with more positive climates, on the other hand, mentioned the quality of interpersonal relations more often than the others. One teacher with a very cohesive peer group with supportive norms first mentioned "relaxed relations," "mutual respect for ideas of others," "kindly attitudes toward each other," and "ability to plan and work in groups and not always with the same people." Another teacher with a positive social climate wrote, "tolerance for individual differences is perhaps the most important condition for positive mental health in the classroom." She went on to elaborate the general concept of individual differences listing over ten related items. Another teacher with positive climate emphasized "warm and stimulating peer relations," and "mutual respect between teachers and pupils." Finally, the teachers with more positive classroom climates enumerated a higher number of linkages between the mental health and academic learning concepts than the other teachers.

Each of the teachers was also asked to categorize his pupils in as many ways as he considered relevant to classroom life. The teachers were given a set of cards with the names of each of the pupils in the class and the following instructions:

In your mind, there are probably many ways in which the children can be seen as similar to and different from one another. Place these cards in piles in as many different ways as might occur in your thinking. Each time you place the cards into piles, you should have some main idea in mind and a descriptive title for each pile.

For instance, in your mind you might divide the class into boys and girls. Then you would sort the cards into two piles, the main idea is "sex differences," and the descriptive titles of the piles are "boys" and "girls." Another division which might occur could be color of hair. Then "color of hair" would be the main idea, and "blondes," "brunettes," and "red-heads," the descriptive titles.

The results showed that the teachers did not differ very much on their numbers of main ideas. They did, however, differ on the extent of their differentiation of these main categories. On the average, teachers with more positive climates used somewhat more than four sub-groupings for each of their main ideas, while other teachers used just less than three. Teachers with less positive social climates tended to dichotomize pupil characteristics such as aggression, self-esteem, and competence; while the teachers with more positive climates saw these as dimensions. Furthermore, teachers with less positive climates emphasized physical attributes of the child more than the other teachers.

Because the teachers differed in their cognitions of pupils and the concept of mental health does not mean that they necessarily behaved differently as classroom teachers. The peer relations reported above might have emerged independently of teacher influences but this is unlikely. One indication that the classroom behaviors of teachers with more positive climates differed from those of the other teachers was in the finding that their pupils perceived them as understanding them more. Other indications were present in impressions gathered from occasional observations of these teachers. The teachers with more positive climates attended to and chatted with a larger variety of students compared with the other teachers. Many of the teachers with less positive climates tended to call on fewer youngsters for classroom participation and seemed to neglect the slower, less involved students. Moreover, the teachers with positive climates tended to reward individuals for helpful behaviors with specific statements such as, "John, you have done a very nice job." They also tended to control behavioral disturbances by making general statements, "Class, it is really very difficult for us to concentrate and to work with all of this noise." The teachers with less positive social climates, on the other hand, tended more often to reward less and to punish individuals publicly for breaking classroom protocol.

In summary, classroom peer groups with nearly an equal distribution of friendship and influence in contrast to those which were distinctly hierarchical had both more cohesiveness and more positive norms concerning the goals of the school. Although the teachers in these two types of classrooms were very similar, they did differ in very significant ways. The teachers with more positive social climates, in contrast to the others, emphasized and were more sophisticated about classroom mental health conditions. They also perceived more linkages between mental health and academic learning concepts than the other teachers. Teachers with more positive climates perceived their pupils' characteristics in a more diffentiated manner and emphasized psychological attributes in contrast to physical characteristics more than the other teachers. Teachers with positive climates appeared to converse often with a wide variety of students and to reward individual students while punishing the whole class. In contrast, teachers with more negative climates conversed often with only a few students, seldom issued reward statements, and often punished individual students publicly.

"TEACHER PERSONALITY" COVERS A LOT OF FACTORS THAT THE teacher carries into the classroom. One prominent factor is whether the teacher is a man or woman. Early childhood teaching has been a sacred area reserved for female teachers. Probably the assumption is that small children need a mother or mother surrogate. Perhaps small children could make good use of more contact with a father or a father surrogate. Certainly it would help little boys through the early perils of establishing identity as a male in a world where the powerful adults who fill their weekday waking hours are women.

Boys who have become more than disenchanted with the world of school learning might drop back in before they drop out if they were asked to "teach" in nursery or kindergarten where help is usually welcome. The tiny boys could have older male contact while the older boys would undoubtedly get more interested in how one learns and see more clearly the value of learning, when they sit in the teacher's chair or even stand in the teacher's spot by the sandbox. This scheme poses an interesting question that could be investigated with some interesting research.

Even if potential dropouts and adult male teachers aren't yet finding their way to nursery school, other males are. The March–April, 1966 issue of CHILDREN reports on one pre-school experiment.[4]

In an effort to find out whether the presence of an adult male in a nursery school could help break the "female-dominated environment" of many classrooms, the University Laboratory School, University of Hawaii, placed four boys, seniors at the university's high school, in each of four nursery schools for 45 minutes a day in the first semester of this school year (1965–66). According to a report on the project in the January 1966 issue of Childhood Education, the nursery school was selected on the assumption that in it "the preschool child is probably at the best age to benefit from benign male influence. . . ." ("Young Men in a Nursery School," by Will Kyselka.)

At the time the article was written, the author points out, the project was still too new (15 weeks) and too limited for positive results. He reports, however, that the boys were enthusiastic and there seemed to be evidence that the children had benefited.

The article is mainly a report on the experience of the boys who, in addition to keeping daily logs, met with a supervisor from time to time in groups and individually. At first, the boys reported, they felt "awkward and unnatural" though the children paid little attention to them. In a few days, though, they were accepted by the children with whom they romped or read stories to, all within the class routine.

The author says the boys took the assignment very seriously. Said one, "Right now it is a very satisfying experience for me because I'm having fun, but I'd like to know if it is really helping them."

TEACHER TRAINING INSTITUTIONS ARE SEARCHING FOR NEW AND better ways to start tomorrow's teacher on the long road of

---

4. Reprinted by permission from CHILDREN.

thinking about what happens between him and his students. Two articles published in the Spring–1966 issue of *The Campus School Exchange* described one such attempt.[5] The first article, by Donald H. Clark, Victor Balaban, Arlene Goldsmith, Leonard Grossman, and Lilyan Ruderman, the staff of the Educational Clinic of Hunter College in the Bronx, a part of the City University of New York, is entitled "An Educational Clinic Goes to School." Part of the article, describing the project, is reprinted here.

When students register for the first educational psychology course, they may register for a traditional section or for an "experimental" section sponsored by the clinic. If a student enrolls in an experimental section he meets two class hours each week with an instructor who is also a member of the clinic staff. During the third class hour he meets in a small group of approximately a dozen students. The small group meeting is led by a mental health consultant on the clinic staff who is not the student's instructor. He is told that his participation in this small group will not directly affect his grade in the course.

Each college student is matched with a child in one of the three campus schools. The matching is done by the clinic and the school and takes into consideration the needs of both college student and child. The Hunter student spends at least one hour each week with the child and discusses the contact in his small group meeting at the clinic.

The college student is not expected to accomplish more than getting to know the child. He is urged to be frank in answering the child's questions about the reasons for his visits. The college student begins by first observing the child in the class. His second step is to move into individual contacts with the child in some activity the teacher or guidance counselor thinks appropriate.

If the child and the college student get on especially well together the question of seeing the child outside of school is raised in small group discussion. The group leader then meets individually with the Hunter student and they plan where, when, and how the contact out of school will take place. School and parental permission is secured and the small group waits anxiously to hear how it went. It may have been a trip to Macy's at Christmas or, more typically, a visit to the Hunter Campus and lunch in the student cafteria. Some junior high school students have been taken to vocational and trade schools.

One of the most difficult aspects of this program is saying "goodbye." For that reason, the small groups begin to consider how to say "goodbye" just after everyone has met "his" child for the first time. Other frequent topics are mutual respect, classroom discipline, and the complexly related roles of teacher, guide, and friend.

LATER IN THE SAME ARTICLE, THE AUTHORS STATE THAT "WHEN college students were asked for an anonymous evaluation of the Hunter Friend Program" a typical response was, "I feel that I have really gained a much better understanding of a child in a classroom situation. I'm sorry I can't be more critical but I have no bones to pick with this experiment. In fact, I found it to be a very rewarding experience and I would like to thank you for making it possible!"

Another typical Hunter Friend said, "I think I got more out of my one day in the clinic and working with a child than I could out of any number of education courses, where you can learn the concepts of psychology and education backwards and forward, but nothing can take the place of first hand experience. . . . What I most received from this clinical experience was the insight into a little of what education entails." This student goes on to explain that before this experience, "I wouldn't have dreamed of working in any neighborhood unless it was middle or upper class—snobbish, I'll admit." Our student has now altered his goals and hopes to teach less privileged children.

The companion article was written by Mr. Joseph Rosen who is principal of P.S. 67 in the Bronx, one of the schools in which the project was being tried. The article was entitled, "When A Fella Needs A Friend." In it he says:

For one session each week, a child has the good fortune of getting this genuine interest, love, concern, and above all, the undivided attention that is his alone for that day. When one thinks about the competition for parental recognition in crowded homes, where parental care and interest is lacking or inadequate at best, one can then realize how strong is the anticipation of this "Friend In Need."

Our children wait impatiently for "their day." They prepare for it. They even dress for it. It is heartwarming and satisfying to see the child after his "pick up" by his personal benefactor. He talks; he communicates; he bubbles over; he radiates enthusiasm, satisfaction, and serenity as he confides the affairs of the week to the interested sympathetic ear. For many children this is their first opportunity to give vent to real feelings, to express their inner fears, to unload problems, to talk out, to emote, to smile. It has been said that he who can relate to even one person is not lost.

In this program, the child has a personal one-to-one relationship that provides him with the adult image. He has a person whom he can emulate, one whom he can trust, one who will understand "his side," "take his part," and "see it his way." Many children are relating now for the first time; this is the essence of personal satisfaction, the first step in social adjustment.

Questions about the home, siblings, teacher, classmates, school work, all generate a better understanding of "What Makes Sammy Run"! "Sammy" now begins to understand himself and can now make himself understood as well. In an overcrowded school, as is P.S. 67 Bronx (triple session, every classroom over-utilized), the major problem faced by school administrators and college supervisors is that of space. Yet, here is an exciting and incredible aspect of this enterprise. There are sixty college students involved in the program. This is in addition to the regular school pupils, student teachers, work experience program students, and a host of construction workers involved in a building alteration. Overcrowded facilities at P.S. 67 would baffle the capabilities of a space engineer. Yet, amazingly enough, the resourcefulness of the college student in this program is undaunted and unlimited. A corner, a staircase, a landing, the schoolyard, a lobby table, a corridor, a lunchroom table, a hallway radiator, a window alcove, anything becomes the improvised "park bench" where mutual trust and long lasting friendships are developed and cultivated.

INNOVATION AND SEARCH ARE HELPFUL BUT NOT SUFFICIENT. THEY too are subject to the tough demands of this decade. They must answer the questions, "So what?" and "Are you sure?" More and more of the search is becoming research. This does not necessarily mean that the search is taking place again but it does mean that the search is being conducted in ways that make it less likely for the investigators to kid themselves about the results. The apparent trend is to admit that while good teaching is a thing of beauty and qualifies as art, investigation must proceed. We are no longer content with the kind of investigation that simply says, "These children turned out well so this is a good teacher." We want to know what "turning out well" means. We also want to know what being a "good teacher" means. And more than anything, we want to know what went on between the teacher and the student. How did it work and how can other teachers learn to do the same thing or something similar?

The creation of oil paintings is an art but the number of art training courses in the world testifies that it involves skills that can be learned. It is probably true that the great artists, whether Renoir, Socrates, Picasso, Annie Sullivan, or Rembrandt would find their way with little or no help. Teaching is, however, a gigantic profession. It cannot rely on the few star artists to do the job. We must have good teachers in large numbers and we must have them now. For that reason, some of our best detectives are now running faster and faster in the investigation of the mystery of teaching.

CHAPTER 9

How Are We Doing?

EDUCATORS ARE ALWAYS IN TROUBLE WITH SOMEONE BUT ONE VIR-tue has never been denied them. They have clung to the virtue of wanting to know how good a job they are doing.

A current issue in the psychology of education is testing. A sample of the furor about testing was seen in the chapter on intelligence. We are now on the verge of getting improved answers to our questions about how we are doing. At least a toe is being put in the door, but the current war about testing may obscure calm evaluation of the proposed method for ob-taining answers. A proposed project is being sponsored by the Carnegie Corporation of New York, and we reprint here their description of it, which was published in the Spring–1966 issue of *The Carnegie Quarterly*. It was entitled, "The Gross Educational Product: How much are students learning?"[1]

The years since Sputnik have witnessed the development of a pastime that threatens to supplant baseball as the national sport. This new game is even more fun than baseball because anybody can play.

The game's simplified name is "How Good Are Our Schools?" (Some players prefer to phrase it "How Bad Are Our Schools?") Ground rules are few, with each player free to propound his favor-

1. Reprinted with permission of The Carnegie Corporation of New York.

ite opinions. He may say: "Kids learned to read better fifty years ago than they do today." Or he may make a generalization of this sort: "Northern schools are pretty good and Southern schools are pretty bad." Or he may differentiate between subjects: "The schools are doing better at teaching math now, but they're still terrible at teaching English."

The beauty of the sport is that anybody can not only play but *win*, since there is no way of proving the truth or untruth of the above and many similar assertions. As a nation—and a very education-conscious and statistic-happy one—we do know a lot about some parts of our educational system. We know how many teachers there are and how old and how tall they are; we have reliable statistics on school buildings and how old and how tall *they* are; we know how many language laboratories are in operation; we can calculate to the penny how much we are spending for education.

The only thing we don't know is what is produced by all these teachers, buildings, laboratories, and dollars. We don't know what the students are learning. We don't know how much most eleventh-graders know about English literature, whether most ninth-graders can read and comprehend a typical newspaper paragraph, whether most high school graduates know more or less about more or fewer things than high school graduates did twenty years ago.

We cannot describe how close our schools come to accomplishing what they aim to accomplish, identify in any precise way the strengths and weaknesses of the system, or measure progress or the lack of it over time. This means that, at a time when the national stake in education is very clearly perceived, our educational achievements are not clearly perceived at all. The schools are attacked and defended without solid evidence to support the claims of either attackers or defenders, and public policy is perforce made largely on the basis of assumption and impressionistic and incomplete evidence.

· It is easy to say that a nation that has hitched its destiny to the star of education and pours billions of dollars into the enterprise is collectively crazy if it does not try to find out what is the result of all this effort. But there are many reasons—some of them good ones—why we have not tried to measure our educational achievements on a national scale. It is a very difficult thing to do from a technical point of view, and there is the danger that the information produced could be misinterpreted and misused. (The same can be said, of course, of information of any kind.)

The question is whether the risks of knowing little do not now outweigh the risks of knowing more, and it was this question that Carnegie Corporation asked a group of national leaders in education to consider more than two years ago. This committee, headed by Ralph W. Tyler, director of the Center for Advanced Study in the Behavioral Sciences, widened its discussions to include school men, university people, experts in testing and measurement, and school board members and other laymen. At great length, they debated whether it would be feasible, and if feasible, desirable, to attempt to make a national assessment of education.

It was agreed that both the theories and techniques of educational measurement have now progressed to the point where such an undertaking would be feasible, although new kinds of measures would have to be carefully constructed. Much discussion centered on how the information to be gathered could be made public in such a way as to be helpful rather than harmful to everyone concerned, in particular the schools. No good purpose would be served by making possible invidious, and probably meaningless, comparisons of individual schools or school systems, but information could be gathered on a regional basis and correlated with relevant socioeconomic data.

There was general agreement that a national assessment would be valuable. For one thing, it is presumably better to know more rather than less about anything, particularly the way we are educating our children. Knowing more would put us in a much better position to make intelligent decisions about the allocation of resources and efforts. From a practical point of view, it is not realistic to expect the national and state legislatures to appropriate increasing amounts of money for a variety of educational programs if they can never find out what the pay-off is. Already, Congress has stipulated that the executive branch must report on the results produced by federal money concentrated in the slum schools, and several state legislatures, including those of California and Pennsylvania, have shown marked interest in doing statewide testing of their school children.

Beyond the immediate implications for public policy, however, there is the possibility of a by-product that could be even more important in the long run. The information compiled in an assessment would make it possible to do research on educational problems and processes that cannot be undertaken without it. It should be possible, for example, to analyze much more closely than we now can the relationship between socioeconomic level and educational attainment. It should be possible to say with greater certainty that investing so much—in terms of money or materials or teachers or time—to attack a particular problem will produce a given result. And new opportunities will develop as time goes on. The construction some years ago of our national economic index, the Gross National Product, made possible a whole series of refinements in our analysis and understanding of the economy. As *The New York Times* said in that connection:

> Thirty years ago our predecessors groped in the dark because national income and product statistics did not exist. Now, with the statistics, we still have no absolute assurance of what to do or where the economy will go. There is still no exact science.
>
> But they do not bleed patients with leeches as doctors used to do. They know better.

WHAT IS A NATIONAL ASSESSMENT?

The idea is to find out what certain groups know about certain things. The groups represent different parts of the country (Northeast, South, Midwest, and Far West), age levels (nine, thirteen, seventeen, and thirty), social environments (rural, suburban, and urban), and economic levels. They include students in public, private, and parochial schools, and youngsters no longer in school. The subjects include reading and writing, science, mathematics, social studies, citizenship, fine arts, and vocational education.

To give the simplest kind of example, it would be possible to say, when an assessment had been made, something like the following: 90 per cent of all American nine-year-olds can distinguish verse from prose, 50 per cent recognize some children's classics such as Mother Goose and Winnie the Pooh, and 10 per cent can distinguish between fiction and nonfiction writing.

Or we could compare groups, and say, for example, that 90 per cent of the seventeen-year-olds who go to school in rural areas know about the land-grant colleges, but only 10 percent of their age group in urban schools know anything about them.

If an assessment were made once every few years, we could trace the growth in knowledge over time. Thus, four years from now we could perhaps say that 90 per cent of the thirteen-year-olds can now recognize free verse, various dramatic forms, and myths and legends, and are familiar with American literary characters such as Tom Sawyer and Ichabod Crane. Furthermore, by comparing what nine-year-olds know four years from now with what nine-year-olds know today, we could measure growth in the quality of the educational system.

This and more sophisticated types of information should be valuable when we consider education in the country as a whole or by region or other classifications. Local school boards and educators would then be in a position to decide to do something about a given situation—or not to do something. Take the example about the land-grant colleges. It would be quite likely that most rural boards would say, "Good—most of our youngsters need to know about those institutions." And it would be perfectly reasonable for an urban board to say, "It really isn't too important that most of our students don't know about the land-grant colleges."

Consider another hypothetical case. Say that we find out that 90 per cent of the seventeen-year-olds have some understanding of the relationships among the legislative, judicial, and executive branches of government. And say that only 10 per cent know how much of Congress and how many of the state legislatures are required to vote to amend the Constitution. Perhaps this kind of outcome wouldn't worry us too much. It's hard to keep straight whether it's two-thirds of Congress and three-quarters of the states or vice versa, and it really isn't very important unless one has it in mind to amend the Constitution, in which case he can turn to the document itself.

But suppose it turned out to be the reverse—that 90 per cent have memorized a series of relatively trivial "facts" about the Constitution but only 10 per cent grasp the fundamental concept on which it is based: the separation of powers and the checks on them. Many of us would be very much disturbed by such a finding. That still wouldn't mean that any school boards or systems would have to take any action, but a lot would probably want to.

TESTING AND A NATIONAL ASSESSMENT

In order to make a national assessment of this sort, it would be necessary to test *some* individuals in each group—probably about one in a hundred—on *some* of the things we want to find out about. No individual would ever take an entire examination. Furthermore, in making the assessments over time it would not be necessary to test at seventeen the same youngsters who were tested at thirteen. They need not even be in the same school or school system. All this is possible because of the sampling techniques so widely used in opinion polling.

The kind of testing that would be done under a national assessment is different in other important ways from much of the testing that goes on at such a rapid clip in our schools today. Dogged readers who last as far as the next article will find that each of our forty million school children takes, on the average, five standardized tests a year. And many adults are given such tests.

In these cases, each individual takes each test in full, and he is then ranked on a norm—his ability or performance is minutely compared with that of thousands or millions of others. The general purpose of these tests is to help decide whether to "do something" to or for or about that individual: have him skip second grade, or take autoshop in high school, or be promoted to corporal in the army. A lot of what happens to a person in his life depends on how he performs on these kinds of tests.

The aim of the assessment is totally different. It seeks to learn only about groups, not individuals, and the point is not to do anything about the groups but to learn something about the educational system. All that could happen to individuals or groups is that their children might get a better education than they did—or better yet, that the schools might improve even during their own school careers.

Another way in which the assessment examinations differ is that they are being constructed to make gross rather than fine discriminations. A college admissions officer, faced with a batch of applicants who are fairly close in aptitude and achievement, wants to know if John Smith is a little smarter, or knows a little bit more math, than Jim Doe. But we are interested in getting a broad picture of the entire country and its regions, so it is more valuable for our purposes to be able to say, "Almost everybody knows this, about 50 per cent know that, only about 10 per cent know the other."

It is necessary to point up these differences because there is legitimate concern about the possible effects of the testing entailed by a national assessment on the students and the curriculum, and thus indirectly upon the ability of local school boards to maintain control of local education.

Our most important concern is of course the welfare of the children. Since only about one in a hundred would be asked to give a half hour to taking part of an examination, probably only once in his life, it is impossible to argue that the practical demands are too harsh. Much more important, no decisions affecting the individual child would be made on the basis of the examination. (In this connection, it is of interest that some school administrators who yearly subject their pupils to a large number of tests that *do* affect their lives are extremely resistant to having their own accomplishments or those of their schools assessed in even the most general terms. And that is all that could result from the assessment—an outline of the level and quality of American education drawn with a very broad brush.)

The standardized tests already in use have been criticized by some on the grounds that the nature of the questions asked determines the curriculum offered by the schools, that teachers try to "teach to the tests" rather than to what they personally or their local districts consider valid educational goals, and that educational innovation is stifled by the entire process. These claims have not been definitely proved in the case of the tests now in use, and there is no reason why the assessment should have such results.

THE CURRICULUM

First, the curriculum. The assessment is not asking any national or "outside" body to say, "This is what kids should know when they are seventeen." The several testing organizations that have been asked to draw up prototype questions (which will later be tried out in a few schools) are being advised by academic subject matter specialists, school administrators and teachers, and lay citizens in all regions of the country. These panels formulate the objectives to be assessed from their respective points of view.

Let us assume that lay citizens believe it is important for most people today to know a little biology, including something of genetics. Biologists might then say that a grasp of the Mendelian law is useful for understanding the transmittal of certain characteristics from generation to generation. The school people would say whether they *do* or *do not* try to teach Mendel's law. The aim is not to find out that the schools are not accomplishing things they don't intend to accomplish in the first place, but simply whether they succeed in teaching what they say they want to teach—things that are deemed important by scholars and laymen also.

Teaching to the tests in the usual meaning of that phrase would seem to be impossible, and to attempt to do so would be a great waste of time to boot. No teacher could know if any of his students were ever going to be part of a sample or what they would be tested on if so, and in addition there would be no feedback on how the particular students did so no one would be in a position to say that a particular teacher had taught well or badly.

As far as innovation goes, at the moment we don't know how

much there has been or what the results have been. An assessment might help find out. There is no reason why it should inhibit further experimentation because it seeks to find out only what people have learned, not how they learned it. It is going to ask how well nine-year-old children can read, not how they learned to read.

NATIONAL ASSESSMENT AND LOCAL CONTROL

Would the kind of information produced by a national assessment have the effect of weakening or strengthening local and state control of the schools? On the premise that you have more meaningful control when you know more rather than less about what you are doing, it should strengthen it. Furthermore, no matter what the information produced by an assessment—if it were revealed, to give a wild for instance, that no school child in the Far West could count to ten—there is no national or federal body that could force the various school boards and systems of the Far West to do anything about it. They would, however, doubtless receive considerable pressure from their constituencies to do something.

This raises another issue. Some superintendents and administrators, who already feel the schools to be the victims of unwelcome attention from local groups, probably fear that an assessment would only increase such pressures. And their fears are understandable. It is likely that an assessment would raise the already considerable public interest in how and what the schools are doing. But as it is now, many school systems are under daily harassment from individuals and groups, some well-meaning and some not so well-meaning, who are not in command of the facts. Surely if the schools are to be the recipients of unsolicited advice it would be better if the advice were directed to real problems and if it were grounded on more solid information than is now available. At any rate, this whole issue is not one of federal control but of increased *local* control.

As for federal control, while it does not exist, no sensible person would hold that there is not considerable national and state *influence* over education. This influence makes itself felt via the purse. Thus, when large sums became available for improving the teaching of science and mathematics under the first National Defense Education Act, there was a definite burst of activity in those fields.

The point here is that both Congress and the state legislatures are already exerting this kind of influence through voting money for specific purposes. The information made available through an assessment should help them make more intelligent decisions, as it should help everybody concerned with education, which means most of us.

For one of the glories of education in the United States is that it never was and never will be fully "controlled" from any single spot. Decisions affecting American education are made every day in a great variety of places—in distant universities and teachers colleges as well as in local school rooms, in foundation board rooms and government agencies, in homes and offices too. If we can construct a kind of Gross *Educational* Product, we will know a lot more than we do now about how we are conducting the nation's most important business. As the *Times* said of the economy so we will be able to say of education: we still have no absolute assurance of what to do or where education will go. But we know more than we used to.

EVEN BEFORE THIS CARNEGIE REPORT APPEARED IN PRINT, CONTROversy appeared in the February, 1966 issue of the *NEA Journal* under the heading, "Opinions Differ on National Educational Assessment." Francis Keppel, who was Assistant Secretary for Education, U.S. Department of Health, Education and Welfare, argued in favor of national assessment. Banesh Hoffman, of Queens College of the City University of New York, author of *The Tyranny of Testing*, described his misgivings. Though there is some repetition of the material reprinted above from *The Carnegie Quarterly*, both men's opinions are printed here in full lest editing in some way unintentionally distort what they have to say.[2]

"WE BADLY NEED IT," SAYS FRANCIS KEPPEL

American education today is woefully short of the basic information needed to carry forward our many educational purposes, to set sound goals, and to work together to reach them.

The U.S. Office of Education, for example, can report on all sorts of things about education: how many teachers we have, how many school children, how many school buildings, and possibly whether the buildings are painted or not. But as yet we do not know how much our children really know, the subjects in which they are strong or weak, the relation between income levels and learning, or a host of other matters.

2. Reprinted by permission of the National Education Association.

One of the topics for discussion last summer at the White House Conference on Education was a proposal to assess our nationwide educational performance in order to acquire the information we need. One might have predicted a calm discourse by educators on how, where, and by what means to proceed with this assessment. Instead, the discussion turned into controversy, and it is not over yet.

Thus far, educators have become embroiled not in the need for *assessment* but in the evils of *testing*. Some have said, and still say, that we have more tests right now than we know what to do with. Others have declared that national testing would ultimately force conformity, or worse, upon all our schools.

The mischievous word here is "testing," and it is this that has generated so much heat. A few comments may help lower the temperature a bit.

Personally I am vigorously opposed to any mammoth national testing of all children. I do not think it is either justified or necessary. At the same time, we do need a far better reporting system than we have ever had on the quality and the progress of American schools.

"Assessment" does not necessarily imply national testing. Today, the science of statistical sampling is well advanced. It can produce answers accurate within 5 percent, even from very small samples. Although we are accustomed to statistical sampling in public-opinion polls, we have hardly begun to employ it in education.

Because I believe that the theory and technology of statistical sampling have developed to a point where they can facilitate educational assessment, as U.S. Commissioner of Education I encouraged the Carnegie Corporation of New York, with private funds, to explore the matter. The Corporation has set out to determine whether a good educational reporting system can be developed by taking samplings of the knowledge of school children—perhaps only 1 percent of the children, but certainly much less than 10 percent.

The Carnegie Corporation has already organized a committee headed by Ralph W. Tyler of the Center for Advanced Study in the Behavioral Sciences. One of its first tasks has been to set forth the purpose of a national assessment program. The committee has said:

A well-conceived and well-executed assessment would, it is hoped, serve several important purposes.
First, it would give the nation as a whole a better under-

standing of the strengths and weaknesses of the American educational system. Thus, it might contribute a more accurate guide than we currently possess for allocation of public and private funds, where they are needed, what they achieve, and decisions affecting education.

Second, assessment results, especially if coupled with auxiliary information on characteristics of the various regions, would provide data necessary for research on educational problems and processes which cannot now be undertaken.

Third, when sampling and testing procedures are adequately developed, international comparisons might be possible.

Several research groups using private funds have undertaken to develop such procedures. They are exploring promising approaches; this spring, they will try some samplings experimentally.

These assessment efforts are not designed to test individual students, or individual schools, or individual teachers. They are designed to report on regional or nationwide educational levels over a period of time.

I believe that this matter of national assessment deserves the full attention of the education profession. We are not now reporting satisfactorily to ourselves, to our states, or to the nation on where we stand in education, where we are going, where we plan to go.

The American people today expect more of American education than ever before. At such a time, isn't it clear to all of us as educators that what we don't know *can* hurt us?

"WILL IT GIVE US A TRUE PICTURE?" ASKS BANESH HOFFMANN

A governmental testing program involving large numbers of students would run the danger of ending as a flawed multiple-choice monstrosity. If it did, the results would tell educators little that current tests do not. Even worse, such a program would set a federal seal of approval on a purblind method of evaluation that exploits ambiguity, rewards superficiality, penalizes depth and originality, frustrates inspired teaching, and corrupts education.

For example, consider this sort of test item:

> Circle the one that does not belong:
> duck, cat, dog, monkey

A Vermont child circled *monkey*, reasoning logically that it was the one creature that did not live nearby. His teacher, however, corrupted by the basic fallacy of "objective" tests that there is only one "best" answer, counted the child categorically wrong for not having circled *duck*.

It is just this mind-stunting type of teaching that is fostered by mechanized evaluation. Moreover, even the best of the machine gradable tests are by no means impeccably constructed. A 1964 sample College Board SAT question [eliminated in 1965] bears this out: In an item testing reading comprehension, the passage said that certain atmospheric layers are "transparent to" the longer radio waves; the wanted answer said that the layers "do not affect" the waves, *which is not at all the same as being transparent to them.* How could eye glasses function if they did not affect the light waves to which they are transparent?

At best, educational evaluation is hazardous. To evaluate our national effort in education solely on the basis of the warped picture presented by mechanized tests would be calamitous. Gifted teachers and educational trailblazers would be rightfully dismayed to have their work federally evaluated by such misleading methods, just as artists would be if their colorful paintings were to be judged by persons who were color-blind or worse.

The situation is not hopeless. While keeping in the background, officials of the U.S. Office of Education are encouraging the Carnegie Corporation to develop a new and ostensibly unofficial national evaluative program. In the purely political sense the program is brilliantly conceived. It will not tread on the toes of any individual, simply because no student, teacher, or school will be individually rated. Only a small sampling of students will be tested, and none of these students will be subjected to more than a small sampling of the total evaluative procedure.

Out of this sampling of a sampling could come a vivid picture of the state of American education, because the purpose is not so much to rate students or schools as to gather evaluational data. Furthermore, the sampling, by greatly reducing the pressure of numbers, would afford a superb opportunity to explore quality in depth.

Will the Carnegie Corporation seize the opportunity to develop a meaningful system of evaluation? I am a little skeptical, for Carnegie has already farmed out details of the task to leading test-making organizations that have been long calloused to the ambiguities and other defects of machine-gradable tests.

In attempting to develop an instrument which will truly evaluate the education of American students, will the test makers do some soul-searching? Will they for instance seek to find out what harm the current emphasis on machine-gradable tests may have done to students' powers of written expression? They could do this easily by giving questions, calling for written responses, and comparing them with those of Canadian students, who have not been brought up on a steady diet of mechanized tests.

If the Carnegie Corporation's sampling procedure is developed with boldness and imagination to probe educational excellences and evils by a broad range of methods, it will provide valuable information about American education—including current evaluative procedures.

Certainly national assessment will exercise coercion—let no one deceive himself about that. Indeed, the coercion will have federal overtones. If wisdom and luck prevail, however, it will be a flexible, enlightening coercion amenable to reason rather than a dogmatic coercion of the blindly numerical sort exercised by such instruments as the TV ratings and IQ scores.

If, however, the Carnegie program ends up as little more than a rehash of current objective tests and interest inventories, let us have none of it. It will do more harm than good.

How ARE WE DOING? THIS IS A QUESTION THAT CAN NEVER BE COMpletely answered. It is also a question we must do our best to answer continually.

Hopefully, the idea of assessment will expand. It would be interesting to have the American educational effort studied by cultural anthropologists, for instance. It might be helpful to have such experts tell us why the natives are sometimes restless and sometimes passive. The natives, of course, include administrators, teachers, and members of boards of education, as well as students. Since all the natives are products of the educational system in which they labor, some questions aimed at teachers might provide follow-up data on what happens to the student's education after he leaves school.

There is little doubt that the Carnegie sponsored assessment program will proceed. The current battle over any and all kinds of tests will nip annoyingly at its heels but in so doing it will keep the assessment planners on their toes.

Any test is only as good as the questions it asks. Hopefully, such a broadly conceived program of educational evaluation will ask more than questions of information. Hopefully, it will investigate the joy of discovery, the satisfaction of intellectual accomplishment, and the dignity of individual self-understanding. We've said for years that it is useless to help our students accumulate "facts" without gaining understanding and wisdom. Now is our chance to find out if we have meant what we said.

CHAPTER 10

The Future

PREVIOUS CHAPTERS OF THIS BOOK HAVE CONTAINED A LIBERAL DOSE of editorial opinion and crystal-ball gazing. This last chapter specifically presumes to look at the future and hazard some guesses about where the psychology of education is taking us.

A front-page article by Leonard Buder, in the July 14, 1966 issue of the *New York Times* reported that the New York City school system had been designated by the education authorities of New York State to develop a "Prototype School for the Year 2000." The Superintendent of the New York City schools, Dr. Bernard E. Donovan, was quoted as saying that he hoped "the initial facilities to implement the new program could be constructed here in five or six years." He was also quoted as saying that consideration would be given to "the type of world anticipated, the range and type of people to be served, the changing needs of these people, the role of community institutions in meeting these needs, the role of formal educational institutions, potential changes affecting education, and the contrast between current and future goals of education." The reader could only gasp and wish "good luck."

The article left one itching to know what such a school will be like. The probable reason is that even the people involved in the planning have the same itch but there's been very little scratching.

The safest prediction is that it will prove impossible to predict the educational needs of children in the year 2000. That does not mean we cannot learn a thing or two in the attempt but it does mean we had better plan to educate the children to meet an unpredictable future. At first, that sounds like double talk. On second thought it sounds impossible. But in the final analysis, it only proves a terribly difficult task.

A simple illustration of how children can be prepared for learning in an unpredictable future would be the teacher who was shopping for interesting toys recently and found one that "explains" how a computer works. Her first response was to recoil in distaste because she was pretty sure she would never understand computers and therefore also pretty sure she would not like or understand the game.

She had gone only a few steps past it when she realized what an opportunity it offered. She bought it and took it to school, explaining to the children that she didn't understand it but thought they and she might have some fun learning about it.

She was able to use the toy to demonstrate by her actions that one need not be ashamed or embarrassed about not knowing something. She was able to demonstrate how one goes about learning because she really had to learn along with the children.

Adults are much more frightened of the unknown than children. Fear is apparently a progressive disease. Classroom demonstrations of facing the unknown, armed only with a desire to learn about it should prove a very effective childhood vaccine, however.

It is likely that there will be a great many changes in the psychological aspects of education long before the year 2000. In the near future, the change will continue to de dominated by the pressures of the civil rights revolution and the accompanying attention to the education of urban children. There is going to be a much broader definition of "talent" and the methods used in its training will be much more creative.

A serious question is what will happen to the teaching profession? It has long offered security and the protection of mediocrity. A person who disagrees with "the system" finds it virtually impossible to climb the administrative ladder and hence influence policy. The pressures now for new talent in teaching may well cause a small revolution here. Salaries are going higher and more people are being attracted to the profession. Until a large corps of superior teachers is established, incentives for superior teachers must be established in ways that are not threatening to the precious security of the conforming mediocre teacher. Chances are that even this kind of teacher will try to change techniques when surrounded by new peers.

One ingredient that will help change the stale air is the volunteer. It is clear that nonprofessionals, such as high-school students, college students, college professors, visiting businessmen, artists, and moms with leisure time, will make more appearances in the classroom to help the teacher who is always a little too busy. The less daring and less flexible educator will probably hide behind the skirts of professionalism and be slow to make good use of these diverse resources at first, but even he will learn.

A teacher is supposedly the intermediary between the uneducated student and the educated world. Too often the teacher simply looks like an untouchable example of that far-off world, rather than a safe bridge. Perhaps teachers will begin to make more use of the "neighborhood specialist," the educated person who has made the trip from the child's neighborhood. This volunteer "teacher" and the classroom professional may connect to form a more sturdy bridge over the rapids. Such specialists may also soon appear in college classrooms where teachers are training.

If this book has followed the trends correctly it would seem more than likely that in the very near future (long before the year 2000) people will be going to school younger and older. An article by Fred M. Hechinger, in the June 5, 1966 issue of the *New York Times* discusses part of this trend. It was called "School for All from Age Four?"[1]

Children of Europe's aristocracy started their schooling almost as soon as they had learned to walk and talk. Governesses and

tutors taught them at an early age, while their less exalted contem-
poraries enjoyed their childhood undisturbed by school until the
age of six.

Although governesses and tutors today are mostly memories, well-
to-do American families have adopted some of the ways of Europe's
nobility of yesteryear—they send their children to nursery school
at age four or sooner. More recently, as part of the battle against
poverty, the so-called preschool movement has begun to offer similar opportunities for early schooling—or a head start—to disadvantaged children.

Last week, the inevitable happened. The Educational Policies
Commission, the ideological branch of the National Education Association, recommended that free public schooling at the age of four
be made available to all children.

The argument is powerful indeed. Out of the nation's 8.4 million
children in the four-to-five-year bracket, about 3.4 million already
enjoy the privilege of schooling. At present, 4.3 per cent of all
three-year-olds and 14.9 per cent of all four-year-olds are enrolled
in some public or private education program. Kindergartens, offered by some school systems and not by others, enroll 58.1 per
cent of all five-year-olds, and another 11.1 per cent of that group
are in first grade.

Newly disadvantaged—educationally speaking—is the middle
group; neither rich nor poor enough.

The Educational Policies Commission, therefore, wants to wipe
out an inequity which, as any student of American educational history knew, was bound to become untenable.

There is a more technical reason for the timing of the recommendation. A major thrust of American psychological research into the
way children learn offers persuasive evidence that children's intellectual and emotional development is capable of greater strides, and
therefore also of more damaging retardation through neglect, during the years before age six than at any time thereafter.

The value of early education has been demonstrated by the work
of sociologist Omar K. Moore, who has used electric typewriters to
teach 3-year-olds to read and write; by the research of Benjamin S.
Bloom at the University of Chicago, who has studied the effect of
early compensatory education on slum children; and by the analysis of the way in which children acquire and retrieve knowledge by
Harvard's Jerome S. Bruner.

Moreover, Dr. Martin Deutsch, director of the Institute of Developmental Studies in New York, has translated this research into

pioneering clinical and classroom work and into new procedures for the training of teachers for preschool programs.

The commission wants to give no aid and comfort to college-admissions-obsessed parents who see in pre-school education yet another device to groom and cram their children for a prestige campus address. It disavows any intent to push the first-grade program down to the kindergarten or nursery school level.

The purpose is not to teach reading, writing and arithmetic, but rather to promote a better understanding of the spoken word and better reactions to other children, and to provide an earlier chance to share experiences and give up the extreme egomania of the untutored child.

For the well-to-do and disadvantaged alike, a temporary escape from the dreadful programming of many so-called children's programs on television—virtually inescapable in the home—will be an added bonus.

Perhaps the commission, being part of the traditional education establishment, tends to go overboard in ruling out an early start at some of the more formal educational experiences—such as reading and numbers—for those children who are ready for it. But in view of the tendency of many parents to push too hard, this caution may be the better part of valor.

There are, however, other pitfalls to be avoided. The commission, which constitutes something of a lobbying group, is already on record as asking for two years of universally available free community college after high school. It now wants two additional years at the lower end of the educational ladder.

The goal is beyond reproach. But merely stretching out the years of public education, without assuring solid financing and staffing, may court disaster. There are already indications, especially in the big cities, that the human and financial resources of public education are spread dangerously thin. Achievements under the existing system are in jeopardy.

A partial answer to such objections is that the earlier start would help to make those achievements more satisfactory, if the program is properly conducted.

That "if" has been troubling such experts as Dr. Deutsch. As even the relatively limited pre-school programs of recent years were getting under way, he has warned against letting good intentions without properly trained staff pave the road to failure.

The most exciting prospect of the new public education proposals is that they might give the American school not merely an earlier but a new start. Some of the ablest of the pre-school experimenters are convinced that the real challenge is not just to add two new years, but to reform the 12 old ones.

THE OPPOSITE END OF THE SAME TREND WAS DISCUSSED BY J. RICH-ard Smith, who is Assistant Superintendent of Adult Education in the Los Angeles city schools. His article, entitled "Daytime, Night-time, Saturday Too" was printed in the March–1966 issue of the *NEA Journal*.[2]

> What Happens to School Dropouts? Some Become Dropins.
> Adult Education: Better Late Than Never.
> Southland's Adult Education Plans—They Thrive by Night!

These recent newspaper headlines reflect a trend: It's *in* for adults to return to school, and large numbers of them are doing it.

Hundreds of day or evening institutions throughout the United States have extended and supplemented the role of the high school by offering a varied curriculum suited to the needs of their new clientele. An adult school in Los Angeles, for example, enabled one of its students to offer Swahili as his language prerequisite for admission to the University of California.

Public adult schools cater to those from age 18 to infinity who for numerous reasons seek information or training through the process loosely termed *lifelong learning*.

Individuals who previously felt little or no need for additional education are coming back to the classroom, urged on by such demands as "Speak better English," "Develop a vocational skill," "Grow culturally," or "Get a diploma."

California's policy that public adult school graduates may receive a high school diploma has contributed greatly to the success of public adult education in our state.

Many of the Californians now seeking a diploma in an adult education institution dropped out of school two or three years ago

---

2. Reprinted by permission of the National Education Association.

and returned after learning that employment possibilities are severely limited without a high school diploma.

In the Los Angeles unified school district, about 2,700 diplomas are awarded to adults each year. Approximately 40 percent of those adults who receive diplomas are persons who dropped out of the day high schools of Los Angeles. Not all students in adult schools are youngsters, however. For instance, one such student was a 72-year-old handyman who recently earned a high school diploma after putting ten children through college.

Even though a majority of the states have not adopted California's policy, the federal government and many of the state governments have shown their awareness of the importance of adult schools by allocating funds to augment local public adult education budgets.

At the federal level, for example, the Social Security Amendments of 1962, Manpower Development and Training Act (MDTA) of 1962, Vocational Education Act (VEA) of 1963, Economic Opportunity Act (EOA) of 1964, and Elementary and Secondary Education Act (ESEA) of 1965 have contributed and will continue to contribute to adult education programs, over two-thirds of which include both academic and vocational courses.

With more students and bigger budgets, some adult schools are making exciting innovations. The success in Dade County, Florida, with classes in English for Spanish-speaking professionals has led to similar experiments in Los Angeles.

The parent-child preschool experience in Los Angeles has shown the rest of the country that low-income families will take part in a child-observation program and can benefit from instruction in family relations.

New programs and new approaches in adult education necessitate new instructional materials. With an eye to a rising market, book publishers are making available more material designed specifically for adults. Holt, Rinehart & Winston's *Adult Basic Education Series*, Macmillan's *English 900 Series*, and Allied Education Council's *Mott Basic Language Skills Program* are prime examples of instructional materials developed for the adult learner.

The rare systems that can afford to experiment in their adult schools are finding that programed textbooks and teaching machines can be effective in achieving educational goals. One Los Angeles "adult study skills center" uses programed instruction in such, required academic subjects as mathematics, economics, government, and English.

Students enrolled in adult education have generally shown that they are eager to learn efficiently and quickly, and want to achieve the elusive satisfaction of learning what they missed during previous experiences. Expanding enrollment in adult education and enthusiastic student reaction support the hypothesis that programed instruction can do much to satisfy these desires. Typical comments are:

"I like being able to learn at my own pace and to know where I am progressing."

"It [programed instruction] gives me time to figure things out and correct them immediately."

Day centers and day branch classes for adults are on the increase in large metropolitan areas. The reason for this is that housewives, senior citizens, expectant mothers, the unemployed, and the handicapped are more inclined to accept educational opportunities if they are offered at the right time and in the right place. Classes housed in recreation halls, churches, rented office space, or even homes, are luring many individuals reluctant to roam from the security of a familiar neighborhood.

In meeting the needs of a community, curriculums must continually change. Though courses necessary for fulfilling graduation requirements comprise the majority of offerings, each year new subjects are added in response to community demands.

Some classes, such as those in machine tool design, meat cutting, practical nursing, transportation, and traffic management, develop because of vocational interests. Others—county government, homemaking, parent education, planning for retirement—spring up because of interest in the home or community. Still others—ceramics, Japanese art, seamanship, and boat safety—are requested because they enhance enjoyment of leisure time.

Adults have also shown interest in a wide range of electives in the academic field. Courses such as Arabic, archeology of Mexico, introduction to humanities, and Swahili have been successful.

As this article suggests, adult learners bring to the classroom a great breadth of experience and diversity of demands. The consequent complexity of the curriculum and the rapid expansion of adult education constitute problems that must be solved in order to forestall the possibility that large numbers of the dropins will become dropouts—many of them for the second time.

Perhaps in addition to stretching education at both ends, we'll soon help it become more flexible in the middle. Some schools now have arrangements whereby students go to school part time and work part time. The pay the youngster earns may be necessary for family support. Whether or not it is necessary, it is certainly attractive. Perhaps we can be flexible enough to permit some youngsters to leave school temporarily for a period of weeks, months, or years when they feel the need to work and earn money. If we do not hang "dropout" signs around their necks and make return to the classroom difficult and humiliating, they may well be present in mind *and* body when they do return. Can there not be individual rhythm in educational need? Posters that tell youths to stay in school in order to get a better job assume a middle-class value that is not present for many potential dropouts. One dollar today is truly worth more than two tomorrow if you have not learned to trust tomorrow.

Most of us are sick unto death with the cliché of "educating the whole child." It looks as if this cliché is at last on the way to becoming reality, however, except that the word "child" will be replaced with the word "person." It looks as if education is going to be concerned with how the developing human learns to cope with his life. Reading, writing, and arithmetic are apparently going to be a very small part of the job.

Educators who want to stick to the three Rs have tradition on their side but that's about all. Certainly they do not have today's needs in mind. Social change is accelerating. Educators pride themselves on being guides and the rear guard is no place for a guide.

An article by Jack Harrison Pollack, in the May–1966 issue of the *NEA Journal*, entitled "Teen-Age Drinking and Drug Addiction" indicated that schools inevitably become involved with the life, dreams, problems, hopes, and frustrations of their students. Excerpts from that article are reprinted here.[3]

3. © 1966 by Jack Harrison Pollack.

The first thing I learned is that alcoholism and drug addiction cannot be considered the same problem. Many educators and mental health experts are convinced that it is a mistake to teach about alcohol and narcotics in a single unit of instruction. Excessive drinking and drug addiction among high school youth often spring from different motivations and have different consequences (claim the experts), and because of these differences, the problems should be assessed separately.

Nearly all states have laws requiring alcohol education. The quality of teaching in such courses, however, is generally mediocre, to the best of my knowledge.

Alcohol education is sometimes taught as a separate course, rather than as a unit in an existing course. Most educators I interviewed disapproved of this approach, believing that it places undue emphasis on the subject. Instead, they favored making alcohol education part of other courses such as health education, driver and safety education, science (especially biology), social studies, family life, or homemaking.

"But schools can't afford to drop it haphazardly into the curriculum just to meet a legal requirement," warns the director of the Cleveland Center on Alcoholism. "It has to be carefully planned with no effort spared to prepare teachers adequately for the job."

In some states (Oregon for one) many teachers now receive special instruction in alcohol education through in-service workshops and summer sessions. Other states have workshops for teachers, and some have given scholarships and college credit for teachers who participate in workshops.

"We will get nowhere until we can replace the image of alcohol education as a bothersome, unimportant or embarrassing fringe item which overloads the curriculum," insists Margaret L. Clay, University of Michigan psychologist. "As long as students believe that this is all alcohol education has to offer, they won't buy it. What they want is information which will help them with their own conflicts."

One organization that educators can turn to for current materials on teaching about the effects of alcohol is the Association for the Advancement of Instruction about Alcohol and Narcotics (212 South Grand Avenue, Lansing, Michigan 48913). Another organization which has published a great deal of material is the Rutgers Center of Alcohol Studies at New Brunswick, New Jersey. Educators may also contact their community Health and Welfare Councils, chapters of the National Council on Alcoholism, Family Service associations, and other United Fund agencies which have vast experience in helping young people cope with special problems. In addition, state and local public health departments can often furnish needed resources for teaching about the effects of drinking.

DRUG ADDICTION

Almost any estimate of the total number of youthful drug addicts or potential addicts must be viewed with skepticism. For instance, a New York newspaper recently estimated that there are as many as a million drug addicts in this country and that "most of them are young people." However, the federal Bureau of Narcotics reported that in 1964 there were 2,029 persons under age twenty-one officially identified as drug addicts. Even if the total number of youthful addicts or potential addicts were ten times greater than the number of known addicts, the total would still be far short of figures quoted by the press.

Most drug users—youthful and adult—are believed to be concentrated in a few large cities, notably New York, Los Angeles, and Chicago. But the problem also exists in other metropolitan centers.

Until now the majority of known teen-age addicts have come from low-income, big city neighborhoods, such as New York's Harlem. In recent years, however, authorities have discovered widespread use of narcotics in some affluent suburbs where in their search for kicks, bored adolescents have turned to marijuana, heroin, and LSD (lysergic acid diethylamide). Indeed, among some well-to-do youngsters, experimenting with drugs has become the "in" thing to do.

Contrary to popular belief, students seldom obtain their drugs from adult peddlers or "pushers." Sociologist Alfred R. Lindesmith of Indiana University, probably America's leading authority on drug addiction problems, told me: "Adult pushers don't generally hang around schools or stand on street corners selling drugs to students. Usually, it is the student's 'best friend' or a classmate who introduces him to drugs."

"The biggest problem we have with narcotics," adds a physician for a large Southwestern school system, "is with dropouts who come on our school grounds and try to sell drugs to students."

Psychotherapist Ernest Harms, who for many years has studied youthful drug addiction in New York, says: "Some of these youngsters [who sell drugs] had no high school education whatever, but they had read considerably on drugs in professional literature which they obtained in secondhand bookshops."

The greatest drug problem among teen-agers is not so much the use of narcotics as it is the indiscriminate swallowing of pep pills (amphetamines) and goof balls (barbiturates). Compared with the number of pill takers, relatively few high school students smoke marijuana or use addictive drugs.

Many youngsters do not realize that indiscriminate use of pills can be just as dangerous as marijuana smoking and even experimenting with some narcotics. Excessive use of amphetamines can possibly bring on convulsions and death. An overdose of barbiturates can likewise be fatal.

Although the drug problem has been widely dramatized, it has received comparatively little attention in the school curriculum. Some school administrators fear that even the slightest mention of narcotics could lead to misunderstanding and unfavorable publicity.

A former New York City Department of Health official says: "A school administrator who is really concerned about the health of his students, rather than just the reputation of his school, must be willing to admit a drug problem exists, if it does, and make the solution educational, not punitive."

Most states have laws requiring some teaching about narcotics, but these are usually vague, such as: "Instruction shall be given in . . . alcohol and narcotics and their effects upon the human system as determined by science."

Some school systems "satisfy" the law with a forty-minute lecture at the end of the student's senior year—which is usually too little and too late. The problem needs to be tackled much earlier and more comprehensively.

Schools often include teaching about the dangers of narcotics, alcohol, and tobacco in a single unit. One superintendent told me: "Because alcohol and tobacco are socially and legally acceptable, many students can easily infer from such a course that there is no difference between them and narcotics."

Many schools invite outside speakers, sometimes ex-drug addicts, but more often police officers, to lecture to students. However, some educators fear that these talks may tend to overdramatize the subject and thus possibly encourage some youngsters to experiment with drugs. "It doesn't help when police officers, in one-shot sessions, show a scare movie followed by a 'Don't Use Drugs' talk," insists one health expert.

Most educators I talked with believe that facts about drug usage and narcotics addiction should be included naturally in some regular course such as health or science. "Any course is worthless that begins with, 'Today we are going to talk about narcotics,'" one outspoken educator told me.

A Westport, Connecticut, report last year recommended that curriculum materials on the dangers of drug addiction be updated and that communications be improved between school officials, police, health officers, doctors, and parents—all of whom tend to keep information about teen-age narcotics usage to themselves.

In some communities, teachers have been urged to look for danger signals which might indicate a student is on drugs: Is he suddenly slipping in his schoolwork? Has he become secretive? Does he suddenly wear long sleeves? Has he stopped being interested in sports or the opposite sex? Has he a new set of friends? Has he lost interest in his appearance? Does he have sudden fits of anger followed by depression?

There are limits, however, to detective work of this sort. As one principal pointed out, "I don't want my teachers rushing a student to me or the school doctor just because he appears drowsy or listless."

The New York City Board of Education gives this advice to teachers. "When suspicions are aroused, it is best to avoid direct accusations. The wiser course is to refer the matter to the school principal, whose responsibility it is to take the next step—referral to the School Health Service."

The Chicago Board of Education warns school personnel to "avoid becoming involved in any way other than to report recognized or suspected incidents of drug users or sellers."

Since the beginning of time, young and old people have searched for euphoria with pills, herbs, and all sorts of weird concoctions. Is it any wonder, then, that today a small percentage of America's youth are experimenting with drugs? The problem, nevertheless, must be taken seriously.

As one superintendent of schools in New York said in a letter to parents: "Let us not seek comfort in the fact that many other communities have a similar problem, probably worse than in our community. Nor should we allow ourselves to be complacent because it now affects only a small hard core of our youth. Drugs and narcotics use by *any* portion of our teen-agers is a potential danger to the entire community."

WE NEED NOT PUSH THE PANIC BUTTON WHEN "DRUGS," "ALCOHOL," or "sex" are mentioned in class. Social issues cannot be avoided in a place that is devoted to helping people learn. Learning is related to living and living involves social issues. Any topic can be approached as "subject matter," not necessarily to be dealt with at that moment but certainly not forbidden within the walls of the school. Education is a search for truth. A teacher can admit that there are pleasures associated with drugs without condoning their use. Drugs have their pleasures but they also have their cost, which is paid in more than money. It is better that a student hear all sides of the story than the one side he may hear from the "in" group who are too busy with "kicks" to think about the future.

Clearly what is needed is not simple stern warnings about dangers. Growing people need to learn how to find the life that will prove satisfying, and that is a larger order than simply avoiding dangers. An editorial addressed to this point appeared in the July 20, 1966 issue of the *New York Times* under the heading "Sex, Tobacco, Dope. . . ."[4]

The recent appeal by the National Association of Independent Schools for development of a sound program of sex education may encourage a sensible approach to a perplexing problem. As the private-school leaders pointed out, today's children and adolescents grow up in an atmosphere polluted by the sordid exploitation of sex. Parental permissiveness, combined with efforts to avoid trouble by not talking honestly about the issues involved, has led to confusion, rebellion, and to charges of adult hypocrisy by the young.

But sex education is not the only area touching personal and social values where instruction should be broadened and intensified; and the N.A.I.S. would have done better to add to its recommendations an emphasis on such other aspects of youthful life today as the use of narcotics and related stimulants, and the harmful effects of smoking on health. Dr. William H. Stewart, Surgeon General of the United States, has disclosed that despite intensive warning campaigns more than half of all teen-agers ignore the scientifically proved dangers to their health and become regular cigarette smokers by the time they are eighteen. The alarming reports about adolescent and collegiate experimentation with drugs under-

4. © 1966 by The New York Times Company. Reprinted by permission.

score similar dangers of ignorance and unconcern, as do statistics of illegitimate pregnancies.

The need is for the kind of teaching that puts into perspective the value of human life as a part of a more meaningful scheme than the instant gratification of whims. Perhaps teaching youth about the nature of growing up calls for a reappraisal of the concept of "the pursuit of happiness" as a mindless justification of all momentary desires.

THAT MAY NOT SOUND LIKE "THE GOOD OLD DAYS" IN THE CLASS-room, but days do change. Once upon a time, youngsters were content to carve hearts in trees and scribble "John hates Mary" on the wall. Scribbled on the wall of a New York City school today are the surprising words "Pablo is a neoclassicist." Many of today's students know about rent strikes and even Picasso. They are products of changing times.

It looks as if teachers are going to be neo-innovators. Problems will be met with more and more innovation and less and less dependence on tradition. A news article in the July 10, 1966 issue of the *New York Times* reported "Ungraded College for Negroes Ends Its First Test Year."[5]

An ungraded 4-year liberal arts college with built-in remedial features and a year-round program for those who need it, has just completed its first experimental year and may have established a blueprint for Negro institutions in the South.

The college is the principal unit of Shaw University, a century-old, predominantly Negro institution in Raleigh, N.C. It is one of the 33 members of the United Negro College Fund.

Details of the plan were disclosed in a recent interview by Dr. James E. Cheek, president of the university, who is also an alumnus. He believes that other Negro colleges may adopt it.

He said that the new plan, which includes a prebaccalaureate program, was necessary to meet the needs of many underprivileged who want to attend college but who cannot make the grade.

"We have found," he said, "that the white colleges are taking the cream of the crop as part of their integration efforts and this leaves us with students who have the desire for a college education but require a good deal of help."

5. © 1966 by The New York Times Company. Reprinted by permission.

Dr. Cheek, who holds a Bachelor of Divinity degree from Colgate-Rochester Divinity School and a doctorate from Drew University in Madison, N.J., said that Shaw had accepted in its prebaccalaureate program 80 students with I.Q.'s of 80 or less and had great hope for them.

The college, Dr. Cheek explained, has no grades, thereby allowing the students to progress at their own pace. They move forward on the basis of national test results and may finish in as little as three years or as many as six.

TEACHERS ARE GOING TO MARCH TOWARD SOME LATE TWENTIETH-century version of the old one-room schoolhouse. They will return to it, however, armed with the lessons of specialization. A great deal has been learned by compartmentalizing, departmentalizing, categorizing, and dissecting the student as well as the educational process. What has been learned will undoubtedly find its way into the new version of the one-room schoolhouse.

The schoolhouse may even be literally one room and that one room may be a storefront. Social agencies have found it necessary to leave their office towers and come down to the street. Educators may follow.

Education's new image is going to be "the helper." The old schools were built to look like impenetrable fortresses. The new schools are more open to the world. The storefront classroom may well be the stepping stone to the school with more rooms.

It's unlikely that most schoolhouses will have only one room, the cost of construction being what it is today, but hopefully they will contain the same maddening and enjoyable elements of heterogeneity. We are beginning to see more clearly that people learn from differences as well as similarities and that they learn from meeting and living with different kinds of people.

The return to the past, armed with the lessons of the present, to meet the demands of the future is a fascinating if not necessarily tranquil trip. Madeline C. Hunter, who is now Principal of the University Elementary School at the University of California, in Los Angeles, gives us some of its flavor in an article entitled, "Teachers in the Non-Graded School" which appeared in the February, 1966 issue of the *NEA Journal*.[6]

Changes and new decisions bother all of us. I was beset with misgivings the moment I found that the ignition switch on my new car was on the left instead of on the right side of the steering wheel as it had been in my former car. These uneasy feelings started to compound as I began to suspect manufacturers of sadistic perverseness. The drive selector on this car was also in a different place, the drive positions were not what I was used to, and I had to set the emergency brake by hand instead of by foot.

As I fought through the maze of new "feels" and places for my hands and feet, with typical human resistance to change, I regretted turning in my comfortable old model. It was too late to reverse my decision, however, so with the skills (and attitude) of a six-year-old with mixed dominance I decided to take my elderly mother for a ride while I got used to the recalcitrant mechanical monster.

"Whatever are you doing?" Mother asked in amazement as I lost my usual complacency and muttered a string of descriptive phrases which are best forgotten.

"I'm trying to decide which drive position to use," I explained snappishly.

"I'm glad that when I was learning to drive, the horse made most of those decisions," she said, primly smoothing her skirts.

Horse sense indeed! But oh how much more comfortable and effective is my new car, now that I am used to it.

I had the same problem of adapting to change when I first started using the "gear selectors" of nongrading. As a teacher in a nongraded school, it was up to me to make recommendations as to how each individual in my present class should be placed next semester. Which of my fellow teachers would bring out the best in Johnny? Should Mary and Sally continue to be in the same group or should they be separated? This decision-making brought into devastating visibility my lack of knowledge of that great middle group in my class—those children who learned just enough and conformed just enough that they never had received my full educational concern.

Once the students were assigned to instructional groups, major learning decisions became the responsibility of individual teachers,

6. Reprinted by permission of the National Education Association and the author.

rather than of the curriculum council or the textbook committee. No longer could the same graded materials be dealt out to an entire class; every teacher had to make professional judgments as to which book and which level of content was appropriate for each child in his class.

The use of educator decisions rather than system decisions is the hallmark of the truly nongraded school. Why do I say "truly nongraded"? Because if you are a teacher in an elementary school that assigns students to a levels program or that groups learners in different classrooms according to ability and achievement, you have eliminated astrology as the guiding principle for placement of children, but you have substituted something not much better. In place of numerals representing the date of birth, you have substituted the numerals from the score of a reading, general achievement, or intelligence test. Such a score is designed to give normative data for large groups; it is not supposed to yield diagnostic data relevant to the optimal placement of individual children in instructional clusters.

Each September, those of us who teach in a nongraded school greet a group that differs radically from those in most other American classrooms. The boys and girls have not all been born within a certain twelve-month period and teachers, therefore, do not have to depend on some fortuitous juxtaposition of the planets at the time of their birth for all to go well. Learners assigned to any one teacher have been diagnosed as responding well to that teacher's style of teaching. Likewise, the sociometric composition of each group has been designed to foster the optimal growth of individual members.

What a refreshing relief it is for teachers to know that each child is beginning the year with a fresh start; that they don't have to brace themselves in anticipation of one of those class groups that moves as an indigestible lump through the school.

Decisions regarding teaching style and peer group that have already been made about class membership help to eliminate such undesirable stereotypes as "worst reader," "poor sport," or "sloppy worker." Similarly, positive reputations such as "best reader," "most popular girl," and "team captain" need to be re-earned in the new group, thereby strengthening an ability that has been manifested.

Everything possible has been arranged in advance to optimize learning and now it's up to the teachers. It is quite a responsibility! No longer can anyone take refuge in the excuse, "He didn't even have fractions in *her* room so what do you expect *me* to do?" Teachers are expected to teach each pupil from wherever he is to as far as they can take him.

No longer is the goal to cover certain material (much of which should be "covered" and appropriately laid to rest). The question changes from, "Has the student done it?" to "Has the student learned it?" We, as teachers, must be able to confidently answer "yes" before moving on.

Selecting for the learner an appropriate task at the correct level of difficulty is the responsibility of each teacher in the nongraded school. This implies assessing the effectiveness of each day's teaching—a task not always conducive to the well-being of one's ego. The fact that a teacher thinks he has taught base ten gives him no license to go on unless he is sure it has been learned.

In a nongraded school, teachers facing, for the first time, a three-year age span of learners are appalled by the anticipated range of abilities. After a few weeks they are further shaken by the realization that they do not know which children are the youngest and which the oldest without looking it up.

After changing to nongrading, one experienced first grade teacher came to her principal complaining, "I can't teach five-, six-, and seven-year-olds in the same class. Why, some of them are not even ready to read, two can read at a third grade level, and one can read at a fifth grade level."

Upon investigation it was discovered that those not ready to read and those reading at third and fifth grade level were all six-year-olds. In the typical first grade class the wiggly, twitchy little six-year-old boys would have been "excused" from the reading group. ("John, take your book and sit over there until you can listen.") The able six-year-old readers would have willingly read "Run, Sally, run" to please such a nice teacher.

Because this teacher was in a nongraded classroom she was forced to the disquieting realization that the typical first grade reading program is inappropriate for some six-year-old children, yet perfectly appropriate for some five- and seven-year-olds. Nongrading does not necessarily assure a wider range of abilities; it does inexorably force teachers to make educational provision for the range they have.

Placement of children, using the criteria of teaching style and peer group composition, presents a new and often unexplored area of decision-making for teachers.

When a teacher in a nongraded school was asked what instructional group she would recommend for seven-year-old Howard in the coming year, she replied, "Give him a teacher who will really get after him. His mother has babied him so that he needs someone who means business."

The next day, however, Howard's teacher amended her recommendation by saying, "I've been watching Howard. When I ran late in my art period and started snapping out orders for cleanup, he just went to pieces. I've decided that he needs a teacher who is not too strict and who will give him support. At the same time, he needs a peer group that will really push him intellectually. He has such a quick mind that the children in his present group never challenge him enough to force him to refine his ideas."

The following day, Howard's teacher came to the office a third time. "Someone told Howard, 'Gee, that was a lousy picture you made' and Howard burst into tears, so I guess he's not ready for too much challenging." She concluded with, "You must think I can't make up my mind, but I'm not used to making these kinds of decisions."

None of us is used to making these kinds of teaching decisions. They represent a new and rigorous dimension in the process of education. These decisions, also, represent the impact of recent research which indicates that a powerful educational environment can make significant and pervasive changes in the individual.

It is not easy to assume the responsibility called for in a nongraded classroom. No longer can the teacher go to the textbook room and check out a set of fifth grade math books. He must begin by assessing at what point each child is able to function, and build the next appropriate skill on a stable foundation. In doing this, the teacher has the satisfaction of knowing that he is not making mathophobes out of the children who are not ready for fractions and that he is not developing indolence and indifference in those children for whom fractions are too easy.

When I used to teach in a graded classroom, I always existed in a frenzy of apprehension for fear I couldn't get place value taught to Johnny before his mother found out he wasn't having long division with the rest of the group.

In a nongraded school, we never have the rigid floors and ceilings of expectations that existed in the traditional graded materials. In a nongraded room, those graded books with dots on the back don't have the power to say, "Everybody should be here." Consequently, children do not need to experience failure and they cannot attain success without effort. As a result, they should become more self-propelling in their learning.

Teaching a nongraded group is based on the same learning principles as good teaching in any group. Teachers present appropriate material at the correct level of difficulty for each child. The difference is that in a nongraded school they do it openly, for it is what they are expected to do, whereas in a graded group some teachers have to bootleg appropriate learning opportunities.

It is easy for a teacher to get caught in a platitudinous trap and wail, "I can't prepare thirty different lessons for thirty different children!" No one expects him to. The tailored education of nongrading does not mean a different lesson for every child, but rather an appropriate lesson for each. With practice, teachers develop skill and facility in modifying academic content and teaching strategies so that they will be in keeping with realistic but rigorous expectations for children. (You should see me drive my new car now!)

EDUCATION IS A BIG JOB IN A CHANGING WORLD. SELECTING AND preparing students for college is a tiny part of the task facing elementary and secondary educators.

Bloom, Davis, and Hess, whose book *Compensatory Education for Cultural Deprivation* was quoted in Chapter 1, say that:

It is difficult at present to determine the exact way in which educational institutions in the United States will be reshaped over he next decade. It is likely that one major change will be a shift in the conception of education from the status-giving and selective system to a system that develops each individual to his highest potential.

THEY ALSO LIST SOME OF THE NEW DEMANDS ON EDUCATION AND indicate that these are "likely to emphasize some of the following goals for education:"

(A) There must be increasing emphasis on the higher mental processes of problem-solving rather than the existing stress on information learning. Only as individuals develop skill in the more complex types of thinking will they be able to cope with the many new problems they must face in their educational and post-educational careers in a rapidly changing society.

(B) There must be increasing emphasis on the basic ideas, structure, and methods of inquiry of each subject field rather than on the minutiae of the subject matter. Individuals must be able to cope with the rapidly expanding and changing body of knowledge in each field and they must be able to find the ways in which the subject fields contribute ideas and tools of thinking necessary for the larger world outside the classroom.

(C) More stress be placed on 'learning to learn' than has previously been true. Each person is likely to have to relearn his own occupation a number of times during his career. Furthermore, learning must continue throughout life, if the individual is to cope with the changing nature of the society, the many new demands on him, and his own possibilities for self-actualization and fulfillment.

(D) Increasing stress must be placed on those aspects of interests, attitudes, and personality which will promote the further growth of the individual, enable him to find satisfaction in the things he does, and help him find meaning and fulfillment in his life. The effects of automation, the shorter work week, urban living, and the fast pace of change on the national as well as international scene, require individual character development which will enable each person to live with himself and with others under conditions very different from those which have prevailed.

ALICE IN WONDERLAND COMES TO MIND, RUNNING TO STAY IN place. But despite the increasing tempo and the new steps, it looks as if we are going to dance further along the road and inspect new terrain. Psychology has tried to help build the best possible house for education. Its attempts have been less than helpful at times. Generally it has profited by mistakes. It is more likely now to work with educators.

Do you remember when Pooh and Piglet built a proper house for Eeyore? They accidentally removed Eeyore's old house from the Gloomy Place in order to build a proper house at Pooh Corner. Eeyore was puzzled to find his house in a new location (though of course he had an explanation). After inspecting it inside and out, he had to admit that it *was* his house and that it was as good as ever; in fact, it was "better in places."

Psychology has been taking education's house apart and now is helping to put it back together. In a new age, most educators recognize it as home. They are glad to have psychologists working with them. The new house is "better in places." It had better be. The family is growing and their educational needs are greater than ever.

Index